VOTING
AND
HOLINESS

VOTING AND HOLINESS

Catholic Perspectives on Political Participation

EDITED BY

NICHOLAS P. CAFARDI

PAULIST PRESS
New York/Mahwah, NJ

Cover design by Sharyn Banks
Book design by John Eagleson

Library of Congress Cataloging-in-Publication Data

Voting and holiness : Catholic perspectives on political participation / edited by Nicholas P. Cafardi.
    p.   cm.
  ISBN 978-0-8091-4767-0 (alk. paper)   ISBN 978-1-61643-140-2
  1. Catholics–Political activity–United States.   2. Christianity and politics–United States   3. Christianity and politics–Catholic Church.   4. Catholic Church–United States–Doctrines.   I. Cafardi, Nicholas P.
BX1407.P63V68 2011
261.7088'28273–dc23   2011040772

Published by Paulist Press
997 Macarthur Boulevard
Mahwah, New Jersey 07430\

www.paulistpress.com

Printed and bound in the
United States of America

Contents

Introduction

This is a book of essays by noted Catholic scholars who apply the teachings of our faith to the political process. The title of this volume, "Voting and Holiness," is itself a bit puzzling, isn't it? We do not normally speak of trying to be holy and voting in the same breath. Yet isn't that what the various public appeals to our Catholicism in seeking our votes are really about? Aren't these appeals, whether they come from bishops or priests or politicians, really saying that, if you seek to be a good Catholic, you must vote for such and so? Being a good Catholic certainly means being a holy Catholic, a pilgrim on the way to heaven, seeking to be guided on the pathways of holiness by our faith. Does how you vote affect that pilgrimage in any way?

In recent presidential elections, undoubtedly prompted by the fact that Catholics were on the national ticket, we have heard that it does affect that pilgrimage. We have heard this primarily from political pundits of the right seeking Catholic votes against Catholic candidates. Do candidates for public office have to be good Catholics before believing and practicing Catholics can vote for them? And who determines who is a good Catholic? Certainly not the political pundits, whose own lifestyles leave their judgments on the virtuous life open to doubt. But increasingly a number of American Catholic bishops have joined this process, saying basically the same things as right-leaning political pundits. And this has raised the stakes.

Our bishops are authentic teachers of our faith. When they say something, it bears listening to. No good Catholic can readily dismiss a proclamation by a successor of the apostles. This collection of essays faces this issue square on: What does our Church authentically teach about Catholic participation in the political life of our nation? After my introductory essay (and it is first only because the essays are in alphabetical order by author), the various contributors each examine this issue from their own perspective and background. These essays will, hopefully, provide a basis for you to consider how your faith affects your political actions. After each essay, I have suggested questions for your further reflection.

Professor Lisa Sowle Cahill in "Voting and Living the Common Good" writes of Catholic participation in the political process, emphasizing that political responsibility is not limited to the voting booth, but impacts how we live our lives in the communities of which we are a part. She focuses first on the 2008 presidential election, but then examines three important moral and political issues in general: racism, abortion, and global justice. On each of these matters, the Catholic Church has been a strong moral voice. It defines both racism and abortion as "intrinsic evils," and the pursuit of global justice is a constant refrain of papal social teaching. Dr. Cahill examines how the consideration of each of these issues should affect a committed Catholic's participation in the democratic process, advocating that our faith should encourage us to bring our Gospel values to our politics.

In "Politics, Morality and Original Sin," Cardinal Georges Cottier examines the moral ground of two prominent 2009 speeches by President Barack Obama: his May 2009 speech to the graduating class at the University of Notre Dame and his June 2009 speech to the students at Al-Azhar University in Cairo, Egypt. The cardinal sees in both speeches an attempt to understand the differences in moral beliefs that exist among people as a result of original sin. He is sympathetic with the president's attempt to seek a "common ground" with those who might perceive morality differently because of humankind's sinfulness, understanding this as a manifestation of "good faith" in the attempt to reach a political solution to difficult issues, such as abortion, that have an undeniable moral dimension.

Dr. William D'Antonio in "Catholic Bishops and the Electoral Process in American Politics" writes of the diverse ways in which the American bishops have intervened in politics, focusing primarily on the period following *Roe v. Wade* in 1973. He focuses on four different kinds of political activity: direct action, political campaigning, lobbying, and infiltration and describes how the American bishops have attempted to use each of these to advance the Church's social justice agenda. Dr. D'Antonio's essay, besides providing a fascinating history of recent political times, is also a good study of what works and what doesn't work in the implementation of the Church's ideals in the raw world of American politics.

In "Prudential Judgment and Catholic Teaching," Dr. Richard Gaillardetz reminds us of the need to exercise the ancient virtue of prudence in our political decisions. He sees this exercise of prudence as rooted in four overarching principles: (1) know the Catholic tradition, in all of its aspects, by immersion in that tradition; (2) identify the fundamental moral principles that must guide your electoral discernment; (3) be careful to distinguish matters of moral principles from matters of prudential judgment; and finally (4) attend carefully to the particulars of political and social contexts in making your political decisions. His essay is an excellent reminder of the need to return to the exercise of prudence in the public order, with a special emphasis on the role of the laity to take the initiative in applying Church teaching to contemporary political problems.

John Gehring in "Not a Single-Issue Church: Resurrecting the Catholic Social Justice Tradition" provides a riveting description of the political partisanship that has roiled our Church in recent elections. Writing admittedly from a "progressive" point of view, Gehring explains that partisanship—of the left or right—emphasizes only those parts of the vast fabric of Catholic social justice teaching that support the partisan's preconceived and prejudged political notions. This approach, namely, the use of our Church for political purposes, not only distorts what our Church teaches, but it will get us nowhere politically, Gehring argues. Rather, he sees the need for thoughtful dialogue, within the Church itself, among the hierarchy and with the laity, as the only way forward in charity and justice, to advance the vast spectrum of the Church's concerns in the political arena. Gehring would also open this dialogue to those of other faith traditions who share the Church's social justice concerns.

Jesuit priest and professor of law Gregory A. Kalscheur, SJ, delves into the Catholic concept of conscience and conscience formation in the first part of his essay, "Conscience and Citizenship: The Primacy of Conscience for Catholics in Political Life." He examines what role the teachings of the church must play in this formation process, carefully distinguishing among the various levels of teaching in the Church and the proper response of the faithful to them. Looking at the concept of the primacy of the conscience, he examines recent hierarchical criticism of this concept as a valid guide to human action, especially political action. From this follows an intriguing discussion of the proposition, put forward by a number of Catholic politicians, that they can draw a line between their personal beliefs as Catholics and their public policy decisions. Here Father Kalscheur examines what Pope John Paul II and Pope Benedict XVI have written on this point. He ends with a discussion of prudential judgment and how that concept might help to analyze these issues.

In "Intrinsic Evil and Political Responsibility: Is the Concept of Intrinsic Evil Helpful to the Catholic Voter?" Professor M. Cathleen Kaveny examines the utility of the concept of "intrinsic evil" to the Catholic voter. She explains the roots of this term in St. Thomas Aquinas's action theory: the morality of an act is determined by the object of the act. But not every intrinsically evil act is a gravely evil act, and some intrinsically evil acts may actually be less grave than other types of wrongful acts. For this reason, the motive and circumstances of an act require moral scrutiny in determining how evil it is, and, as a result, the claimed political responsibility of Catholics to prevent "intrinsically evil" acts is not always the easy answer it appears to be. Dr. Kaveny believes that the term "intrinsically evil" is more valid as prophetic language in combating the evil that we confront than it is as an analytical tool for the Catholic voter.

In "A Moral Compass for Cooperation with Wrongdoing" Dr. Gerald Magill offers an explanation of Catholic moral theology in the area of "cooperating with evil." He starts by examining both illicit formal cooperation with evil and licit material cooperation, clearly establishing the critical difference between the two. The first is never morally licit; the second may be in certain circumstances. Then Dr. Magill turns to the mission of the Church and what political means might be used to accomplish that mission, referencing back to his introductory principles of "cooperation with evil." With these basic principles established, the question of the Catholics cooperating with evil is analyzed, first from the point of view of the Catholic legislator and then from the view of the Catholic voter. He ends with a deft application of these principles to Canon 915 of the Code of Canon Law, which states that Catholics who obstinately persist in manifest grave sin should not approach the Eucharistic table.

Father Bryan Massingale's "A Parallel That Limps: The Rhetoric of Slavery in the Pro-Life Discourse of U.S. Bishops" deals with a delicate matter, the comparison of the evil of abortion in America to the evil of slavery in America and the use of this comparison in the political/moral debate. This comparison is used by the bishops to support their stance that the only way to deal with abortion is to make it illegal. It is a comparison that rules out any alternative approach to the evil of abortion. For example, it rules out any approaches that, instead of focusing on overturning *Roe v. Wade*, seek to provide a better social safety net for women so that abortion, while possibly remaining a legally available choice, is in fact not the choice that women would make. In this context, Father Massingale points out that the historic record of the church's opposition to slavery in the United States is not a felicitous one and that in making the slavery-abortion analogy the bishops are rewriting this history, and weakening their own anti-abortion argument.

Dr. Vincent J. Miller begins his "The Disappearing Common Good as a Challenge to Catholic Participation in Public Life: The Need for Catholicity and Prudence" by explaining how the notion of the common good has been central to the Catholic vision of the political life, from Aquinas to Benedict XVI. He then examines how, in the era of the "citizen as consumer," both political parties in our country have lost sight of the common good, how they have gone from seeing the role of government, not as promoting the common good, but as promoting the private economic activity of individual citizens. Our social mores enforce this political individualism: the way we live apart from each other, the consumer culture we have created, erode a sense of community that supports the common good. In place of the pursuit of the common good, which is the traditional Catholic approach to political life, Dr. Miller writes that Catholics have become "values voters," but focusing on a narrow range of values, subject to easy political manipulation. Dr. Miller ends his essay with a consideration of the Catholic theological principles of cooperation and prudence and how they might be used to restore the common good as a political value.

In "Can You Sin When You Vote?" Professor Maureen O'Connell writes of two spaces, the confessional and the voting booth, and the moral perspectives that we must bring to both. Rather than focusing on the negative, she rephrases the question: How can we be holy, how can we love when we vote? Dr. O'Connell sees two implications in this question. First, that our divine creation makes us free, rational beings with moral agency and moral responsibility. Second, that since human love is a relational experience, how we comport ourselves within the larger society in the "ordinary time" between elections is morally significant. From this basis, Dr. O'Connell goes on to analyze notions of both personal sin and social sin. Dr. O'Connell concludes with the implications of this analysis for voting and loving, finding that voting is an expression of conscience, which must be well formed, that the moral view is the long view in which voting is not an isolated act, and that voting requires a vision beyond the personal, but one sharpened and focused by others, by what we learn from revelation, tradition, social sciences, and experiential wisdom.

Father Anthony J. Pogorelc turns back the pages of history to the 1980s, when the American bishops were writing *Economic Justice for All*, their famous pastoral letter on the American economy, in his "Lessons from the U.S. Bishops' Economic Pastoral Letter: Modeling the Way of Holiness." Father Pogorelc describes the consultative process that the bishops used in preparing that document, seeking comments from experts, consulting the laity, publishing early drafts and soliciting comments, even holding public hearings. In this process, Father Pogorelc writes, the bishops were guided by the fact that they were not experts in the field of economics, but that they had a need to speak on economic matters authoritatively because of the clear moral dimensions of so many economic issues. In order to do this effectively, and noting that the Holy Spirit speaks to the whole church, they entered into a consultative and collaborative process with the laity that resulted in a pastoral letter that had greater exposure, being cited and responded to in the secular media, and greater credibility among the laity than it would have otherwise had. Father Pogorelc allows that this method of collaboration and consultation with the laity, which has fallen into desuetude, could serve as a model for the bishops to address the thorny social justice issues that confront the Church in the United States in the twenty-first century.

Professor Stephen F. Schneck writes of the formative value faith has on political life in the concrete circumstances of the only Catholic to have been elected president of the United States. In "President Kennedy and Archbishop Chaput: Religion and Faith in American Political Life," he takes as his starting point Chaput's criticism that candidate Kennedy's speech to the Houston Ministers Conference initiated a separation between faith and political life that has harmed our national discourse ever since. First, Scheck roots Kennedy's speech in its historical circumstances of political anti-Catholicism, explaining that the setting and the denominational divisions of the times cannot be forgotten in interpreting Kennedy's words, while at the same time criticizing Kennedy for downplaying "faith's imprint on conscience." He next analyzes the assertion that we have always been a religious nation and should remain so, despite the opposition of an alleged militant secularism. Finally, using St. Thomas Aquinas and Pope Benedict XVI's recent encyclical *Caritas in Veritate* as his guides, Schneck arrives at a relationship between faith and politics in which each properly informs the other.

In "How Would Jesus Vote? or, the Politics of God's Reign," Dr. Terrence W. Tilley writes that Christians are obliged to consider political issues, such as how they vote, in the light of their religious beliefs. How does this get done when we are told that Christians cannot vote for certain politicians because of their position on school vouchers, the legality of abortion, same-sex marriage, or the use of military force. In answering this question, Dr. Tilley looks at two diverse approaches, the confrontational, countercultural approach and an approach favoring engagement and communication. In considering the countercultural approach, Dr. Tilley argues that we are a diverse nation, not just inter-religiously, but intra-religiously, noting that the Catholic Church comes in many flavors in the United States and that the ways of "being church" vary by location. Because we are so diverse, the confrontational approach will have dubious effects. Diversity demands engagement and communication. Dr. Tilley points out that reconciling practices have been, from the start, at the heart of the Jesus movement, and that the most effective form of communication is, as the early Church knew, personal witness. In deciding how to vote as Christians, Dr. Tilley suggests that these reconciling values are the ones we should reinforce.

It is my hope that you will enjoy reading and contemplating this volume as much as I did in editing it. The authors are committed to the notion that our faith has much to offer to our politics and that we should embrace, and not be paralyzed by, that possibility.

ONE

Voting and Holiness

Nicholas P. Cafardi

When Mother Teresa won the Nobel Peace Prize, a reporter, cameras rolling, asked her if she was a holy person. She looked right at him and said, "It's my job to be holy. It's your job to be holy, too. Why do you think God put us on this earth?" I belong to what was probably the last generation to be taught from the Baltimore Catechism, and the lines drilled into my memory by the good Sisters of Mercy linger still: "Why did God make you? He made me to know Him, to love Him and to serve Him, in this world and to be happy with Him in the next."

It is our job to be holy, to be holy in everything that we do, including when we vote. These are the two ideas that I want to explore in this essay: holiness and voting. How can we be holy when we vote? How can we transcend this world (which is what holiness calls for) and at the same time be a part, immanent in this world (which is what voting is all about)? We know we can do it, be both transcendent and immanent, because our faith teaches that the Lord whom we worship is himself both a transcendent God and an incarnate human.

Most of the time when we vote in America, we are voting on candidates for public office. There is a choice between two, sometimes more, candidates. Sometimes we vote in a referendum, in which one very specific issue is on the ballot for voter approval: we want a new sales tax or not; we want to issue public bonds to build a new sports arena or not; we want to revise our state constitution to say something or not. Those are one-issue votes, and their moral value is more susceptible to discernment than when we are voting in elections for public office.

When we choose one candidate over another, which is by far the more common kind of voting, it is unlikely that we are making our decision based on just one reason or one issue. I suppose it is possible that a voter could say, "I am voting for X because . . ." and then go on to cite only one reason, but normally the basis on which we choose one candidate over another is multifaceted, just as life is multifaceted. We weigh the candidates against each other, agreeing with some of the candidates' positions, perhaps not agreeing on others, but preferring one candidate over another on a basis of weighing complex alternatives.

Our bishops speak in *Forming Consciences for Faithful Citizenship*, their guide to Catholic participation in the political process, of the one-issue voter. They say, in no. 34, that "a Catholic cannot vote for a candidate who takes a position in favor of an intrinsic evil, such as abortion or racism, if the voter's intent is to support that position. In such cases, a Catholic would be guilty of formal cooperation in grave evil."[1]

If you grant this premise, that a candidate takes a position in favor of outright evil, and that the only reason a particular Catholic voter chooses that candidate is in order to advance that evil, then the bishops' conclusion follows as well. The Catholic voter has done something terribly wrong. But how likely are those facts—that a voter chooses to vote for a candidate for one reason and one reason only and that that reason is an evil one? Human nature is hardly ever that simple.

In their defense, the bishops do say in that same document, *Forming Consciences for Faithful Citizenship*, no. 42, that Catholics should not be one-issue voters when they are weighing candidates, one against another.

This essay is about the more typical kind of voting that we do, not single issue referendums, but votes in which we are choosing one candidate over another. When we are weighing alternatives, when we are conducting a deliberative process informed by our Catholic faith and values, when we are weighing the good positions of one candidate against those of another, the bad positions of a candidate against those of another, in such a moral calculus how can we be holy? How can we pursue the purpose of our existence, placed in us by our Creator?

So that's voting. What does it mean to be holy? We know Jesus' answer: "Love the Lord your God with your whole heart, your whole soul, and your whole mind; and love your neighbor as yourself" (Mark 12:30–32). I have always been struck by how the Lord defines holiness in terms of love. And if you want to be holier still, "Sell all your goods, give the money to the poor and come follow me" (Mark 10:21). This is love in the extreme, completely selfless love.

That last part is tough. Not too many of us chose to divest ourselves of all worldly goods in order to pursue holiness. But some people do, some very admirable people do, the men and women in religious life, and in doing so, they are imitating the Lord who was offered all the kingdoms of this world by Satan—and turned the devil down.

On a very basic level, we know that holiness requires the imitation of Christ, every day, day in, day out. What is the mind and heart of Jesus, and what does it require me to do in these circumstances? That prayerful conversation with Jesus is so very essential to holiness. We must seek to imitate Christ in the circumstances by "reflecting on faith from the historical present and reflecting on the historical present from faith."[2]

I am going to hazard a number of propositions that I think holiness requires in the voting process, examples drawn from the Gospel stories of Jesus, because holiness requires that we should do as he would do. These are not the only propositions, but they are the ones that have affected me personally.

1. HOLINESS DOES NOT ASSUME WE HAVE INSTANT ANSWERS TO COMPLEX POLITICAL QUESTIONS

Not that complex issues should paralyze us or lead us to believe that every answer is equally correct, but we do have to strive to be holy in discerning those answers. Holiness requires us to inform our consciences in weighing complex political choices. As our bishops have said, "Conscience is the voice of God resounding in the human heart, revealing the truth to us and calling us to do what is good while shunning what is evil."[3] Or, as stated in the *Catechism of the Catholic Church*, "Conscience is a judgment of reason whereby the human person recognizes the moral quality of a concrete act. In all he says and does, man is obliged to follow faithfully what he knows to be just and right."[4]

So consciences must be informed. Untethered feelings are not conscience. Conscience is based on truth: the Scripture, the Church's traditions and teachings, the guidance of the Holy Spirit. We are obliged to apply all of these to moral choices such as voting.

Because holiness is not a matter of readily apparent answers to complex political questions, we cannot use our Church as a political answer machine. When the scribes and the Pharisees tried to trick Jesus into getting involved in a political debate about Roman power, to which there was no good answer, he refused to get involved. He refused to give a specific answer. Instead, he said, "Render to Caesar what is Caesar's; and to God, what is God's" (Mark 12:17).

We need to learn from this because when our Church has tried to act like a political answer machine—when it has acted more like Caesar than Christ—the consequences have led us away from holiness, away from the imitation of Christ. We do not have to go very far back in history to find some tragic examples of this. Pius IX asserted in the 1864 Syllabus of Errors that it violated the natural law to teach that "the Roman Pontiff can, and ought to, reconcile himself, and come to terms with progress, liberalism, and modern civilization."[5] In the twentieth century, in 1933, the Vatican signed a concordat with Nazi Germany in which it acquiesced to the disbanding of the German Catholic Center Party, the only viable political opposition to a complete Nazi dictatorship.[6] And more recently, in Latin America, it was the Vatican's choice to dismantle liberation theology, thus maintaining the Church's century-old connection with the aging political power structures of those countries.[7] This was a political answer by the Church whose repercussions were felt by the Jesuit and Maryknoll martyrs of El Salvador. They were, in effect, abandoned by their Church, which appeared to be choosing one political side over another in the El Salvador conflict. Is it any surprise that their enemies thought that these men and women religious were vulnerable, that the Church would not defend them?

The Church has to preach, even when that preaching has a political aspect to it, as so many moral issues today do. But in holiness, our pastors, when they speak to the morality of an issue, should not choose political sides. The perception of political partisanship on the part of the Church is destructive of holiness. The Church must leave the political answer—the how of solving political problems, even when those political problems have a moral component—to the informed consciences of the laity. Political strategy is not a question of holiness, or even of faith. It is a question of effective political means, not ends, and the Church is not a political answer machine.

2. HOLINESS DOES NOT LET US DEMONIZE THE OTHER

Holiness does not demonize those candidates we do not like, those people on the other side of a political issue with whom we disagree. Yes, I know, I am talking about the man who occasionally called his opponents "whitened sepulchers" (Matt. 23–27), and some other choice phrases, but he had to be extremely agitated to do that. It was not the normal way of the Lord, who said more than once, "Love your enemies and pray for those who persecute you" (Matt. 5:44), who is "humble, patient and loving, who suggests but does not demand, who remains nailed to the cross even when we tell him to come down."[8]

In this regard, I think that holiness should lead us to question the tactic of condemnatory labels that are sometimes used in the political process. There is one label that I find particularly troubling. I don't know anyone who is "pro-abortion," that is, someone who thinks abortions are a good in themselves and ought to be pursued as a value of our society. On the other hand, I do know some people who, while they consider every abortion a tragedy, do not favor criminalizing abortions in general, putting doctors, nurses, and perhaps even mothers, in jail. That makes them pro-choice, not pro-abortion. I have never heard anyone suggest that women should become pregnant so that they can help them kill their unborn child. That's what the word "pro-abortion" means. It is an ugly word and it should be used only in situations where it truly applies.

As believing Catholics, it may be difficult for us to accept that there are people who do not agree with our Church's teaching that abortion is wrong in every instance, with no exceptions. But those people who disagree with us on this issue are not, by that fact, pro-abortion. And demonizing them with the "pro-abortion" label is not holiness. The use of such inexact, deprecating terms coarsens the political dialogue and creates situations where, in the minds of some, it becomes acceptable to do things like carry guns to political rallies or even kill those who disagree with us, because, after all, they are "pro-aborts," they favor killing the unborn, so what could their own lives be worth? Jesus would weep. Recall that he specifically said, "God sent his Son into the world, not to condemn the world, but that through him the world might be saved" (John 3:17).

3. HOLINESS DOES NOT MISUSE THE LORD IN THE EUCHARIST AS A WEAPON

Not the Lord who said, "I am meek and humble of heart" (Matt. 11:29), not the Lord who said, "I desire mercy, not sacrifice, for I have come to call not the righteous but sinners" (Matt. 9:13). Politics in the American Catholic community has taken the form of what has cynically been called the "Communion wars." An archbishop of a major Midwestern see said during the 2004 presidential campaign that if John Kerry came to his archdiocese to campaign, he could not receive Communion there because he was not sufficiently anti-abortion. The same thing happened again in the 2008 election, only the target then was the Catholic vice-presidential candidate, Senator Joe Biden.

A bishop is well within his rights to challenge the actions of his ecclesiastical subjects, the Catholics who live in his diocese. There is no doubt about that. He is their proper pastor, and that is his duty. I would suggest that both justice and charity require that such challenges should not be part of the public discourse, but should occur in private. While canon 915, the canon that deals with admission to Communion, is not pristinely clear in such situations, canon 220 is very clear.[9] Under canon 220, all baptized persons have the right to their good name and to their privacy. The condition of people's souls should not be publicly discussed by their sacred pastors.

And a distant bishop has no right to call out another bishop's ecclesiastical subject—that is, someone who lives in another diocese—and say, "If that person comes to my town, he or she better not come to me for Communion." Why doesn't he have this right? First of all, because jurisdiction in the Catholic Church is territorial. That politician has a proper pastor and proper bishop back in his or her home diocese. The politician is their ecclesiastical subject, not the ecclesiastical subject of the overreaching bishop in a remote city where the politician may or may not visit, where the politician may or may not go to Mass, where the politician may or may not attempt to receive Communion.

I don't know what to call this other than "overreaching." This remote bishop is making a judgment he has no right to make. If he wants to deny Communion in his diocese to a campaigning politician who is not from his diocese, he needs to follow the rules. The rules are that he must first contact that person's proper pastor and determine whether it is that pastor's determination that the politician is disqualified from receiving Communion. And that's whose judgment it is—the person's proper pastor, not the bishop of the remote diocese who wishes to see his name in the papers.

And the grounds for disqualification, according to canon 915, are that the politician "obstinately persist in manifest, grave sin."[10] Because canon 915 is restrictive of rights granted elsewhere in the Code of Canon Law—in this case, canon 912, which says that "any baptized person not prohibited by law can and must be admitted to holy Communion"— it must be given its most restrictive interpretation.[11] Let's take the requirements apart. "Obstinately persist" means knowing it's wrong and doing it anyway with consistency. "Manifest grave sin" means a sin that is public (manifest) and of sufficient seriousness as to sever the Catholic's relationship with God (grave).

Abortion rights in the United States exist by fiat of the U.S. Supreme Court and not by legislative or executive action. The only way abortion issues come before legislatures and the executive today is in abortion control legislation or abortion funding legislation. Does voting for abortion funding legislation constitute "obstinately persisting in manifest grave sin"? One vote is not obstinacy; a single act is not obstinate. Perhaps if the legislator were to consistently do so, it could be considered obstinate. But is such a vote a "manifest grave sin"? What if the measure were simply one item in a state budget of a thousand items that also funded many other social goods—unemployment insurance, assistance for poor families, medical insurance for those without— which is typically how the state budgets its money? Our own bishops have regretfully accepted the language of the Hyde Amendment, which, while preventing federal funding of abortion in most situations, does allow such funding for abortions to save the life of the mother and in cases of rape and incest.[12] Can a Catholic legislator look at this example and say, "If the bishops can endure some evil to achieve a greater good, then I can accept some evil in this budget bill to achieve a greater good"?

What about failing to vote for abortion control legislation? Is this manifest grave sin? If a governor vetoes an abortion control bill passed by the state legislature—is that manifest grave sin? What if the legislator who votes against it or the governor who vetoes it believes that such legislation imposes the type of "undue burden" on abortion rights that is prohibited by the U.S. Constitution according to our Supreme Court? In other words, the vote against it or the veto of it is not because the politician disagrees with the idea of abortion control, but believes that this embodiment of it is ineffective, and will involve the state in spending tight tax dollars defending a law that it is bound to be overturned by the courts, given the framework the U.S. Supreme Court has placed on such laws? This is what happens when we try to apply absolute moral principles to the messiness of human politics. The principles are clear; the application not so.

One bishop I know, in a diocese where Senator Kerry was a frequent visitor during the 2004 campaign, refused to tell the senator, "Don't show up for Communion in my diocese." When I asked him why, he told me that he disagreed with the fundamental premise, that it was far from clear to him that legislators who failed to vote for abortion control laws were in manifest grave sin, and so the conditions of canon 915 were not even met.

We saw another sad example of ecclesiastical misbehavior with the funeral of Senator Ted Kennedy. He was buried with a Catholic requiem Mass, the cardinal archbishop of Boston, Sean O'Malley, presiding. The cardinal was severely criticized for this by some, including at least one American archbishop now assigned to Rome. The criticism was that Senator Kennedy was unworthy of a Catholic funeral because he failed to fight the abortion wars. Cardinal O'Malley defended himself quite well on his blog, but any canonist knows that the conditions of canon 1184 on the denial of a church funeral are not met if the deceased person gave some sign of repentance before death.[13] Let's assume for the sake of argument that Senator Kennedy was a manifest sinner because of his opposition to abortion control laws, an assumption that is far from clear, as my bishop friend noted. As long as Senator Kennedy's proper pastor had decided that he had repented—and this did not have to be a public repentance because private final confession to a priest suffices—then the objections by other bishops are moot. Those with jurisdiction have spoken. And those who speak without jurisdiction do great harm to the Church.

4. HOLINESS DOES NOT ALLOW ITSELF TO BE USED AS A POLITICAL OR ELECTORAL TOOL

After the last presidential election, we heard some priests and bishops say that persons who had voted for one candidate had to go to confession before presenting themselves at the Communion rail. Even during the 2008 campaign, I heard reports—and these were from people who I know to be credible, including a priest and a woman in religious life—that some priests were asking persons in the confessional how they planned to vote for president. This kind of conduct is unprecedented, at least in the United States. It recalls the in-house holy men, the court prophets of King Ahab, whom the true prophet of the Lord, Micaiah, condemned in First Kings (22:23).

During the Italian elections of 1948, when it seemed like the communists were about to take power democratically, Italian priests made similar requests in the confessional, and Pius XII even said that he would excommunicate Catholics who voted for communist candidates in that election.[14]

Italy has come a long way since then, and perhaps we can learn from its example. In Italy, abortion has been legal since 1978. Their law is not as permissive as the mandates of *Roe v. Wade*. It allows unrestricted abortions only through the first ninety days of pregnancy; abortions are paid for with tax dollars because medicine is socialized in Italy. In 1981, at the impetus of Pope John Paul II, Italy had a national referendum to overturn this law. That was a one-issue vote, the kind I described earlier with a clear moral component. But the referendum lost by more than two to one. Sixty-eight percent of all the people voting—and the majority of those would self-identify as Catholics—did not want to abolish Italy's law on legalized abortions.[15]

There were national elections in Italy in April of 2008, seven months before our own 2008 elections. One enterprising Italian politician, Giuliano Ferrara, sought to revive the abortion issue, and he created what he called a pro-life list of candidates for parliament in the 2008 Italian national elections. He presented his pro-life list to the Italian bishops conference for their endorsement, and they turned him down. They said that "beyond his noble intentions, the end of such a ploy would be to mistakenly inject a moral theme into the electoral competition." They also said that his list carried "a serious risk of extremization, and of ghettoization, of one part of the Catholic world on such a delicate matter."[16]

I should note that when Italians speak of ghettoization, they are not speaking of the racial discrimination that disfigures so many American cities. They are speaking of the prior errors of the Church in Italy that forced people of a different faith, Italian Jews, to live in squalor and poverty in walled-off sections of Italian cities for centuries. It was a terrible sin committed by the Church, not to be repeated or forgotten.

The Italian bishops knew that they were being used, that the Church was being used, as a political tool in the national elections, and they refused to participate. And their choice of the word "ghettoization" is telling. Focusing on one moral issue to the exclusion of all other moral issues results in ghettoization. Insisting that your moral view, and only your moral view, is binding on all others results in ghettoization. And ghettoization on moral issues is ineffective. The larger society has to be engaged on these issues; it has to be converted, not condemned.

"The new heaven and the new earth promised by Christ will not come about by cutting ourselves off from the rest of the world, by forming Catholic ghettos" where certain people and certain ideas are not welcome. "It will not unfold through the triumph of ecclesiastical power. It will come about only as we follow the footsteps of the crucified one, descending into the darkness of this world, and rising in the transcendent power of love."[17] The Italian bishops knew that electoral lists of Church-approved candidates would not accomplish that. As I said, holiness does not allow itself to become a political tool.

But in the United States, holiness—"I am a better Catholic than you" or "I follow the Church's teachings more faithfully than you do"—has become a political tool. There is a website now where Catholics can sign petitions against named Catholic elected officials asking that a politician's bishop declare the politician ineligible to receive the Eucharist. At least they got that last part right: the petition is directed to the politician's proper pastor. But I think that everything else about such a tactic is mistaken and in violation of canon 220, which I have already cited, guaranteeing all baptized persons a right to privacy and to their good name.

Holiness does not seek to control others. We cannot take away free will, the rights of conscience. We can seek to persuade people, to convince them; but holiness does not disrespect the religious and civil liberties of others. Our church used to teach that error had no rights, and, as a philosophical proposition, that may still be true today in the abstract. But in the concrete it is not. "Persons in error, consciences in error, do have rights," rights that Catholics, especially Catholics seeking to be holy in the political process, cannot ignore.[18] In doubt, we bring faith, not coercion. And we bring faith, primarily by example, by our respect for those who disagree with us, who do not share our faith or our values or our conclusions. "Truth can only be proposed. It cannot be imposed without violating the sanctity of the individual person and subverting the truth itself."[19]

This is the classic dilemma for American Catholics. "We are committed, on one hand, to religious principles that we hold to be absolute truths. But, on the other hand, we are also committed to the U.S. Constitution, which not only guarantees our freedom to hold and practice these beliefs, but also guarantees to others the right to disagree with those beliefs."[20]

So to sum up, holiness does not lead us to think that there are easy or readily apparent answers to complex political issues; it does not make our Church into a political answer machine; it does not demonize the other; it does not use the Lord as a weapon; it does not let itself become a tool, used to control others.

How does all this play out in voting? Let me use myself as an illustration—not as a moral paragon but as a committed Catholic trying to be holy in the political process. There were a number of issues in the 2008 national elections that I considered to be very important: the war in Iraq, whether it was just or not, whether it should be continued; the condition of the poor and homeless both in the United States and in Iraq, where the war had made four million people homeless; the need for adequate health care for everyone in our country; the burning concerns of the unemployed in America; the deteriorating financial situation and the lack of adequate regulations on financial profiteers. And especially the life issues.

When I weighed these concerns in the 2008 election, the protection of human life, in all of its aspects, was the most important issue. As a believing Catholic, I would very much like to end the evil of abortion. But on a strategic level, I happen to think that a coercive law is not the best way to achieve this. Coercive laws work very poorly in curbing social evils, as our legal system's complete lack of success with alcohol and drug control laws demonstrates. This will be even more the case with abortion control laws now that abortions can be done at home with pills and not in abortion clinics.

There was an article in the *New York Times* two years ago that described how having an abortion was truly looked down on by the people of the Dominican immigrant community in New York, as one would hope, given the overwhelming Catholicism of the Dominican people. So instead of going to an abortion clinic, Dominican women who are pregnant but who secretly do not wish the child to be born go to a neighborhood pharmacy and ask for something "to bring down my period." The pharmacist, understanding this code language, gives them five pills of misoprostol, an ulcer medication, known to cause spontaneous abortions when taken in that dose.[21]

How does the law possibly stop that? Do we make a law against ulcer medicines? Now one could say that it does not matter if the law will be unenforceable or if it will be ignored. It is still the law, and the law has an undeniable didactic value. Our law should teach the value of human life by prohibiting all abortions. But it is still good Catholic legal philosophy that writing unenforceable laws causes people to ignore all laws, and that unenforceable laws can subvert the entire legal system.[22]

When I wrote in 2008 that I believed we Catholics had lost the legal battle to stop abortion, I was pretty roundly criticized, at least by my political opponents, but this is what I was talking about. I did not mean to imply that we should stop pursuing the moral battle against abortion. That battle should be pursued until victory. We should never give up trying to change the hearts and minds of our co-citizens on this issue. Imagine if we could do that through our example, our kindness, our charity, our lack of shrillness, and our lack of condemnations. Then it would not matter if abortion were legal or not, because we Catholics, through the conversion of our neighbors' hearts and minds, would have made abortion, not unlawful, but unthinkable and unacceptable. "See these Christians, how they love and care for one another!"[23] How very far the current rhetoric is from that.

In my 2008 essay, I also did not accept that the best way to prevent abortions is to overturn *Roe v. Wade*,[24] which is the consistent position of one political party and, evidently, of our bishops. Keep us in power, these folks say, until we can get another Justice on the U.S. Supreme Court who thinks like us. Then we will have the elusive fifth vote to overturn *Roe*.

There are two problems with this. First, overturning *Roe* will not make abortions illegal. Let's look at history. There was never a time when abortions were completely illegal in the United States. Before *Roe v. Wade*, abortions for psychological reasons, the classic "health of the mother," were available in about a fourth of the states.[25] So there is no abortion-free, pre-*Roe* world to return to. But suppose that a Justice who is specifically dedicated to overturning *Roe* reaches the U.S. Supreme Court, what would be accomplished if the elusive fifth vote were garnered and *Roe* were overturned?

Quite simply, the matter would be left to the individual states—where it was before *Roe*. And what would that mean? Overturning *Roe* would not abolish abortion. Read the survey data, even among people who say that they are Catholic. There is no societal consensus for banning all abortions. According to every poll that I have ever seen, the majority of Americans want to see exceptions for the life and health of the mother, for incest, and for rape.[26] Now that is not the teaching of our Church, which admits no exceptions, and I faithfully accept that teaching, but our Church has not done a good job of convincing the larger society, not to mention all Catholics, of the correctness of our position.

So, without *Roe*, where would the United States be on abortion? It would be highly regulated in some states and less regulated in others, depending on the political climate in each state and what the state legislature could be persuaded to do. And the number of abortions in the United States would not change one bit as long as interstate travel was still possible.

And the second problem with this "fifth Justice" strategy is that this same U.S. Supreme Court, while waiting for that hypothetical abortion case in order to overturn *Roe*, is deciding actual cases in the meantime, cases that, by my lights at least, do great violence to other aspects of Catholic social justice teaching.

How can Catholics, or any religious person, ignore the fact that the author of the U.S. Supreme Court decision that has done the most harm to religious groups in the United States in recent years, *Employment Division v. Smith*,[27] is the great anti-abortion Justice Scalia? Prior to the *Smith* case, religious people were protected from state laws that adversely impacted the practice of their faith by the "compelling state interest" test. That test required the government to demonstrate a compelling interest, a reasonably high burden, before it could enforce laws that adversely impacted individuals in the practice of their religion.[28] That protection, after the *Smith* case, written by Justice Scalia, is gone, although Congress did try to patch it up with the Religious Freedom Restoration Act.[29]

Or that the Supreme Court did great harm to women's rights in the *Ledbetter* case.[30] This opinion limited the recovery period for discriminatory acts only to those acts occurring within 180 days of when the complainant filed the charge, thus wiping out the possibility of back pay recovery for all but the last six months of the woman's employment, even though she may have been receiving a discriminatory pay rate, as compared to male employees, for years. Congress had to correct this decision with a new law after the 2008 elections.[31]

Or that this Supreme Court failed to protect minority voters' rights when it upheld Indiana's restrictive voter identification law in the *Crawford* case?[32] That result was later undone by the Indiana state superior court[33] but is now under state supreme court review. Ironically, the first persons turned away from the polls in Indiana because they lacked adequate identification were a group of older Roman Catholic nuns who did not have driver's licenses.

Or that this Court in the case of *Davis v. Federal Election Commission* did great damage to the electoral process itself by voiding campaign spending laws that prevented wealthy persons from using huge amounts of their own riches to fund their own personal electoral campaigns?[34] After the *Davis* decision, the super-rich can basically buy elective office with their personal wealth by freely spending on ads and other promotions that bury or drown out their opponents. Or that the same Court in *Citizens United v. Federal Election Commission* has done even greater damage to a fair electoral process by permitting corporations to deploy their great wealth, without limits, in our elections?[35]

Or that, with its new and expansive interpretation of the Second Amendment in *District of Columbia v. Heller*, on the right to bear arms, this Court has made it practically impossible to stop the murder epidemic in our nation's capital by striking down as unconstitutional Washington D.C.'s gun control ordinance?[36] And that the same Court in the case of *McDonald v. Chicago* has extended this precedent to all the states, thus guaranteeing that forever forward thousands of people a year will be murdered or commit suicide with guns in the United States?[37]

And none of this is to mention the same Court's consistent upholding of the death penalty in all but the most egregious circumstances. Astonishing though it may seem, Justice Scalia is on record in the *Herrera v. Collins* case saying that the U.S. Supreme Court has "*never* held that the Constitution forbids the execution of a convicted defendant who has had a full and fair trial but is later able to convince a habeas court that he is 'actually' innocent."[38] In other words, mere factual innocence is no reason not to carry out a death sentence properly reached. This, from the great protector of unborn human life. What about born human life?

Waiting for the fifth vote against *Roe* on this Court and keeping one particular political party in power, indefinitely, in order to get that fifth vote, is too great a price to pay in justice and in holiness for far too uncertain a promise.

So if a coercive law is not the answer to the scourge of abortion, what is? Let me tell you a "parable" from my own life. After our first son was born, my wife and I invited my parents to dinner at our apartment. We were running behind schedule. My parents got there early, a lot early, in order to spend as much time as possible with their first grandchild. My wife, who worked full time as a physician, was a wreck in the kitchen. I was holding a three-month-old who was colicky and would not stop crying. I was exasperated. My wife was exasperated. I said something stupid; my wife said something stupid; and then I said something mean. My father, who was my hero, put his little finger out for my son, Chris, to grab, and Chris did, clasping the fingers of his small hand around his granddad's finger, the way babies instinctively do. My dad leaned over and whispered to me: "Do you love your son?" I said, of course. He replied, "Then you need to take care of his mother."

That parable points out the best way to deal with the evil of abortion. If we love that unborn child, as we profess to, then we have an obligation to take care of the child's mother. If we want a legal solution to abortion, those kinds of laws work, laws that provide medical care for pregnant women and support for those women with children. We know they work—not in America, because we have barely tried these kinds of laws—but in other advanced countries, primarily in Western Europe, where the law mandates a stronger social safety net, where pregnant women and their children, preborn and following birth, get health care and maintenance income from the state. In those countries, the abortion rate is much lower than it is in the United States.

So let me suggest that, if we are serious about ending abortions, we need, in justice and holiness, to take care of the mother and the child. We need to put our resources where our preaching is; as the Lord said, where your treasure is, there your heart is also. One political party proposed this kind of an attack on abortions, not "Help us stay in power in order to get *Roe* reversed" but rather, "Let's take legal steps now to care for that mother and child."

As a committed Catholic, was I allowed, according to long-established principles of Catholic ethics, to make that prudential judgment, to give preference to the legal approach that I thought would work over one that I knew would not, and vote accordingly? I am sure that I was. Was I allowed, according to the same long-established principles of Catholic ethics, to consider as social justice issues what I thought would be the disastrous consequences of the "fifth Justice" strategy on other aspects of American law? I am sure that I was.

Our bishops are very clear in *Forming Consciences for Faithful Citizenship* that the evil of abortion outweighs every other evil. I had honestly wrestled with this question and decided that neither party had the perfect approach to abortion, but one approach was more likely to work more effectively and more quickly, without any disastrous side effects, than the other. Once I got to that point, then all the other factors weighed in: the wars; the financial meltdown; the need to care for the poor, the powerless, the unemployed; the need for universal health care. At that point, the choice was self-evident, at least to me. And I made that choice with an informed conscience, honoring everything that my Church teaches.

Where does that bring us? To my final proposition.

5. THE WORLD IS IMPERFECT AND IMPERFECTABLE

The kingdom is here and not yet here. The transcendent interacts with the immanent, but the immanent endures. Holiness understands this and puts up with it. This is perhaps the devil's greatest tool. He has brought us to a place in our politics where the only choice is a Hobson's choice, where no matter what we do, it is not right. We either participate in a political process that allows wrong choices, some might even say immoral choices, or we withdraw from our democracy. Trying to control someone with a morality they do not perceive is not holiness. It certainly is not reflective of the Lord who "summons and asks but does not impose himself,"[39] the Lord who said, "Take the log out of your eye before you tell your brother to remove the splinter from his" (Matt. 7:3).

Human freedom, given to us by our Creator, is the proper intermediary of holiness. So in the final analysis holiness in the political process endures acts that are wrong or maybe even evil, because to do otherwise means that we violate the consciences and the God-given freedom of others.

There is a scene from *A Man for All Seasons* in which St. Thomas More is arguing with his son-in-law, William Roper, his wife, Alice, and his daughter, Margaret, who want him to arrest Richard Rich, the king's spy whose perjured testimony will eventually condemn More to death.

ROPER	Arrest him.
ALICE	Yes!
MORE	For what?
ALICE	He's dangerous!
ROPER	For libel; he's a spy.
ALICE	He is! Arrest him!
MARGARET	Father, that man's bad.
MORE	There is no law against that.
ROPER	There is! God's law!
MORE	Then God can arrest him.
ROPER	Sophistication upon sophistication!
MORE	No, sheer simplicity. The law, Roper, the law. I know what's legal, not what's right. And I'll stick to what's legal.
ROPER	Then you set man's law above God's!
MORE	No, far below; but let me draw your attention to a fact—I'm *not* God. The currents and eddies of right and wrong, which you find such plain sailing, I can't navigate. I'm no voyager. But in the thickets of the law, oh, there I'm a forester. I doubt if there's a man alive who could follow me there, thank God . . . *(He says this last to himself)*
ALICE	*(Exasperated, pointing after RICH)* While you talk, he's gone!
MORE	And go he should, if he was the Devil himself, until he broke the law!
ROPER	So now you'd give the Devil benefit of law!
MORE	Yes. What would you do? Cut a great road through the law to get after the Devil?
ROPER	I'd cut down every law in England to do that!

MORE	*(Roused and excited)* Oh? *(Advances on* ROPER*)* And when the last law was down, and the Devil turned round on you—where would you hide, Roper, the laws all being flat? *(He leaves him)* This country's planted thick with laws from coast to coast—man's laws, not God's—and if you cut them down—and you're just the man to do it—d'you really think you could stand upright in the winds that would blow then? *(Quietly)* Yes, I'd give the Devil benefit of law, for my own safety's sake.
ROPER	I have long suspected this, this is the golden calf; the law's your god.
MORE	*(Wearily)* Oh, Roper, you're a fool, God's my god. . . . *(Rather bitterly)* But I find him rather too *(Very bitterly)* subtle . . .[40]

So goes *A Man for All Seasons*. I am not sure if that is all St. Thomas More or rather the imagination of Robert Bolt, who wrote the play. Bolt did base the play heavily on More's letters.

But it makes my point. The Lord is subtle. Be wary of anyone who tells you that he knows exactly what God wants you to do. Revelation ended when the last apostle died. Our sacred pastors can tell us the ethical and moral principles that should govern human behavior; they can tell us the values that should be defended; and we must learn from them on these matters in order to inform our own consciences. We also have an obligation to look at Scripture, the teachings and traditions of the Church, the people of God, over the centuries. And we need to pray, to ask the Spirit for guidance. None of this can be dodged. You cannot be holy in voting and fail to do these things.

But once your conscience is properly formed, then I would paraphrase St. Augustine, who said, "Love and do what you will"[41] and say (keeping in mind that "love" means to be holy):

"Love and vote how you will."

QUESTIONS FOR FURTHER REFLECTION

1. What does it mean in today's context to "Render to Caesar what is Caesar's and render to God what is God's"?

2. When our sacred pastors are speaking of a moral issue and that issue has a political component to it, can they help but choose a political side? Would such a choice make their moral teaching any less true? Would it make their moral teaching any less effective?

3. How does the author define what it means to be holy in the political process? Which parts of his definition do you agree with? Which parts would you throw out? What would you add?

4. How in my life can I become more holy in voting? By what standard would I make that judgment?

5. If, as the author says, one vote by a legislator in favor of abortion rights does not qualify as "obstinately persisting in manifest, grave sin," how many votes does it take? What if, without even voting in the legislature, the legislator simply campaigns as "pro-choice"? Is that obstinately persisting in manifest grave sin?

6. If a legislator votes for a bill that restricts abortion rights but that also cuts public funds for aid to poor mothers or poor families with children, has she or he performed a morally defensible act?

7. What if the situation were reversed and the legislator voted for a bill that failed to prevent abortions but that also provided public funds for aid to poor mothers or poor families with children, has she or he performed a morally defensible act?

8. Is seeking to gain control of others through "holiness" ever sinful?

9. Is it realistic to think that we can prevent abortion through love and kindness? As a society do you think will we ever reach that point?

10. Do you agree that coercive laws are not successful in regulating morally offensive behavior? If not, what harm do such laws do—in other words, why not at least try them?

NOTES

1. *Forming Consciences for Faithful Citizenship: A Call to Political Responsibility from the Catholic Bishops of the United States* (Washington, DC: United States Catholic Conference, 2007).

2. Jose Sols Lucia, "The Legacy of Ignacio Ellacuría, Ten Years after Martyrdom," 10. *www/fespinal.com/espinal/lib/en86.pdf.*

3. USCCB, *Forming Consciences for Faithful Citizenship*, November 2007, Section 17.

4. *Catechism of the Catholic Church,* No. 1778.

5. Pius IX, *Iamdum cernimus*, March 18, 1861, Syllabus of Errors, no. 80 in *Dogmatic Canons and Decrees of the Council of Trent and Vatican Council I plus the Decree on the Immaculate Conception and the Syllabus of Errors of Pope Pius IX* (New York: Devin-Adair Company, 1912; republished by Tan Books and Publishers, Rockford, IL, 1977).

6. *Reichskonkordat*, 1933, Articles 31, 32.

7. Congregation for the Doctrine of the Faith, "Instruction on Certain Aspects of Liberation Theology," August 6, 1984.

8. Louis Evely, *The Gospels without Myth* (New York: Doubleday, 1971), 28.

9. Canon 220 of the 1983 Code of Canon law says, "No one is permitted to harm illegitimately the good reputation which a person possesses nor to injure the right of any person to protect his or her own privacy."

10. The text of Canon 915 of the 1983 Code of Canon law reads, "Those upon whom the penalty of excommunication or interdict has been imposed or declared, and others who obstinately persist in manifest grave sin, are not to be admitted to holy Communion."

11. Canon 18 of the 1983 Code says, "Laws which prescribe a penalty, or restrict the free exercise of rights, or contain an exception to the law, are to be interpreted strictly."

12. The current version of the Hyde Amendment, which is Public Law 111–8. H.R. 1105, Division F, Title V, General Provisions, says:

SEC. 507. (a) None of the funds appropriated in this Act, and none of the funds in any trust fund to which funds are appropriated in this Act, shall be expended for any abortion.

(b) None of the funds appropriated in this Act, and none of the funds in any trust fund to which funds are appropriated in this Act, shall be expended for health benefits coverage that includes coverage of abortion.

(c) The term "health benefits coverage" means the package of services covered by a managed care provider or organization pursuant to a contract or other arrangement.

SEC. 508. (a) The limitations established in the preceding section shall not apply to an abortion

(1) if the pregnancy is the result of an act of rape or incest; or

(2) in the case where a woman suffers from a physical disorder, physical injury, or physical illness, including a life-endangering physical condition caused by or arising from the pregnancy itself, that would, as certified by a physician, place the woman in danger of death unless an abortion is performed.

(b) Nothing in the preceding section shall be construed as prohibiting the expenditure by a State, locality, entity, or private person of State, local, or private funds (other than a State's or locality's contribution of Medicaid matching funds).

(c) Nothing in the preceding section shall be construed as restricting the ability of any managed care provider from offering abortion coverage or the ability of a State or locality to contract separately with such a provider for such coverage with State funds (other than a State's or locality's contribution of Medicaid matching funds).

13. Canon 1184 of the 1983 Code of Canon Law says, "Unless they gave some signs of repentance before death, the following must be deprived of ecclesiastical funerals:

1. notorious apostates, heretics, and schismatics;

2. those who chose the cremation of their bodies for reasons contrary to Christian faith;

3. other manifest sinners who cannot be granted ecclesiastical funerals without public scandal of the faithful.

§2. If any doubt occurs, the local ordinary is to be consulted, and his judgment must be followed."

14. The *Osservatore Romano* of July 15, 1948, published a decree that excommunicated those who supported communism. The Italian national elections were held on April 18, 1948, and the Popular Democratic front, a union of the communists and socialists, had received 31 percent of the vote.

15. "One event that has strongly conditioned the pro-life movement in Italy is the 1981 referendum on the abortion law. The referendum, heavily promoted by the church, failed, with only 32 percent of Italians voting to repeal the law" (John Thavis, *Vatican Letter*, October 15, 2004, Catholic News Service).

16. Editorial, Davide Rondini in *L'avvenire* of February 21, 2008. *L'avvenire* is the daily paper of the Italian episcopal conference, known as CEI (Conferenza episcopale italiana).

17. This and the previous quotation in this paragraph are the words of Ilia Delio, OSF, in "Confessions of a Modern Nun," *America*, October 12, 2009.

18. Mary C. Seegers, "Murray, American Pluralism and the Abortion Controversy," in *John Courtney Murray and the American Civil Conversation*, ed. Robert P. Hunt and Kenneth L. Grasso (Grand Rapids: Eerdmans, 1992), 246.

19. Charles J. Chaput, *Render unto Caesar* (New York: Doubleday, 2008), 115.

20. This is a close paraphrase of Thomas P. Ferguson, *Catholic and American: The Political Theology of John Courtney Murray* (Kansas City, MO: Sheed & Ward, 1993), vii.

21. Jennifer Lee and Cara Buckley, "For Privacy's Sake, Taking Risks to End Pregnancy," *New York Times*, January 4, 2009, A15.

22. "To have made the moral argument against abortion, for example, is not necessarily to have made the legal argument as well. St. Thomas Aquinas himself had insisted that if civil laws laid too heavy a burden on the 'multitude of imperfect people,' it would be impossible for such laws to be obeyed and this, in turn, could lead eventually to a disregard for all law. Moreover, unenforceable laws are worse than no laws at all. And without a sufficient consensus within a society, no law is enforceable. Civil laws, therefore, can demand no more than a pluralistic society can agree upon" (Richard McBrien, *National Catholic Reporter*, April 23, 2004).

23. This was a pagan observation about Christians recorded by the second-century Christian author Tertullian.

24. 410 U.S. 113 (1973).

25. Ruth Bader Ginsburg, "Some Thoughts on Autonomy and Equality in Relation to Roe v. Wade," 63 *North Carolina Law Review* 375 (1985).

26. In the Gallup Poll from 2000 on, the percentage of Americans who want to see abortion legal "in certain circumstances," typically taken to be rape, incest, or the life or health of the mother, has consistently surpassed 50 percent. See *www.gallup.com/poll/1576/abortion.aspx*.

27. 494 U.S. 872 (1990). Smith was recently cited by the Supreme Court in *Christian Legal Society v. Martinez*, 130 S. Ct. 2971 (2010) in support of the proposition that the Hastings College of Law, a public law school, had no constitutional obligation to exempt the Christian Legal Society from the school's rule that, in order to get official recognition (and funding), it had to accept anyone as members, and not just those who professed its Christian beliefs.

28. *Sherbert v. Verner*, 374 U.S. 398 (1963).

29. USC §2000bb; but see *City of Boerne v. Flores*, 521 U.S. 507 (1997) in which the U.S. Supreme Court struck down the Religious Freedom Restoration Act as it applies to states and local governments. After Flores, RFRA applies only to the federal government.

30. 550 U.S. 618 (2007).

31. The Lilly Ledbetter Fair Pay Act, 42 USC §2000e–5.

32. *Crawford v. Marion County Election Board*, 515 U.S. 181 (2008).

33. *League of Women Voters of Indiana et al. v. Todd Rokita, Indiana Secretary of State,* 915 N.E. 2d 151 (Ind. App. 2009); recently overturned on standing grounds, but leaving alive as applied challenges, 929 N.E.2d 758 (Ind. Sup. 2010).

34. *Davis v. Federal Election Commission*, 554 U.S. 724, 128 S.Ct. 2759 (2008).

35. 558 U.S.____, 130 S.Ct. 876 (2010).

36. 554 U.S. 570 (2008).

37. 561 U.S.____, 130 S. Ct. 3020 (2010).

38. 506 U.S. 390 (1993) at 427.

39. Evely, *The Gospels without Myth*, 35–36.

40. Robert Bolt, *A Man for All Seasons*, copyright © 1960, 1962 by Robert Bolt. Used by Permission of Random House, Inc.

41. *"Dilige et quod vis fac"* (St. Augustine from the Seventh Sermon on the First Letter of St. John).

TWO

Voting and Living
the Common Good

Lisa Sowle Cahill

Political participation in a democratic society is one of the most important ways in which human beings can fulfill their human dignity, live their vocations as members of society, and contribute to the common good and global justice. Political participation is also a requirement of Catholic social ethics. We are created to be in relationship with God and others, to join with others in care for human life and stewardship of the earth. Though human history is marked by evil and sin, we are also redeemed by Jesus Christ to renew life in community and to serve our neighbors and even our enemies. We are called especially to forgive, to reconcile, and to reach out to those whom society has forgotten or rejected. The modern papal social encyclicals make clear that everyone has social duties and rights and a responsibility to work for justice and the common good.

In his first encyclical, *Deus Caritas Est* (2005), Pope Benedict XVI reminds Catholics of the connection between Gospel values and political participation: "Charity must animate the entire lives of the lay faithful and therefore also their political activity, lived as 'social charity' " (no. 29). In their 2007 guide to Catholic voting, *Forming Consciences for Faithful Citizenship*, the U.S. bishops therefore say, "In the Catholic tradition, responsible citizenship is a virtue, and participation in political life is a moral obligation" (no. 13). The bishops then outline several interdependent issues that define Catholic political responsibility.

Responsibility on these issues does not begin and end with personal conscience, nor is it limited to the voting booth. Responsible political participation is a broad social reality that engages us on many levels and in many spheres. It should be part of our way of life, our relationships, and the communities of which we are a part. It is not enough to vote the common good; we must also live and act the common good, on a number of issues, in a number of ways.

This calls for personal investment, in our local communities, in our churches, and with other partners. It calls for state and federal advocacy for legal and policy changes on issues that we care about, but it also means making a difference in the ways immediately open to us personally, large or small. We can cooperate with and learn from others in the process, even those with different political viewpoints and different practical priorities.

This essay will approach these questions by first taking a look at the 2008 presidential election, the role that Catholics played in it, and the outcome in terms of the national political climate and relations in the church.[1] Then it will look at the broader picture of three issues that were identified as priorities in *Forming Consciences for Faithful Citizenship*: racism, abortion, and global social justice. It is important to seek greater understanding of the issues, of others' views and values, and of what concrete steps will bring greater justice in our society and in the world. One resource is initiatives and programs of the U.S. Catholic bishops, to be evaluated and applied in light of the requirements of justice; the political realities and possibilities; and the insights of other, diverse groups within the church as a whole.

THE 2008 PRESIDENTIAL ELECTION

The 2008 election season was tumultuous, divisive, exhilarating, and historically unique. It yielded the first American president of African ancestry, Democratic candidate Barack Hussein Obama,[2] with the first Catholic vice president Joe Biden. Republican counterparts were John McCain, a decorated war hero, and Sarah Palin, governor of Alaska, potentially the first woman vice president.

Obama's campaign to empower his message at the "grassroots" was massively effective. It registered new African American, Hispanic, and young voters, all of whom strongly favored Obama. Using frequent email appeals, Obama raised over six hundred million dollars from over three million donors. Obama won 53 percent, compared to McCain's 46 percent. Catholics were 54 percent to 45 percent. Yet (non-Hispanic) whites overall favored McCain 55 percent to 43 percent, with a narrower gap among white Catholics—52 percent to 47 percent. This means that Latinos, two-thirds pro-Obama, gained him the Catholic vote. Still, Obama did better with white Catholics than the two previous Democrats (Gore in 2000, Kerry in 2004).[3]

Though U.S. political and legal traditions separate church and state (government cannot establish a religion, nor directly fund religious activities), America is a religious country. Only 6.3 percent of Americans self-identify as "secular" and "unaffiliated" with any religion.[4] Religious leaders and groups are politically active and influential. The religious beliefs of candidates (all Protestant except Biden) were scrutinized by the media and voters. Catholics, a quarter of the electorate, were courted by both parties.

Prioritizing issues like economic equity, education, employment, and health care, Obama summoned all to the common good and galvanized many young voters with his messages of change and hope. McCain also named issues of national importance, issues that resonate with many Catholics. He promised to win the Iraq war, and identified himself as "pro-life," although he does support embryonic stem-cell research. Defense of life is central to Catholic moral tradition; it especially appeals to Catholics for whom "pro-life" serves as a Catholic identity marker.[5]

What did the episcopal leadership in this country have to say about the issues? Since 1975, the national bishops' conference has issued political advisories. In November 2007, it overwhelmingly approved *Forming Consciences for Faithful Citizenship* to guide but not to "tell Catholics for whom or against whom to vote" (nos. 7, 58). It is no secret that the public and the media see abortion as "the" Catholic moral and political issue, followed closely by stem-cell research and gay marriage. According to the bishops, taking innocent life is not "just one issue among many" (no. 28). Still, "other serious threats" including racism, the death penalty, unjust war, hunger, health care, and immigration "are not optional concerns" (no. 29). Abortion is an "intrinsic evil," but "racism" falls in the same category (no. 34), along with genocide, torture, and targeting noncombatants in military conflicts (no. 23). *Forming Consciences for Faithful Citizenship* places all these issues on the table, and calls voters to prudential discernment and "the art of the possible" (John Paul II, *Evangelium Vitae*, no. 73). Catholics must neither advocate intrinsic evil, nor be single-issue voters (no. 34).

In light of the need to consider an array of important issues in making political decisions, members of many faith traditions are trying to figure out better ways to make progress on interconnected aspects of justice. A novel U.S. development is a bipartisan and ecumenical "progressive" coalition combining social justice and ecology with traditional "pro-life" causes. This movement connects through Internet media, public events, and religious activism. A leader here has been the evangelical theologian Jim Wallis, with his organization, website, and magazine called *Sojourners*. Another visible evangelical figure is Rick Warren, author of *The Purpose-Driven Life* and pastor of Saddleback Church in Orange County, California. Warren is pro-life, and has also dedicated his influence and wealth to an attack on global poverty, AIDS, illiteracy, and disease. He hosted a widely televised presidential debate and was chosen by President Obama to offer an invocation at the inauguration.[6]

A surge of Catholic publications and organizations advances a similar "common good" agenda. Leading activists encouraged voters: "There has scarcely been a better opportunity for members of our church who are passionate about the common good to embrace their identity as Catholic Americans, and to help bring the light of our faith's message of justice and dignity to the farthest reaches of our nation and our world."[7] These spokespersons, Chris Korzen and Alexia Kelley, are the authors of *A Nation for All: How the Catholic Vision of the Common Good Can Save America from the Politics of Division*. Kelley and Korzen founded Catholics in Alliance for the Common Good and Catholics United, Catholic political organizations that aim to reach a new audience through the Internet as well as public events such as the Convention for the Common Good held July 2008 in Philadelphia.[8]

Did the election of Obama signal a new politics of social justice? Seventy-one percent of Catholics support policies that "protect the interests of all and promote the common good," compared to 13 percent who focus on abortion and same-sex marriage.[9] Yet Catholic voters did not obviously favor "solidarity" and the preferential option for the poor over their families' welfare, especially economic security and health care.[10] Political participation is crucial to healthy democracy and justice; the election enfranchised oppressed and disillusioned populations. The Gospel mandate to love one's neighbor as oneself remains a challenge, however, in view of competition for economic resources, overt racism, negative stereotyping of Muslims, and constricted interest in foreign policy obligations.

As the campaign went on, it became all too clear that abortion was a very divisive issue among Catholics, despite the apparent effort of *Forming Consciences for Faithful Citizenship* to bring Catholics together under a bigger political tent. Catholics prioritizing poverty, war, health care, immigration, or the environment; or limiting their abortion advocacy to socioeconomic measures, met swift and firm repudiation from some bishops branding Obama unacceptable. Garnering less media attention were bishops insisting on symmetry of issues or stressing "intrinsic evils" like racism. One of the voices in this latter category was Blase Cupich, bishop of Spokane, Washington, then-bishop of Rapid City, South Dakota, who recalled the example of Archbishop Joseph Rummel of New Orleans, who in the 1960s excommunicated critics of Catholic school desegregation. Cupich reiterated the categorization of racism as an intrinsic evil, declaring that to vote against a candidate solely on the basis of race is just as bad as voting for a candidate solely because he or she supports abortion.[11]

In the election controversies, the term "intrinsic evil" was often used as a trump card. But it is obvious even from the fact that both abortion and racism are called intrinsic evils that the term is complex. Political responsibility does not consist in individual decisions alone. *Forming Consciences for Faithful Citizenship*'s paired condemnations of abortion and social sins remind us that all agency is socially embedded, that individuals are responsible for social evil, and that acts are not more "directly" or "intrinsically" evil than practices and institutions.

The precise significance and political implications of this term may not always be easy to tie down.[12] Perhaps "intrinsic evil" is not best understood as a technical term that tells us exactly what to do. It can function as a "prophetic" category. When we call racism or abortion an intrinsic evil we are identifying a social practice against which we must ardently struggle. But this does not mean that there is only one path to the end. It does not exclude the possibility that, in the process, some of our own attitudes and actions, or the institutions in which we participate, will still be burdened by the same evil that we are attempting to eliminate. To call something "intrinsic evil" does not resolve all the moral questions.

In the run-up to the election, some bishops disparaged Democrats, warned Catholics away from Obama, and advised dissenters to refrain from Communion. A few demurred,[13] and many were silent. But bishops were not the sole shapers of Catholic politics. Catholics of every stripe were remarkably active, going beyond academic publications, mainstream media, and Catholic magazines, to produce parish and campus panels, local action committees, websites, and blogs reaching a huge new audience. This too is a healthy development, despite frequently divisive rhetoric.

Obama promised a bipartisan administration. U.S. Catholics deserve a bipartisan Church—for Democrats and Republicans, traditionalists and progressives, and older and younger Catholics uninterested in reliving or reinventing the liberal-conservative hostilities of an earlier era.[14] Obama's April 2008 campaign speech on race was hailed for its honesty, its empathy with fears and grievances of blacks *and* whites, and its call for forgiveness.[15] Catholic ethics and politics should resist the "culture wars," forging a dynamic vision from constructive debate, respectful criticism, practical commitment, and a hermeneutic of generosity toward others' value priorities.

A closer look at three issues may assist toward these goals.

RACISM

Catholics are integrated into the American mainstream, yet Catholic identity is still stamped by nineteenth- and early-twentieth-century immigrant experiences.[16] Some recall or imagine a "vibrant culture of the Catholic

ghetto" existing pre–vatican II.[17] They resent lingering anti-Catholic senti-
ment that immigrant forebears evoked. Waves of new immigrants can be met
with mistrust, fear, and suspicion, especially when economic times are tight
and old ways of life seem under threat.[18] Yet Catholic ethnic enclaves can be
tainted by defensiveness and racism. Catholic calls for justice have not always
been inclusive.[19] During the years of the Second Vatican Council and the civil
rights movement, Catholics were often resistant to integration, including the
nonacceptance of blacks in white immigrant parishes. Here is one illustration.

Misled by their pastors' affirmation and insistence that segregation was not
wrong, many ethnic Catholics in Chicago resisted the admission of African
American Catholics to their parishes and schools. The movement of one single
family into an ethnic Catholic neighborhood or parish was often cause for protest. In such a crowd, one Catholic man was heard to say, "I don't want those
jigs sitting in the same pew with me!' A seventeen-year-old quickly responded
that "those niggers don't join the church anyhow." The phenomena of "changing parishes" and the migration of ethnic Catholics to the suburbs were fueled
by ethnocentrism, economic prosperity, and racism.[20]

The bishops now have a track record in identifying racism as an intolerable
sin, even though that record is not as publicly visible as their record on the so-
called "life" issues. The Council document *Gaudium et Spes* notes that racial
injustice denies equality, rights, and the mutual responsibilities of all human
beings (no. 29). In the 1979 pastoral letter *Brothers and Sisters to Us*, the
U.S. bishops take their strongest stand against racism.[21] Just as *Forming Consciences for Faithful Citizenship* says that taking innocent life is not one issue
among many, so *Brothers and Sisters to Us* says, "Racism is not merely one
sin among many, it is a radical evil that divides the human family and denies
the new creation of a redeemed world." In 1988, the Pontifical Commission for
Justice and Peace released a document called *The Church and Racism*, which
praised *Brothers and Sisters to Us* as "the most important document of the
decade," for speaking out so clearly against racial prejudice, along with racist
political ideologies and racist practices.

Yet racism in fact still shadowed the 2008 campaign, and it is an issue on
which Catholics have had a mixed record. Obama's speech on race urged that
America cannot afford to ignore the issue of race, confronted anger on both
sides, named the racial stalemate in which we find ourselves, and called Americans to bridge the racial divide and "continue on the path of a more perfect
union."

While about 13 percent of Americans are black, only about 3 percent of
Catholics are African American. African Americans may be a minority in
the Catholic Church, but they have a long history behind them and many

contributions.[22] The USCCB subcommittee on African American Affairs connects this group with larger issues, events, and roles in the church, while recognizing the distinct interests and sociocultural attributes of African Americans. It serves the goals of "ministry, evangelization, social justice, [and] worship" for black Catholics.[23] For example, it calls African Americans to rally against abortion and all acts of violence, recognizes and celebrates the St. Peter Claver Society, and announces the curriculum at the Institute for Black Catholic Studies at Xavier University in New Orleans, a historically black Catholic institution. Yet most Catholics would recognize that there is still de facto segregation in most of our parishes and neighborhoods. It is essential that Catholics of all races become aware of and committed on the issue of racial discrimination. White people in particular can have a hard time imagining what it is like for others to live in what is still in reality a "white supremacist society": racial equality receives verbal and legal recognition, but the "normal" and "expected" are defined from a white perspective. Whiteness is the norm, "minorities" are exceptions. Even the title of the bishops' otherwise prophetic letter illustrates the problem of us-them thinking: "Brothers and Sisters to Us." Who is the "Us" and who is thought of as related to "us," but not the main referent of "our" identity?

The USCCB *Cultural Diversity in the Church* website also addresses the roles and needs of Asians and Pacific Islanders, Native Americans, Hispanic or Latino Catholics, and other migrants, immigrants, and refugees. Latinos are perhaps the most important immigrant group from the standpoint of the Church, due to their large and growing numbers and the youthfulness of the Latinos. Hispanics have contributed 71 percent of the growth of the Catholic Church in the United States since 1960. Hispanics account for more than 35 percent of all Catholics in the United States, but more than 50 percent of all Catholics under the age of twenty-five.[24] Because of the youth of the population and new immigration, those rates are likely to rise, despite declines in observance after the first generation, and conversions to evangelical denominations.

The Cultural Diversity in the Church Committee includes the Office for Hispanic Affairs. Hispanic Catholics have traditionally organized themselves through a communitarian, consultative, and inclusive process called "Encuentro," now supported by the national office. Almost 80 percent of all archdioceses have Hispanic ministry coordinating staff; about 20 percent of parishes have Hispanic ministries as well. Many Latinos are recent immigrants, not all of them legally authorized. Most work hard to educate their children and frequently send remittances back to their home countries. It is often a struggle to learn a new language, adapt to a new culture, and find work that supports a family. Like blacks, many Latinos have become American success stories. In

2009 Judge Sonia Sotomayor, of Puerto Rican descent, became the first Latina Supreme Court Justice, rising to the top of U.S. achievement, in good part thanks to her widowed mother's dedication to providing for and educating her two children in New York.

Latinos are the face of tomorrow's Church. The integration and success of this projected Catholic majority is the responsibility of all Catholics. The words of Alejandro Aguilera-Titus, assistant director of the Catholic Bishops' Hispanic Affairs Office, apply to us all: "I invite you to share, with even more generosity, your vision, perspectives, gifts and values in building the reign of God. . . . Let us continue being bridge-people. . . . Let us live in joy today and tomorrow the call of John Paul II to 'make the Church the home and the school of Communion.' "[25]

Creating bridges among all the different cultural, racial, and ethnic groups in our churches is not easy. Yet it is possible to reach out to neighbors, to fellow students on college campuses, to families in our children's schools, in our places of work, and in our parish liturgies and ministries. Many of us who are members of long-established U.S. families can use a little imagination to picture what it might have been like for our forebears to arrive on new shores where the inhabitants did not always seem welcoming, nor the way ahead smooth. Where are the various racial, ethnic, and cultural groups in my Catholic "circles"? Is my parish, prayer group, Bible study group, young adult group, or women's group ethnically homogeneous or diverse? Do we generally keep a polite distance or interact easily? How well do we work together? Is there anyone who is being hurt by stereotypes or exclusion? What can I/we do to build on and improve relationships? These are questions on the table for every parish pastoral council, every parish ministry or committee, every Catholic educational institution, every lay organization, and every individual Catholic.

ABORTION

Some people see abortion as Catholicism's signature issue. Along with racism, *Forming Consciences for Faithful Citizenship* defines abortion as an "intrinsic evil." In their *Pastoral Plan for Pro-Life Activities: A Campaign in Support of Life* (2001), the bishops "proclaim that human life is a precious gift from God; that each person who receives this gift has responsibilities toward God, self, and others; and that society, through its laws and social institutions, must protect and nurture human life at every stage of its existence."[26] The USCCB Office of Pro-Life Activities presents several quotations from the pope and bishops regarding the sacredness of life, the rights of the unborn, and the evil of abortion, embryonic stem-cell research, euthanasia, and assisted suicide.[27] The pro-life action campaign of the USCCB, People of Life, calls for active protest against all destruction of innocent life, and mandates the involvement of all dioceses and parishes.[28]

In 2008, some bishops reclaimed abortion to define Catholic politics, equated opposition to abortion with commitment to make it illegal, and excluded the possibility of Catholics supporting Obama.[29] But judging the morality of abortion is logically and ethically distinct from choosing political strategies to combat it, and distinct from judging morally or religiously those who choose differently. Therefore Catholic opposition to abortion permits different choices of candidates and permits other issues to be prioritized along with abortion. Though most Americans and a majority of Catholics do support legal abortion,[30] most (81 percent) want abortion reduction.[31] There is more than one way to move toward this goal, and different efforts are not mutually exclusive.

In general, the pro-life movement is focused on reversing the 1973 Supreme Court decision making abortion legal, *Roe v. Wade.* Yet both prudence and realism question single-minded determination to reach this one goal. Is it feasible? What would it accomplish, and are there equally or more effective options available? Even with pro-life appointments by a Republican president, the Court would maintain its bias toward established law (*stare decisis*). Overturning *Roe* would return the matter to the states, and most would allow abortion. Furthermore, data show that abortion rates decline as social programs rise. Latin American countries banning abortion still have high rates due to poverty and women's low status. Northern European countries with permissive abortion law and expansive programs of health care and family support have much lower rates than the United States.[32]

A 2008 study (conducted by Catholics in Alliance for the Common Good) of abortion reduction measures found that in the United States, the abortion rate among women living below the poverty level is more than four times that of women above 300 percent of the poverty level. Data from all states from 1982 to 2000 indicate that social and economic supports such as public assistance to low-income families and benefits for pregnant women and mothers have contributed significantly to reducing the number of abortions in the United States over the past twenty years.[33]

It is not enough to offer pregnancy crisis counseling or short-term help during pregnancy or immediately thereafter. Pregnant women and families need education, jobs, housing, and health care in order to raise families. A most important yet largely unmet responsibility is to pair Catholic advocacy for the unborn with advocacy for women, and to make the latter loud and clear.[34] When abortion activism focuses exclusively on the rights of fetuses, the rights, needs, and dignity of women seem to be forgotten. Pro-choice advocates usually do not think of themselves as pro-abortion but as pro-woman. The political work of pro-life advocates has much greater appeal when it makes the welfare of women and girls as important as the welfare of the unborn.

A bipartisan effort in Congress, the Pregnant Woman Support Act (H.R. 3192 and S. 2407), proposes to reduce abortions by promoting pregnancy assistance, health care insurance coverage for pregnant women and newborns, adoption, child care, nurses' visits, and educational and other support for pregnant students and new mothers. Cardinal Justin Rigali, chair of the Committee on Pro-Life Activities for the U.S. Conference of Catholic Bishops, commented that "the Pregnant Women Support Act reaches out to women with a helping hand when they are most vulnerable, and most engaged in making a decision about life or death for their unborn children." It offers "an authentic common ground, an approach that people can embrace regardless of their position on other issues." As Rigali stated, "no woman should ever have to undergo an abortion because she feels she has no other choice, or because alternatives were unavailable or not made known to her. An abortion performed under such social and economic duress meets no one's standard for 'freedom of choice.' "[35]

Abortion is rarely if ever a stand-alone decision or option. Women, couples, and families facing pregnancy and abortion come to their situations and make choices as a result of many intersecting cultural, social, and economic factors. These include access to jobs, housing, education, health care, and childcare; cultural ideas and pressures around sexuality, gender, and parenthood; and social attitudes of disapproval or support concerning birth control, teen pregnancy, abortion, adoption, and single parenthood. Whether one believes abortion should be legal or illegal, reduced or protected as an option, accepted in some circumstances or never at all, it is important not to stop at voting one's conscience. One must also listen respectfully to other approaches, support options beyond abortion, and work to make our families and communities places where it is easy to welcome children, not unduly difficult to give them the love and care they need.

GLOBAL JUSTICE

Half the people in the world — nearly three billion people — live on less than two dollars a day. Twenty percent of the population in the developed nations consume 86 percent of the world's goods. By contrast, about 790 million people in the developing world are chronically undernourished.

However briefly, it is important to frame religion and politics in the United States in the context of global problems, recalling statements that have been issued by the pope and Vatican immediately before and after the election. As U.S. Catholics move forward, it is essential to put our own national and ecclesial dilemmas alongside those of the human family, and to remember the criteria of justice and the preferential option for the poor that are so key to the big picture of Catholic social teaching. In fact, this big picture and the call for global justice, solidarity, and hope seem more important to Benedict XVI than the recent divisive history of religion and politics in the United States, with its focus on abortion. This obviously is not to say that the pope and Vatican have lost interest in this issue. In December 2008, the Congregation for the Doctrine of the Faith released *Dignitas personae*, on abortion and other biomedical life issues.[36]

Yet, in his 2008 U.S. visit, Benedict XVI called for action on war, poverty, and the environment. Days before the election, Archbishop Celestino Migliore, papal nuncio to the U.N., called for protection of the global climate, food security, human rights, a moratorium on the death penalty, basic health care, education, economic development, and all other "necessary efforts . . . to create a society in which life is respected at all stages of development."[37] In the election, Americans, including Catholics, subordinated global concerns to domestic ones, especially the economy, the war in Iraq, universal health care, and energy policy.[38] Benedict XVI reminded the new president, and with him, his Catholic constituency, that the American good is part of the universal common good. He sent Obama a congratulatory message, identifying "peace, solidarity and justice" as the "special issues" on which his administration should make progress.[39]

In his World Day of Peace message 2009, Benedict XVI reflected on the theme, "Fighting Poverty to Build Peace."[40] He called for global solidarity to combat factors such as social and economic marginalization due to globalization, pandemic diseases, food shortages, and the connection between nuclear and military build-ups and poverty. Later in the year, he released a new encyclical, *Caritas in Veritate*.[41] In it, he highlights the intrinsic connection between Christian charity and work for justice (no. 7), and argues that capitalism and markets, while valid and even necessary ways of organizing human productivity, must be subject to moral constraints (no. 35). The global economic meltdown of 2008–09 made it abundantly clear that we are all interconnected, and that domestic problems are never isolated from global ones.

CONCLUSION

The laity has shown that it is ready and able to join political discourse and action on "Catholic" terms. Targets include health care, economic recovery, poverty, energy, trade policy, immigration, Iraq and Afghanistan, nuclear reduction, improved racial and ethnic relations, and abortion reduction via programs that empower women and support families. Much can be accomplished through synergy among lay spokespersons and agencies, Catholics in public office, offices of the national bishops' conference, local dioceses and parishes, Catholic-sponsored education, Catholic political groups, and fellow citizens of every tradition and faith.

QUESTIONS FOR FURTHER REFLECTION

1. Can a Catholic simply throw up his or her hands and say, "Both parties support immoral things, and so I see no reason to engage in politics, or even to vote"?

2. How do you understand "the common good agenda"? Is this something that a Catholic could/should support politically? Is the "common good agenda" in any way a devaluation of the importance of abortion as a political issue for Catholics?

3. How do you understand the term "intrinsic evil"? Are there other intrinsically evil acts beyond abortion? How should politics deal with intrinsically evil acts?

4. How has our Church and how have our fellow Catholics dealt with the evil of racism in the past? What is your view of racism? Is it an evil on a par with abortion?

5. How does the fact of the increasing Latino population of American Catholics help us confront the racism issue? Is anti-Hispanic racism any different for Catholics than racism against African Americans?

6. Could a Catholic support a politician or a political party that endorsed racial divisions, even tacitly or subtly? Is immigration a racial issue, or is it a national security issue, or is it both?

7. Is the fight to make abortion illegal the only way, or even the best way, to fight the evil of abortion?

8. Are there other morally permissible ways to fight the evil of abortion?

9. Do you agree that when anti-abortion activism focuses exclusively on the rights of the fetuses, the rights, needs, and dignity of women seem to be forgotten?

10. Should "global justice" be a political concern for American Catholics in deciding what political party to support? How do you understand "global justice"? In Catholic teaching? Where does the need for global justice stand on your moral spectrum with the need to fight racism and oppose abortion rights?

NOTES

1. An earlier and briefer version of this essay was published as an analysis of the election, "Religion and Politics: USA," *Theological Studies* (March 1, 2009). No perspective is context-free; I served on the Catholic Advisory Committee of Barack Obama. I am also committed to diversity of political affiliation among Catholics and to respectful dialogue about differences. Thanks to Thomas J. Reese, SJ, for many constructive suggestions on this essay.

2. Although Obama is frequently characterized as African American, that term has in the past been reserved for descendents of slaves, not recent immigrants or their children. That may be changing. Obama was born in Hawaii, but his father was Kenyan and he is bi-racial. He was raised by his white mother and grandparents after his parents divorced.

3. See the Pew Forum survey, "How the Faithful Voted," at *http://pewforum.org/docs/?DocID=367*. See also Mark Silk and Andrew Walsh, "A Past without a Future? Parsing the U.S. Catholic Vote," *America*, November 3, 2008; and Peter Steinfels, "Catholics and Choice (in the Voting Booth)," *New York Times*, November 8, 2008.

4. Pew Forum, "U.S. Religious Landscape Survey," at *http://religions.pewforum.org/reports*.

5. On countercultural pro-life commitment see Jennifer Fulweiler, "A Sexual Revolution," *America*, July 7–14, 2008, 11–13.

6. See Jim Wallis, *God's Politics: Why the Right Gets It Wrong and the Left Doesn't Get It* (New York: HarperCollins, 2005); E. J. Dionne, Jr., *Souled Out: Reclaiming Faith and Politics after the Religious Right* (Princeton, NJ: Princeton University Press, 2008); Amy Sullivan, *The Party Faithful: How and Why the Democrats Are Closing the God Gap* (New York: Scribner, 2008); Sojourners Christians for Peace and Justice website (*www.sojo.net/*); Matthew 25 Network website (*http://matthew25.org/*); and evangelical pastor Rick Warren's website (*www.rickwarren.com/*).

7. Chris Korzen and Alexia Kelley, *A Nation for All: How the Catholic Vision of the Common Good Can Save America from the Politics of Division* (San Francisco: Jossey-Bass, 2008), 123. See also Clarke E. Cochran and David Carroll Cochran, *The Catholic Vote: A Guide for the Perplexed* (Maryknoll, NY: Orbis Books, 2008); and Gerald J. Beyer, "Yes You Can: Why Catholics Don't Have to Vote Republican," *Commonweal*, June 20, 2008.

8. Chris Korzen and Alexia Kelley founded Catholics in Alliance for the Common Good (*www.catholicsinalliance.org/*); and Catholics United (*www.catholics-united.org/*), respectively. Another web-based organization is Catholic Democrats (*www.catholicdemocrats.org/*).

9. See "Religion in the 2008 Election: Post-Election Survey," by Catholics in Alliance, Faith in Public Life and Sojourners, November 14, 2008; at *www.faithinpubliclife.org/content/post-electionpoll/*.

10. See n. 37 below.

11. Bishop Blase Cupich (Rapid City, SD), "Racism and the Election," *America*, October 27, 2008, 5.

12. See M. Cathleen Kaveny, "Political Responsibility: Is the Concept of Intrinsic Evil Helpful to the Catholic Voter?" *America*, October 27, 2008, 15–19; and Amelia J. Uelman,' " 'It's Hard Work': Reflections on Conscience and Citizenship in the Catholic Tradition," *Journal of Catholic Legal Studies* 47 (2008): 338–39.

13. See Archbishop John C. Favalora (Miami), "Why We Don't Take Sides on Candidates," September 12, 2008, pastoral letter, at *http://www.miamiarchdiocese.org/Statement.asp?op=Column080912&lg=E*.

14. A resource for achieving greater political understanding and cooperation among Catholics is the Catholic Common Ground Initiative, started by Cardinal Joseph Bernardin of Chicago to heal divisions in the church through respectful dialogue (*http://www.nplc.org/commonground/characteristics.htm*).

15. Barack Obama, "A More Perfect Union," Philadelphia, March 18, 2008, at *http://www.npr.org/templates/story/story.php?storyId=88478467*.

16. See James M. O'Toole, *The Faithful: A History of Catholics in America* (Cambridge, MA: Harvard University Press, 2008).

17. Michael Sean Winters, *Left at the Altar: How the Democrats Lost the Catholics and the How the Catholics Can Save the Democrats* (New York: Basic Books, 2008), 70. Winters rails against John F. Kennedy's relegation of religion to the private sphere and finds hope in the influx of Latino Catholics.

18. See Kristen E. Heyer, "Welcoming the Strangers: What Christian Faith Can Bring to the Immigration Debate," *America*, October 13, 2008, 13–15.

19. E. J. Dionne, Jr., "There Is No Catholic Vote—And It's Important," in *American Catholics and Civic Engagement: A Distinctive Voice*, ed. Margaret O'Brien Steinfels (Lanham, MD, and Boulder, CO: Rowman & Littlefield, 2004), 258–59.

20. Jamie Phelps, "Racism and the Church," in Dwight Hopkins, ed., *Black Faith and Public Talk* (Maryknoll, NY: Orbis Books, 1999), 57; citing John T. McGreevey, *Parish Boundaries: The Catholic Encounter with Race in the Twentieth-Century Urban North* (Chicago: University of Chicago Press, 1996). An excellent resource on Catholicism and race is a thematic issue of the *Journal of Catholic Social Thought* 3, no. 1 (Winter 2006).

21. For a discussion, see Phelps, "Racism and the Church," 60–62.

22. M. Shawn Copeland, ed., *Uncommon Faithfulness: The Black Catholic Experience* (Maryknoll, NY: Orbis Books, 2009).

23. *http://www.usccb.org/saac/*. See also "African American Catholics in the United States," a backgrounder prepared by the USCCB Department of Communications (*www.usccb.org/comm/backgrounders/african_american.shtml*).

24. See "Hispanic Catholics in the United States," USCCB Backgrounder (*http://www.usccb.org/comm/backgrounders/hispanic.shtml*).

25. Secretariat for Hispanic Affairs Home Page (*www.usccb.org/hispanicaffairs/*).

26. United States Conference of Catholic Bishops, "Pastoral Plan for Pro-Life Activities: A Campaign in Support of Life," 2001, "Introduction" (*www.usccb.org/prolife/pastoralplan.shtml#intro*).

27. *http://www.usccb.org/prolife/tdocs/popebquotes2008.shtml*.

28. *http://www.usccb.org/prolife/peopleof life/involved.shtml*.

29. For example, Cardinal Justin Rigali and Bishop William Murphy, "Joint Statement," October 21, 2008, accessed in pdf format, November 16, 2008, at the website *usccb.org*; for a counterpoint, see Winters, "Why They Didn't Listen."

30. See *The Faith and American Politics Survey: The Young and the Faithful*, available at Faith in Public Life website, *http://www.faithinpubliclife.org/content/faps/*.

31. See "Religion in the 2008, Election: Post-Election Survey," by Catholics in Alliance, Faith in Public Life, and Sojourners, November 14, 2008, at *http://www.faithinpubliclife.org/content/post-electionpoll/*.

32. See Joseph Wright and Michael Bailey, *Reducing Abortion in America: The Effect of Social and Economic Supports*, sponsored by Catholics in Alliance for the Common Good, 2008, available at *http://www.catholicsinalliance.org/*.

33. Catholics in Alliance for the Common Good, *Reducing Abortion in America: The Effect of Economic and Social Supports*, August 2008 (*www.catholicsinalliance.org/files/CACG_Final.pdf*).

34. Feminists for Life seeks to put abortion in the context of the larger needs of women (*http://www.feministsforlife.org/*).

35. USCCB News Release, "Pregnant Women Support Act provides life-affirming support for pregnant women and their unborn children," May 12, 2009 (*www.usccb.org/comm/archives/2009/09-105.shtml*). The act was passed as part of the "Patient Protection and Affordable Care Act" in 2010.

36. Congregation for the Doctrine of the Faith, *Dignitas Personae*, Instruction on Bioethical Questions, September 8, 2008 (*www.vatican.va*). Interestingly, this document was finished well before the election, but published after it.

37. Catholic News Service, "Nuncio's talks to UN committee focus on global climate, human rights," October 29, 2008, at *http://www.catholicnews.com*.

38. Jackie Calmes and Megan Thee, "Voter Polls Show Obama Built a Broad Coalition," *New York Times*, November 5, 2008. On Catholics, see Patricia Zapor, "Catholic voters mirror general electorate in support for Obama," Catholic News Service (*www.catholicnews.com/data/stories/cns/0805649.htm*).

39. Cindy Wooden, "Pope Sends Congratulatory Message to Obama," Catholic News Service (*http://www.catholicnews.com/data/stories/cns/0805616.htm*).

40. *www.vatican.va*. See also Howard J. Hubbard, "Fighting Poverty to Build Peace: Pope Benedict's Challenge to the World," *America*, February 9, 2009, 11–14.

41. Benedict XVI, *Caritas in Veritate*, June 29, 2009 (*www.vatican.va*).

THREE

Politics, Morality, and Original Sin

Cardinal Georges Cottier, OP

In 2009 Barack Obama gave two important speeches in two very different university contexts. On May 17 he spoke at the University of Notre Dame, the Catholic university in Indiana, where he had been invited to receive an honorary degree on graduation day for twenty-nine hundred students. On June 4 in Cairo he gave a long speech addressed in particular to the Islamic world at the Al-Azhar Islamic University, considered the main center of religious teaching in Sunni Islam.

I don't want to make a political comment, which does not come within my sphere of competence, but I was struck by many aspects of the two speeches by the president of the United States. Apart from the individual topics touched on, they gave a glimpse of politics that can be usefully compared with fundamental elements of the social doctrine of the Catholic Church.

In the speech at Notre Dame, I was already struck by the words that Obama addressed to young people at the very beginning. The president pointed out that we are going through a particular historical moment and described the fact as a *privilege* and a *responsibility* for young people. Already in that positive approach there is something Christian. The tasks of each generation are tasks from which the Providence of God is not absent.

To fully evaluate the import of the two speeches one must take two premises into account. First, it should be said that his speeches concern the problems of temporal society. And the Church has recognized—not least in important encyclicals and pronouncements of the Magisterium—the autonomy of temporal society. Autonomy does not mean separation, antagonism, isolation, or hostility between temporal society and the Church. The Church simply acknowledges that temporal society has an entity of its own, with its own purposes. In dialogue with that entity, the contribution offered by the Church—which represents the Gospel and the values of grace—does not dim or deny but on the contrary exalts the autonomy of temporal society.

The second premise is that Obama talked about the world as it is today. His words referred to the United States, but with the great movements of peoples over recent decades, his words can be applied to all areas of the world—in particular in the West—now inhabited by pluralistic societies. Obama is a head of government called upon to handle a pluralist society. This is a fact to consider if one really wants to understand his words.

In fact, the speech at the University of Notre Dame seems littered with references taken from the Christian tradition. There was, for example, an expression that came up frequently, "common ground," which corresponds to a fundamental concept of the social doctrine of the Church, that of the *common good*.

There is a tendency in current mentality to think that morality concerns only the sphere of private life and relationships, whereas the quest for the common good calls upon reference to moral criteria and norms (cf. *Pacem in Terris*, no. 80). Morality is always the same; it does not change depending on whether it applies to the public or the private sphere. But morality always takes account of the reality to which it applies. In this case, it is a matter of the quest for the common good in a pluralistic society.

The problem is complex in the extreme: how to seek together the common good in a society where there are different and even conflicting ideas about what is good and what is evil. And how to proceed together in this quest without anyone being forced to sacrifice any of their essential beliefs. I think that we can agree with Obama's way of setting out the search for solutions, not least because in proposing it Obama took his cue precisely from a principle always recognized and taken into account in the Christian tradition: the consequences of original sin. As Obama said at Notre Dame, "Part of the problem, of course, lies in the imperfections of man—our selfishness, our pride, our stubbornness, our acquisitiveness, our insecurities, our egos; all the cruelties large and small that those of us in the Christian tradition understand to be rooted in original sin."

At a certain point in his speech Obama warned: "The ultimate irony of faith is that it necessarily admits doubt. . . . It is beyond our capacity as human beings to know with certainty what God has planned for us, or what He asks of us, and those of us who believe must trust that His wisdom [the wisdom of the Lord, *ed.*] is greater than our own." There are, in appearance, words in this passage that seem to go against the teaching of the Church. As St. Thomas writes, the faith as gift of God is infallible. There is no doubt in faith. One can't be wrong. But believers can err when their judgment does not proceed from faith. Moreover, it is a fact that believers, especially when faced by various practical choices, wonder how to act, wonder what criteria the faith suggests. And in the face of the concrete situations of life, these criteria may not always seem so clear and crisp. Cases of conscience may well arise.

The second part of the sentence makes clear the meaning that Obama meant to give to his words: certain knowledge of what God wants from us "is beyond our capacity as human beings," but we "must trust that His wisdom is greater than our own. "

For its part, the Catholic Church maintains and teaches that God, the beginning and end of all things, may be already known with certainty by the natural light of human reason with created things as the starting point. But in the historical conditions in which we find ourselves, however, we experience many difficulties in fruitfully using this natural ability to gain through its own strength alone a true and certain knowledge of God as personal, as also of the natural law inscribed by the Creator in our souls. As the *Catechism of the Catholic Church* explains in paragraphs 37 and 38, which cite the encyclical *Humani Generis*, humankind needs to be enlightened by the revelation of God not only on what exceeds its understanding but also on "religious and moral truths which of themselves are not beyond the grasp of human reason," because in the current condition of the human race, "hampered by . . . disordered appetites which are the consequences of original sin," such truths cannot be known "with ease, with firm certainty, and with no admixture of error."

In Christian doctrine, heeding the consequences of original sin does not mean becoming accomplices of sin, or refusing to offer all humankind moral truths, knowledge of which, in the real historical situation experienced by humankind on this earth, appears blurred to many.

Nor in his speech did Obama suggest hiding one's moral certainties, as if to maintain the existence of objective truths were to be considered impossible or at least inappropriate in the context of a pluralistic society. He merely pointed out that the experience of our limitations, of our weakness, of our misery, "should not push us away from our faith," but should simply "humble us," remaining "open and curious" even in situations of challenge and opposition on ethically sensitive issues.

Thus, the traditional teaching on original sin itself suggests an approach to human reality that can turn out to be useful in the present historical circumstances experienced in pluralistic societies.

Every pluralistic society suffers tensions, conflicts, and divisions over what is just and what is unjust. But there's a democratic way of experiencing them that Obama described in his speech and that can be in harmony with a Christian understanding of the relationships among people. Obama says: we must be persuaded, as pre-judice (for once giving a positive meaning to the word) that the other is in good faith. Even those who do not think like me. We must avoid caricaturing the other, respect the other, not demonize the other. Democracy lives by this inspiration of an inwardly Christian kind. When I read the speeches, I immediately thought of that very fine encyclical from Paul VI, *Ecclesiam Suam*, in which Pope Paul VI wrote that the way of human relations in society is that of dialogue, even on vital truths for which one may go so far as to give one's life.

This is not a matter of dragging these speeches into our camp, but of looking for points of encounter. The speech at the University of Notre Dame also reminded me of *Dignitatis Humanae*, a great text of the social doctrine of the Church, which recognizes the duty of individuals to seek the truth that is a duty before God and springs from human nature. Thus, when I respect the other, I respect in the other this capacity for truth.

Another issue that sometimes causes tension in pluralistic societies is the demand for religious freedom made by individuals before the State. This demand does not make religious indifference an obligatory choice for the State, but requires awareness of the limits of its powers.

I was struck by how Obama did not dodge the thorniest issue, that of abortion, on which he had received so much criticism, not least from the U.S. bishops. On the one hand such reactions are justified: nonnegotiable values are involved in political decisions about abortion. For us what is at stake is the defense of the human person and the person's inalienable rights, the first of which is precisely that to life. Now in a pluralistic society there are radical differences on this point. There are those who, like us, consider abortion an *intrinsece malum*, there are those who accept it, and even some who claim it as a right. The president has never taken the latter position. On the contrary, I think he has made positive suggestions—something also stressed by *L'Osservatore Romano* of May 19, 2009—proposing again in this case the search for common ground. In this search, Obama points out that nobody should censor their beliefs, but on the contrary maintain them and defend them in the face of all. His position is not the misunderstood relativism of those who say that it is a matter of contrasting views, that all personal opinions are subjective and uncertain, and thus it is better to set them aside when speaking of these things.

In addition, Obama recognizes the tragic seriousness of the problem, that the decision to abort "is a heart-wrenching decision for any woman." The common ground that he is proposing is that we all work together to reduce the number of women seeking abortion. He adds that any legal regulation of the matter must guarantee in absolute fashion conscientious objection for health workers who do not want to engage in the practice of abortion. His words go in the direction of diminishing the evil. The government and the State must make every effort to ensure that the number of abortions is minimized. It is, of course, only a *minimum*, but a precious *minimum*. It reminds me of the attitude of the early Christian legislators who did not repeal the Roman laws tolerating practices that did not comply with or even went counter to natural law, such as concubinage and slavery. The change was arrived at by slow degrees, often marked by setbacks, as the number of Christians in the population increased and with them the impact of the sense of the dignity of the person. At first, to obtain the consent of citizens and preserve social peace, the so-called imperfect laws were left in force, which prevented persecution for acts and behavior contrary to natural law. Even St. Thomas, who had no doubt that the law must be moral, added that the State should not make laws too severe and "lofty" because they would be despised by those incapable of applying them.

The realism of the politician recognizes evil and calls it by its name. It recognizes that we must be humble and patient, fighting without the presumption of eradicating it from human history by means of legal coercion. It is the parable of the wheat and the weeds, which also applies at the political level. On the other hand, this does not become justification for cynicism and indifference to it. The effort to decrease evil as much as possible remains persistent. It is a duty.

The Church has always perceived the illusion of eliminating evil from history by legal, political, or religious means as unattainable and dangerous. Recent history is also full of disasters produced by the fanaticism of those who aimed to dry up the sources of evil in human history, ultimately transforming everything into a vast cemetery. The communist regimes followed exactly this logic. So does the religious terrorism that kills even in the name of God. When a doctor who favored abortion was killed by militant anti-abortionists—as happened recently in the United States—one has to admit that even the highest ideals, such as the sacrosanct defense of the absolute value of human life, can be corrupted and turn into their opposite, becoming slogans at the disposition of an aberrant ideology.

Christians are bearers in the world of a realistic temporal hope, not of a vain utopian dream, also when they give witness of their loyalty to such absolute values as life. St. Gianna Beretta Molla, the doctor who died by refusing treatment that might have hurt the baby she carried in her womb, touches the hearts not only of Christians with her ordinary and quiet heroism; she reminds everyone of the common destiny to which we tend. It is a prophetic form of the evangelical style of Christian witness.

In his speech at the University of Notre Dame, Obama made a very important remark precisely on this point. He spoke of when he was involved in a social work project in the slums of Chicago—funded by some Catholic parishes—in which Protestant and Jewish volunteers also participated. On that occasion he happened to meet welcoming and understanding people. He saw the performance of good works nourished by the Lord among them. And he was "drawn—not just to work with the church, but to be in the Church. It was through this service," he concluded, "that I was brought to Christ." He also gave a moving eulogy of the great Cardinal Joseph Bernardin, who was then archbishop of Chicago. He described him as "a lighthouse and a crossroads," lovable in his way of persuading and in his continuous attempt to "bring people together always trying to find common ground." In that experience, Obama said, "My heart and mind were touched by the words and deeds of the men and women I worked alongside with in Chicago." The spectacle of charity, which comes from God, has the power to touch and attract the minds and hearts of humankind. And it is the only seed of real change in human history. Obama also quoted Martin Luther King, of whom he feels he is a disciple.

That only forty-one years after the assassination of King he himself is president of the United States is a sign and proof of the historical efficacy of trust in the *power of truth*. In these decades we have seen so many ideologies base their pretense to change on violence, from revolutionary programs to the project of exporting democracy by military force. And we have seen only tragic failures and retrogression. Obama's humble realism opens up new vistas also at the geopolitical level, as evinced by his speech at the Islamic Al-Azhar University in Cairo.

In that speech Obama also sought to identify a "common ground" on which the complicated relationship between Islam and the Western world, in particular the United States, might make progress. In this search, according to the president, we are all called upon to look within our own tradition to rediscover the core values and shared interests on which to build mutual respect and peace. This approach represents a radical refutation of the notion of a clash of civilizations and an antidote to the tendency to apply negative stereotypes to others. In a speech heard by hundreds of millions of Muslims, Obama took an entirely different line, with full confidence in the good faith and ability to judge of his hearers. For that very reason he was able to touch on all the controversial points with clarity and courage: the violent extremism—which affects everyone, starting with the Muslims—the Western missions in Afghanistan and Iraq, the use of torture, the Israeli-Palestinian question, on which he reaffirmed the right of both peoples to live in safety in their own homeland and described the situation of the Palestinian people as "intolerable," in tune with what the pope had said during his recent visit to the land of Jesus. On the theme of nuclear power, in reference to Iran, Obama said that no one can be denied the right to use nuclear energy for peaceful purposes, reaffirming that we must aim at a situation in which no country—beginning with his own—develops the project of making recourse to nuclear power in the military field. In his speech in Cairo, the U.S. president also reiterated that democracy cannot be imposed from outside and that on the path to democracy all peoples must find their own way. He stressed that religious freedom is fundamental for peace. And on Islamic soil he also spoke of women's rights. Among his quotations from sacred texts—the Torah, the Koran, and the Bible—I was struck that the biblical text he chose to quote was the Sermon on the Mount. That discourse is addressed directly to the disciples of Christ. It was not made *in primis* for temporal, political, and civil society. But Obama has perceived its positive meaning and its inspiration for the life of the *civitas*. That reminded me of the insight of John Paul II on the political meaning of forgiveness and requests for the purification of memory. One sees no way of coming out of intolerable situations, such as those experienced in the Middle East, if people's pain from the malice and wrongs they suffered is not dissolved by the reconciling power of forgiveness.

I imagine that this man, Obama, felt all these things when he had to prepare his two speeches. This surprises me. It seems to me an interesting fact, even in terms of the political commitment of Christians in our pluralistic and globalized world.

QUESTIONS FOR FURTHER REFLECTION

1. What does the autonomy of temporal society mean? Does it mean that the Church has no role to play in temporal society? If the Church does have a role to play, what is it, how should it be carried out, and is this role simply one for Church leadership or should individual Catholics play a part? Should the Church try to influence or control temporal society?

2. There is a tendency to think that morality covers only the private acts of individuals. Does it cover more than that? If so, what would that be?

3. How is the "common good" a Catholic concept? More importantly, how does a pluralistic society, with people of many faiths and no faith, establish what their common ground is? What should be the role of the Church in this process?

4. How do you relate the concepts of common ground and common good? Are they the same?

5. Can a Catholic agree that faith necessarily admits doubt? Is there any sense of that phrase that could be Catholic in meaning or perspective?

6. What is the effect of original sin in human attempts to know God and God's laws? Is this ever a morally valid excuse for Catholics to accept disagreement with others in the political process?

7. How should the presumption of good faith affect the way Catholics seek the common good in a pluralistic, democratic society?

8. What common ground does the author see President Obama proposing on the abortion issue? Does the author think that a Catholic should participate in this search? Are there any limits on what a Catholic could agree to in this process?

9. The author writes that "the Church has always perceived the illusion of eliminating evil from history by legal, political, or religious means as unattainable and dangerous." What does that mean to you in terms of current-day American politics?

10. How does the author think that the insights of Pope John Paul II on the political meaning of forgiveness and requests for the purification of memory entered into President Obama's speech at Al-Azhar University? Should this make a difference in the way Catholics perceive the other positions of the president?

FOUR

Catholic Bishops and the Electoral Process in American Politics

William V. D'Antonio

It has become a commonplace to say that "religion has always been a major force in U.S. politics, policy, identity, and culture."[1] This is no less true today than it was in the time of the Founding Fathers. One reason for the active role of religion in the American electoral process may be precisely because these Founding Fathers disestablished religion from government with the First Amendment to the Constitution.

The First Amendment says only that Congress shall not establish any religion or restrict the free exercise thereof. Thus, one's beliefs, religious or other, should not be a qualification for public office. It also says nothing about what religions might or might not do regarding the public square. And therein lies the story of the influence of religion in American public and political life.

In this essay I propose to focus on the way in which the U.S. Catholic bishops have participated in the electoral process during the time period beginning with the *Roe v. Wade* Supreme Court decision of January 1973, which gave women the legal right to abortion, and up to and including the national elections of 2008. My focus will include the bishops' interaction with candidate Jimmy Carter in 1976, their absence from the 1980 campaign, and then an increasing public presence beginning with the 1984 Democratic Party candidacy of Geraldine Ferraro. I will review data on how the Catholic membership in the U.S. House and Senate has changed in this same time period, as well as changes in roll call voting of Catholics in the U.S. House and Senate on the abortion issue. I will also include data showing the changing nature of the Catholic laity's support for the Democratic and Republican parties in this same time period and suggest relationships between the attitudes and behavior of the bishops in the public square and the reactions of the Catholics as seen in their voting behavior, especially in the 2008 national elections.

BACKGROUND

Most of the Founding Fathers were themselves religious, at least in the sense of identifying with one or another religious denomination. Episcopalians had a majority of the seats in the first House and a plurality of the seats in the first Senate, and President Washington himself was an Episcopalian. Presbyterians and then Congregationalists were second and third in size, respectively, in the first House and Senate (1789–90). And from the beginning, Catholics have been among the founders and members in the House and Senate. At the same time, a minority of members of the First Congress in both House and Senate gave no religious affiliation. So it cannot be said that, as a group, the founders were particularly religious or anti-religious.[2] They feared control by one or another religious group, and sought in the First Amendment to avoid the dangers they saw in the European experience of giving one religion preferred status; for example, in England it was the Anglican Church, in Sweden it was the Lutheran, and in Spain it was the Catholic Church. Indeed, almost every president has used religion to foster social solidarity and national cohesion and, in recent times, to ask God to bless America. And it is generally recognized that for most of the first two hundred years of this nation, a strong Protestant ethos dominated the culture and politics.

If it is true that no religious group or denomination is privileged by the government in the United States, it is also true that religions across the board have over time learned to use a variety of methods or processes to pursue their interests with the government with regard to legislation, including funding to support social programs central to their interests. For example, religious groups may apply for and receive financial support from the federal government for some of their activities. Catholic, Lutheran, and Jewish charities are among these groups. They receive money as 501(c)(3) tax-exempt organizations because they follow specific government guidelines defining such organizations.

Over time four major methods or processes have emerged by which Americans as individuals and as groups or associations may try to influence the federal government, especially in the political realm. Kenneth Wald has identified four processes as central to the pursuit of political objectives by religious individuals and groups.[3] Throughout this essay I will refer to these four processes within the context of recent political events as they pertain to the Catholic bishops. The four processes are:

Direct action: Examples range from peaceful marches for civil rights, such as those undertaken by Dr. Martin Luther King Jr., to cross burnings and synagogue bombings carried out by the KKK and other violent groups.

Political campaigning: This should be distinguished from lobbying. A well-known example is the very open campaigning for or against John F. Kennedy on the basis of his being a Catholic. Some feared that he might take orders from Rome if elected. As it turned out, Kennedy used his being Catholic effectively. With Catholic crowds, he insisted they should not vote *for* him just because he was Catholic. With Protestant crowds, he asked them not to vote *against* him just because he was Catholic. George W. Bush's use of his born-again Christian experience to great advantage in his presidential campaigns is another example of this process of religious influence.

Political lobbying: More than 120 religious groups devote time annually to lobbying Congress and the president on a wide range of issues. Religious groups are as free to lobby as are business, labor, and other associations. The only restriction facing religious groups is that they cannot lobby directly for a particular candidate or party. They can and do support or oppose legislation, or parts of legislative bills, and can be critical of candidates' support for particular issues.

Infiltration: The decision to run for public office is the classic example of this process of influence. Anyone from a deist like Jefferson to born-again Christians like George W. Bush and Sarah Palin may run for office, making whatever use they can or wish to of their beliefs and practices. One consequence of this openness is that in the more than two hundred years since the first elections were held, we have had people elected to Congress from more than thirty different religious denominations and sects, as well as people who claimed no affiliation with any denomination.

The First Amendment has indeed allowed religion to flourish in the United States.[4] In the course of time, the four processes made possible by the First Amendment have led to both civic engagement and confrontation. This was shown in a classic manner in the most recent national elections, to which I now turn my attention.

CATHOLICS IN THE CONTEXT OF WALD'S FOUR PROCESSES

The focus of my concern is the more and more openly hostile attacks against candidates for public office, especially but not exclusively at the national level.

The criticisms began in 1984 when Cardinal John O'Connor of New York and other bishops criticized Geraldine Ferraro, the Democratic Party's vice presidential candidate, for her position on abortion;[5] these attacks gradually escalated into more concerted attacks against candidate John Kerry in 2004, and most recently against Barack Obama and Joe Biden in 2008, continuing into 2009.

How effective have these attacks been? In what ways may we measure their effectiveness? How, if at all, do these attacks reflect our attempt as Catholics to live our lives as Christ would have wanted? It is not only the attacks by bishops and some priests, but what is implied in these attacks, as well as their immediate and long-term consequences that we must begin to address. I begin with an examination of the way in which Catholics have used the four processes cited by Wald.

DIRECT ACTION

In recent years, the most publicized direct action taken by Catholics is their participation in the Right to Life March, held in January every year to mark the anniversary of the January 1973 U.S. Supreme Court decision *Roe v. Wade*, granting a woman a constitutional right to an abortion. The march has from the beginning been led by citizens committed in their opposition to abortion.[6] In its early years Catholic lay groups were most visibly present, but over time it has drawn people from across the religious spectrum. The Catholic bishops have become more and more supportive in their efforts to raise the consciousness level of all Americans about the Church's teaching that abortion is an intrinsic evil, a violation of the moral law; and they have put increasing pressure on the executive and legislative branches of government to vote against financing of abortions, with the long-term goal still to overturn *Roe v. Wade*.

In recent years, the support for the march by a growing number of bishops has been accompanied by an increase in the numbers of young people in these marches. The March for Life has taken on national significance, with students and people of all ages and religions coming to Washington, DC, by car, bus, and train.

Presidents have sent letters of support to be read, and members of Congress have appeared in person to express their support for the march. The march essentially is a peaceful effort to stir the nation to rethink *Roe v. Wade* in the hopes of eventually overturning it and in the interim finding ways to restrict it.

Recent reports by the Pew Forum and the Gallup Organization[7] show a decline in support for abortion rights, a change from the situation some twenty years ago in which a majority of Americans including Catholics were supportive of abortion rights.

POLITICAL CAMPAIGNING

In the 2004 presidential campaign, candidate John Kerry, a churchgoing Catholic, was openly criticized by more than a dozen bishops, most prominent among them Archbishop Raymond Burke, then of St. Louis, who openly stated that he would not permit him to receive Communion were he to appear at the altar rail in Burke's archdiocese. Almost as many bishops, led by Cardinal Theodore McCarrick of Washington, DC, and Cardinal Roger Mahony of Los Angeles, stated their opposition to the use of Communion as a sanction. Even Cardinal Ratzinger was brought into the debate; his nuanced letter was seen by both sides as supporting their position. It is difficult to say how much Kerry was hurt by these attacks, but they put him on the defensive, and a large percentage of Catholics saw his Catholicism as questionable.[8]

The Republican Party formed a special National Committee of Catholic Republicans, with a budget of several million dollars, used to publicize the virtues of George W. Bush and the faults of Kerry. People were encouraged to visit Internet sites with titles like "Kerry Wrong for Catholics" and "Kerry Wrong for Mormons."

In the 2008 campaign, more bishops, including Joseph Martino of Scranton, Charles Chaput of Denver, and Joseph Finn of Kansas City, Missouri, attacked Obama and vice presidential candidate Catholic Democrat Joe Biden for their pro-choice stand on abortion, declaring in increasingly shrill voices that abortion trumped all other considerations and that Catholics were putting their eternal salvation at risk by supporting the Obama-Biden ticket. Again, as more bishops joined in the confrontation, they argued that abortion was not a political issue but a moral issue and that the laity could not in good conscience vote for a pro-choice candidate. Candidate, now President Obama, is a member of the United Church of Christ, a liberal Protestant denomination; its teachings provide support for a woman's right to an abortion under a variety of conditions. It is interesting to note that none of the Mainline Protestant churches and the Jewish groups that support abortion raised their voices in defense of Obama's position as having its own moral weight and thus deserving of respect in a pluralistic society.

The protests against Obama did not cease with his victory in November 2008. When it was announced in March 2009 that the University of Notre Dame had selected now President Barack Obama to be its commencement speaker and that it was also going to give President Obama an honorary degree, a widespread attack on Notre Dame brought direct action to a new level of confrontation. Before it was over, a significant minority of bishops (about eighty) openly criticized Notre Dame, its president, and its trustees for offering President Obama an honorary degree. In their view, Notre Dame's action was in violation of the American bishops' directive that Catholic schools should not confer honors on people who are pro-choice on abortion, since abortion is seen as an intrinsically evil act, impermissible in all situations.

Some radical groups, like the one headed by Randall Terry (a Catholic convert), took more direct action, putting up rows of crosses on campus and threatening to disrupt the commencement exercises. Eventually, Notre Dame alumni groups and others campaigned in defense of the university and the issue gained national attention for more than a month. Even non-Catholics were polled about whether they thought Obama should receive an honorary degree in light of his position on abortion and stem-cell research. No bishops spoke out in defense of Notre Dame until well after the event was over.

Some Consequences of Direct Action and Political Campaigning

1. The generally peaceful Right to Life marches in January of each year, accompanied by statements from the hierarchy about the sacredness of all life from conception till death, may be one factor in the decline of support among Catholics and others for a woman's right to an abortion in all or some cases. These marches are accepted as part of an American political process that permits direct action to influence political decision-making.

2. The campaigns of 2004 and 2008 politicized the position of the bishops to such an extent that abortion effectively became a non-negotiable issue, focused mainly against Democratic Catholic candidates for public office.[9] The movement began at the national level with the candidacy of Geraldine Ferraro in 1984 and reached a crescendo in the 2008 campaign and the follow-up that included the Notre Dame commencement address and award of an honorary degree to President Barack Obama. It seems to have had several consequences. In 2004 it placed almost as many bishops in opposition to Candidate Kerry as in his support, while raising serious issues about publicly denying Communion to Catholic candidates. For example, the actions of some U.S. bishops stood in contrast with the response of Pope John Paul II in the aftermath of Italy's referendum on a woman's right to an abortion. Pope John Paul II had given Communion to the mayor of Rome when it was well known that the mayor had been one of the supporters of Italy's law granting Italian women the right to an abortion.[10] The pope also gave Communion to Prime Minister Tony Blair

of England, at the time known to be a pro-choice Anglican. (It should be noted that in the United States, some Catholic bishops said they did not see Communion as an appropriate way to address the abortion issue.)

In the case of the 1984 election, it is generally agreed that the financial activities of candidate Ferraro's husband were a more significant factor in the Democratic Party loss than was the criticism of her on the abortion issue. In the 2004 election, about the same number of Catholic bishops opposed the use of Communion as a negative sanction against candidate Kerry as openly stated their threat to refuse him Communion in their diocese. But the headline war was won by those opposing Kerry and his pro-choice position. Kerry suffered from an unwillingness to address the religion issue directly and from the perception that he was not a devout, church-attending Catholic. But there were more faults than this with his campaign, and he ended up losing the Catholic vote to George Bush by four points, 48 percent to 52 percent

The results from the 2008 election tell a different story. Overall, Obama-Biden won the Catholic vote 54 percent to 45 percent. The voting patterns in the dioceses headed by the bishops who spoke out most strongly against Obama-Biden offer an important indicator of the bishops' efforts to influence the election. Let's take a look at those:

In Denver, Colorado, the archdiocese headed by Archbishop Charles J. Chaput, the Obama-Biden ticket won 75 percent of the vote; McCain-Palin won 25 percent.

In Lackawanna County, Pennsylvania, which includes Scranton, the diocese headed by Bishop Joseph Martino, who openly stated he would deny Obama Communion, the Obama-Biden ticket won 63 percent of the vote; McCain-Palin won 37 percent.

In Kansas City, Missouri, headed by Bishop Robert Finn, who feared for the souls of those who would dare to vote for Obama-Biden, the Obama-Biden ticket won 78 percent of the vote; McCain-Palin won 22 percent.

Other indicators were to be found in the states that went Democratic:

In Colorado, not only did Denver go overwhelmingly for Obama-Biden, but the state, which had not supported a Democrat since 1992, went Democratic by a vote of 54 percent to 45 percent.

The New England and mid-Atlantic states from Maine to Maryland, most with significant Catholic populations, all went Democratic, with the Pennsylvania percentage (54 percent to 46 percent) for Obama-Biden being almost as large as that of New Jersey (57 percent to 43 percent).

It appears that where the bishops spoke out most strongly against Obama-Biden, most Catholic voters either ignored them or simply followed their conscience and voted for the persons they expected to provide the leadership on issues of most importance to them.[11] And the issues most important were the economy-jobs and health care.

Notre Dame in Retrospect

The Vatican's response to the tumult at Notre Dame over the invitation to President Obama was much more nuanced, especially when contrasted with the harsh criticisms of Notre Dame by some eighty American bishops. Pope Benedict preferred to emphasize the desire for dialogue and finding areas of common ground with the Obama administration. By all accounts the U.S. public and Catholics in particular supported the Notre Dame decision to honor President Obama. Several bishops, led first by retired archbishop John Quinn of San Francisco and then by Archbishop Michael Sheehan of Santa Fe, finally spoke out against the attacks on the president, criticizing them as not being helpful to jointly addressing serious issues like abortion, stem-cell research, and same-sex marriage.

POLITICAL LOBBYING

The United States Conference of Catholic Bishops has an Office of Government Relations, which officially represents them before the U.S. Congress on public policy issues of concern to the bishops. Like most religious groups that lobby before the federal government, lobbying activity is only a small part of their budget. Under 501(c)(3) rules they are able to continue to be a tax-exempt organization as long as they restrict their lobbying activities below a substantial amount of their overall activities, usually determined by what percent of their overall budget goes to pay for lobbying activities. The formal lobbying activity of the USCCB's Office of Government Relations is not the concern here. Rather, it is the more informal lobbying activity of the bishops carried out on their own, and not through the USCCB, that is the focus.

It would be a misreading of U.S. history to see the lobbying activity of the bishops in recent years as typical of their approach to central issues. A look back provides context for the changing nature of lobbying activity by the bishops, priests, and laity during the last century. They have lobbied on behalf of Church issues ranging from financial support for parochial schools, housing for the poor, raising the minimum wage, lifting the embargo against Cuba, etc. In much of this activity their activities were and are not substantially different from the other religious groups that lobby Congress on many if not most of these issues. For example, they have been successful in defeating efforts by pro-choice supporters to provide public funding for abortions.

The nature and tone of the lobbying activity have changed over time. For example, the bishops were unhappy with candidate Kennedy because he opposed federal aid to parochial schools, but the Kennedy family had friends among the hierarchy, most of the hierarchy and priests were Democrats, and the overwhelming desire to elect a Catholic as president took precedence over other matters.

There was more than a little outcry against electing Kennedy from Protestants, including such distinguished leaders as Norman Vincent Peale, Billy Graham, and "Protestants and Other Americans United for the Separation of Church and State."[12] Despite their efforts, Kennedy won the election with 78 percent of the Catholic vote, with 70 percent of the black vote, and with minimum support from white Protestants.

The relationship of the bishops to the Democratic Party began to change in the 1970s. The *Roe v. Wade* decision, guaranteeing a constitutional right to an abortion, was announced by the U.S. Supreme Court in January 1973. In March 1974, representatives of the U.S. Catholic Conference gave testimony on a "Constitutional Amendment Protecting Unborn Human Life" before one of the Senate's subcommittees on the Judiciary. In November 1974, the Vatican Congregation for the Doctrine of Faith, with the formal approval of Pope Paul VI, published its *Declaration on Procured Abortion*, in effect validating the earlier action of the U.S. Conference of Bishops.

In the campaign for the presidency in 1976, Democratic candidate Jimmy Carter was known to be opposed to abortion. And there was strong pro-life support among Catholics in both the House and Senate. George McKenna provides a detailed account of the process by which the Republicans became the pro-life party and Democrats the pro-choice party.[13] He argues that the Democrats, with their commitment to social justice programs that were at the heart of Catholic teachings, would have seemed more appropriately the pro-life party while the Republicans seemed more committed to the values that fostered population control. McKenna recounted the efforts of several U.S. Catholic prelates, including then-Archbishop Bernardin, in meetings with candidate Carter to convince him to come out in support of a constitutional amendment to outlaw abortion. Carter saw that as a bad strategy. Instead, Carter emphasized the areas of social justice in which the Democratic Party and the bishops were in accord.

McKenna reported that Archbishop Bernardin was adamant that abortion was a moral, and not just a Catholic, issue, and even expressed "outrage" at the Democratic Party's failure to support a constitutional amendment to outlaw abortion. Ultimately, Carter and the bishops went their different ways. The bishops were very much aware that, across the board, it was the Democrats who supported the kinds of legislation that most closely reflected the Church's social teachings. Besides, as McKenna pointed out, most bishops and priests were still Democrats, and apparently unwilling to align themselves with Republican leaders. The Republican stance on abortion in 1976 was ambiguous, and there appears to be no evidence that the bishops made a concerted effort to convince President Ford, who was known to be pro-choice, to include a plank in the Republican platform to outlaw abortion.

In 1980, President Carter continued to take a personal stance against abortion, while the Democratic Party, through labor, women's groups, and other forces, was moving in a pro-choice direction. McKenna asserted that the bishops had given up attempting to change Carter's mind and stood aside. Meanwhile, candidate Ronald Reagan, the very pro-choice governor of California, decided to become the pro-life candidate of the Republican Party. Instead of going to the Catholic bishops, with whom he had very major differences on social justice issues, Reagan arranged to have Bill Brock, the head of the Republican Party, and Catholic priest Father Don Shea, then working as the director of Urban Affairs for the Republican National Committee, meet with members of the Moral Majority through the help of the Majority's national field director, Charles Moore.[14]

Through a series of negotiations designed to ensure that the Evangelicals would give their support only to the Republicans, the party's platform addressed a series of moral and political issues important to the Evangelicals, culminating with the now-famous "Anti Abortion Plank" that has become a core element in the Republican Party platform ever since. Several members of the Moral Majority were named to the platform committee and three to subcommittees. Since 1980 the Republican Party has been the "Pro-Life" party and the Democrats increasingly the "Pro-Choice" party.

In the process, Reagan also attracted to the Republican Party wealthy Catholics who supported a strong military, opposed abortion, and opposed taxes to support social justice concerns. They affirmed the principle of subsidiarity by which concerns for helping the poor were best handled at the local level and through personal acts of charity—and not by the federal government. Reagan also attracted conservative working-class Catholics who were put off by the liberal moves of the Democrats on racial issues, not least what they perceived to be reverse discrimination against them brought on by the Democrats' social legislation. These mostly Democratic voters feared that such laws gave blacks preference over their own rights, and Reagan was able to cultivate that fear.[15]

One consequence of this was the beginning of polarization across as opposed to within parties over the abortion issue.

In the 1980s, the American bishops attempted to reenter the public arena with two important pastoral letters. The first was in May 1983, *The Challenge of Peace: God's Promise and Our Response: A Pastoral Letter on War and Peace,* also known as the Peace Pastoral, with its opposition to the continued arms buildup and the possession and use of nuclear weapons. The second was in November 1986, *Economic Justice for All*, also known as the Pastoral on the Economy, questioning many of the nation's economic policies, and seeking to promote more economic justice and equality. Both pastorals were contested and critiqued by Catholic members of the Reagan administration and political conservatives like Michael Novak. And these criticisms did impact the drafting of both letters. The letters were meant to stir up the laity and increase their participation in the political arena.[16]

In December 1983, and again in the spring of 1984, Cardinal Bernardin put forth and refined his idea of a "Consistent Ethic of Life" in order to open a dialogue on life issues. He proposed protecting all of life as a "seamless garment" from the moment of conception until natural death. But Cardinal Bernard Law and others insisted that there could be no public dialogue on the beginning of life, that the idea of a dialogue about abortion was not possible. At this point, we begin to see the beginnings of the polarizing position that led to some bishops' attacks on candidates Ferraro, Kerry, and Obama-Biden.

INFILTRATION

Catholics have had a growing presence in the U.S. House and Senate since at least the New Deal Era. In 1971 there were some seventy-nine Catholic Democrats and twenty-two Catholic Republicans in the House. In the Senate in 1971 there were nine Catholic Democrats and two Catholic Republicans. Roll-call votes on abortion issues before Congress during the period following *Roe v. Wade* showed that Catholic Democrats in the House and Senate were more pro-life than pro-choice in the late 1970s through the first years of the Reagan administration.[17] In the Ninety-fifth Congress (1977–78), only 30 percent of Catholic Democrats and 10 percent of Catholic Republicans in the House were pro-choice in their roll-call votes on abortion; in the Senate 45 percent of the Catholic Democrats and 20 percent of Catholic Republicans were pro-choice. By 1987–88, the tide had turned, especially among Catholic Democrats, with two out of three in the House, and close to 80 percent in the Senate pro-choice. Among Catholic Republicans in the House the pro-choice vote varied between 10 percent and 20 percent before dropping to its present level of 2 percent.

Among Senate Republicans the pro-choice Catholic vote ranged between 1 percent and 10 percent, with the 110th Congress (2007–08) showing 2 percent pro-choice.

To help show how party came to trump religion on the abortion vote, the voting patterns of the Mainline Protestant Democrats in the House are illustrative. They were pro-choice throughout the period, increasing the average percentage from 66 percent to 80 percent, by 2008. In the Senate the pro-choice votes of Mainline Protestant Democrats never dipped below 75 percent and have hovered around 80 percent in the most recent sessions.

The most dramatic change has come among Mainline Protestant Republicans: their pro-choice vote hovered around 70 percent before Reagan; by 1987–88, it had dropped to 50 percent and continued its decline to a level of 10 percent in the 110th Congress (2007–08).

The point to be noted is that during the period beginning with the presidency of Ronald Reagan, the Catholic Democrats in the House and Senate have moved from being primarily pro-life to strongly pro-choice. While Catholic Republicans have always been more pro-life than pro-choice, their pro-choice numbers have dropped to very low levels. Since the same pattern emerged with the Mainline Protestants in both parties, what we find is that political party now trumps religion on the abortion vote. Despite the bishops' increasing attacks on Catholic candidates for public office, it appears that more and more Catholics elected to the House and Senate on the Democratic Party ticket have been pro-choice. At the same time these Catholic Democrats have also been strong supporters of the Church's other social teachings, especially as they reflect Democratic Party ideology. Nevertheless, it seems the case that the Republican Party has been more successful in recruiting candidates who toe closely to the party line on abortion. The Democrats, on the other hand, have been willing to accept candidates like Bob Casey of Pennsylvania, a pro-life Senate Democrat, because he provides so many votes on other issues and because the party decided it was better to win with Casey than to have a very conservative Republican continue in the Senate.

There is one anomaly in this pattern. Among House Catholic Democrats, there has continued to be a strong minority of pro-life Catholics, ranging around 30 percent to 33 percent. Many of them come from traditional Catholic areas in Pennsylvania, Ohio, Indiana, Michigan, and Illinois. It appears that many if not most of the Catholics in the House from these states support Democratic Party legislation that is in line with the bishops' positions on housing, the poor, the elderly, and so forth.

Rep. Bart Stupak (D-MI), one of the pro-life and social justice Catholics, pressured by the bishops, with support of forty-two Democrats and all of the

Republicans, passed an amendment to the Health Care Bill that prevented funding for abortions from government-supplied funds. This led to a four-month struggle between the House and Senate, enough time for the Republicans to defame the bill while the bishops continued to oppose it. The Stupak Amendment provided the Republicans four months of negative attacks, creating fear in the hearts and minds of senior citizens that the bill would take away their Medicare benefits and somehow bankrupt the society.

On the other side, we also witnessed the defeat of a conservative Republican candidate in upstate New York's Twenty-third District. The local party leaders had selected a moderate Republican (pro-choice among other moderate to liberal leanings), and the more orthodox Republicans decided to run a conservative independent candidate in the race. National conservatives like Sarah Palin and Governor Pawlenty of Minnesota denounced the Republican moderate, Dede Scozzafava, and urged Republican voters in the Twenty-third District to consider the conservative candidate, Dan Hoffman, as the true Republican candidate. The conservatives forced the moderate Republican candidate, Scozzafava, to withdraw from the race, but she then threw her support to the Democrat, Bill Owens, who won by three percentage points, the first time a Democrat had won in that district in more than a century. Clearly, there are limits to party control, as was seen in some of the House votes on health care legislation.

DISCUSSION AND CONCLUSION

In this essay I have described and analyzed a variety of processes that U.S. Catholics and their bishops have used to pursue their interests in the public arena, and especially as those interests involve moral issues, politics, and legislation.

The laity who organized and motivated pro-life groups led the way with their annual March for Life, going as far back as 1973. Their peaceful style of protest and demand for legislation banning abortion is a core example of taking direct action in pursuit of their goal. The bishops have come aboard more recently, and gradually this movement has gained momentum, with the addition of Protestant Evangelicals in the 1980s. This movement may be one reason for recent polls showing a decline in support for abortion rights as noted by the Gallup Organization and the Pew Forum polls in the summer of 2009.

Political campaigning and lobbying by the bishops have taken several routes during the past thirty-six years: some have been low key and face to face with political leaders, while public criticism and open attacks reached a peak with the verbal attacks on Notre Dame and President Barack Obama in the late winter through the spring of 2009. Attempts to convince candidate Jimmy Carter to adopt a plank in the Democratic Party platform in 1976 did not work; attacks on pro-choice Catholic candidates for national office seem primarily to have helped raise the level of polarization between pro-life and pro-choice forces. The voting results in the dioceses where bishops spoke out most critically of the Obama-Biden ticket seem to have backfired, perhaps in large part because the public, both Catholics and non-Catholics, were focused on the issues that confronted them daily, which were the economy, jobs, and health care.

When the bishops attempted to address national and international issues with their peace and economy pastorals in 1983 and 1986, they were strongly contested by the Reagan administration. The pastorals soon were reduced to historical documents. What is most interesting about the bishops and about their subsequent revival in the presidential campaigns of 2004 and 2008 with their documents on responsible citizenship, is that abortion remains for them a non-negotiable issue, while jobs, housing for the poor, and even health care are matters of prudential judgment, best left to dialogue and compromise.

QUESTIONS FOR FURTHER REFLECTION

1. How do you understand the idea that "religion has always been a major force in U.S. politics, policy, identity, and culture"? Do you agree or disagree with that idea? Is it a good thing that religion plays a role at all in U.S. politics? What about the opposite: Should politics play a role at all in religion? Do you think that it does in the United States?

2. In what ways or methods does the author say that religion has tried to influence politics in the United States? Do you agree with him? Would you add any other ways to the list? Where, for example, on his list would you put denying Communion to a dissenting politician?

3. When the author talks about these methods of religion influencing politics, who does he say the actors are—the church hierarchy itself, its pastors, or lay persons who are church members?

4. Do you agree with the author that, as a form of direct action, the annual March for Life has had an effect on American politics? What effect has that been?

5. Does it make sense to you that there should be a "National Committee of Catholic Republicans" or a "National Committee of Catholic Democrats"? How would you feel if bishops or priests were members of such groups? What about prominent Catholic lay persons? Is there a danger that such groups put

politics ahead of faith in their tactics and decisions? Is there a danger that such groups make a political use of our faith?

6. The author presents some interesting election results in areas where the local Catholic bishop took what some perceived as a political stand during the election. Do you agree with the conclusions that the author draws from these statistics?

7. Do you agree with the author's history of how the two major political parties came to take their stands on abortion? Do you think these stands are values-driven or have simply been used by the parties to attract votes? What other stands can you think of that the major political parties take that are more a result of partisan advantage seeking than firmly held party beliefs? Must a party take action on its abortion stand, rather than just publicly espouse it, for its stand to be credible to voters?

8. How would you describe the "infiltration" of Catholics into the U.S. House and Senate, to use the author's term? Do these elected representatives appear to be more loyal to their party or their Church? Given that they represent states or districts where Catholics are not a majority, how should their faith affect their votes? If their states or districts were majority Catholic, should that make a difference in how they vote?

NOTES

1. Walter Russell Mead, "God's Country: Evangelicals and Foreign Policy," *Foreign Affairs* (September/October 2006): 24.

2. For an overview of the First Amendment and some of its consequences, see W. V. D'Antonio and D. R. Hoge, "The American Experience of Religious Disestablishment and Pluralism," in *Social Compass* 53, no. 3 (2006): 345–56. John T. Noonan Jr. has provided a brilliant analysis of the epic struggle among the Founding Fathers to establish the principle of religious freedom as written into the First Amendment. See *The Lustre of Our Country: The American Experience of Religious Freedom* (Berkeley: University of California Press, 1998).

3. Kenneth D. Wald, *Religion and Politics in the United States,* 4th ed. (Lanham, MD: Rowman and Littlefield, 2003).

4. One of the most widely accepted analyses of the consequences of the First Amendment is provided by Roger Finke and Rodney Starke, *The Churching of America, 1776–1990: Winners and Losers in Our Religious Economy* (New Brunswick, NJ: Rutgers University Press, 1992). They found that in 1776 only 17 percent of Americans were formally churched, that is, members of a church congregation. By 1980 this figure had risen to 60 percent and in recent years has stabilized around 65 percent. They explain this growth as a response to the openness provided by the disestablishment of religion. With no federal funds to support them, religions created a marketplace where they competed openly for members.

5. See "Pressing the Abortion Issue," *Time,* September 24, 1984.

6. See Kristin Luker, *Abortion and the Politics of Motherhood* (Berkeley: University of California Press, 1985).

7. See The Pew Forum Survey, October 1, 2009, "Support for Abortion Slips." Also see USA Today/Gallup Survey, August 4, 2009. Their mid-July survey found that 47 percent of Americans were pro-life, and 46 percent pro-choice.

8. See John K. White and W. V. D'Antonio, "Catholics and the Politics of Change: The Presidential Campaigns of Two JFKs," in *Religion and the Bush Presidency,* ed., Mark J. Rozell and Gleaves Whitney (New York: Palgrave/Macmillan Press, 2007).

9. The anti-abortion campaign may well have prevented Tom Ridge, a pro-choice Catholic and the popular Republican governor of Pennsylvania, from becoming George W. Bush's running mate.

10. The first referendum supporting legal abortion was passed by a two-to-one vote; the second one, requested by John Paul II in 1981, was approved by a four-to-one vote.

11. See "American Catholics and Church Authority" for a detailed analysis of the growing gap between the laity and Church leaders regarding the locus of moral authority on key sexual issues. Catholic laity look less and less to the bishops on these matters. See D'Antonio et al., *American Catholics Today: New Realities of Their Faith and Their Church* (Lanham, MD: Rowman and Littlefield, 2007).

12. See Shaun A. Casey, *The Making of a Catholic President* (New York: Oxford University Press, 2009), 110–12.

13. George McKenna, "Democrats, Republicans, and Abortion," *Human Life Review* (Summer–Fall 2006): 57–79.

14. See *Moorereport.com/mrpl_plank.html,* "How Did the Pro-Life Plank Become a 1980 Republican Party Platform?"; for a broad understanding of the role of the Evangelicals in American politics, see *Evangelicals and Democracy in America*, ed. Steven Brint and JeanKeith Schroedel (New York: Russell Sage Foundation, 2009). See especially chapter 9, "Moral Values and Political Parties: Cycles of Conflict and Accommodation," by Kimberley H. Conger; and Chapter 11, "Of Movements and Metaphors: The Coevolution of the Christian Right and the GOP," by Clyde Wilcox.

15. See McKenna, "Democrats, Republicans, and Abortion," 57–80; also Mary Meehan, "Democrats for Life" *Orthodoxy Today* (Summer 2003): 63–81, *Orthodoxytoday.org.* David Leege et al., *The Politics of Cultural Differences* (Princeton, NJ: Princeton University Press, 2002).

16. For an account of how the two pastorals were received by the Catholic laity, see D'Antonio et al., 1989, *American Catholic Laity in a Changing Church* (Kansas City, MO: Sheed & Ward, 1989).

17. W. V. D'Antonio, S. Tuch, and J. K. White, "Catholicism, Abortion, and the Emergence of the Culture Wars in the U. S. Congress, 1971–2006," in *Catholics and Politics*, ed. Kristin E. Heyer, Mark J. Rozell and Michael A. Genovese (Washington, DC: Georgetown University Press, 2008), esp. 139–40.

FIVE

Prudential Judgment and Catholic Teaching

Richard R. Gaillardetz

Over the last few decades, the quadrennial presidential election campaigns have been accompanied by a parallel drama enacted within the American Catholic community. The public has witnessed rancorous debates among Catholics regarding the relationship between their religious convictions and their civic obligations as voters. In order to help guide Catholics in their negotiation of this tension, in this essay I will offer some prudential "imperatives" that I think Catholics must attend to as they exercise their dual obligations as Catholics and American citizens. But first it might be helpful to explore in a little more detail what we mean by "the Catholic voter."

APPEALING TO CONSCIENTIOUS CATHOLICS

Clarke and David Carroll Cochran have divided the so-called "Catholic vote" into three different groups. First are the "nominal Catholics," that is, Catholics who self-identify as Catholics but "whose affiliations with the church and its Catholic social teaching are tenuous at best."[1] Their political viewpoints are influenced far more by their social, cultural, and ideological convictions than by their religious convictions, and they seldom articulate their political views in the language of their religious tradition. A second group we might refer to as "ideological Catholics." Their policy positions are primarily driven by ideology, whether from the political left or the right. These Catholics will appeal to church teaching but only as it has already been filtered through prior ideological commitments. They will cite church teaching, but selectively, appealing only to those teachings that support their prior ideological agenda.

Last are those whom Cochran and Cochran refer to as "faithful Catholics," or whom I will refer to as "conscientious Catholics," namely, those Catholics "who strive to embrace Catholic social teaching as a whole and who work to have their Catholic faith shape their political attitudes and behavior, including voting."[2] The American bishops have tried to nudge more American Catholics toward this third category. In their document *Forming Consciences for Faithful Citizenship*, which they approved in November 2007, the bishops wrote:

> As Catholics, we should be guided more by our moral convictions than by our attachment to a political party or interest group. When necessary, our participation ought to transform the party to which we belong. We should not let the party transform us in such a way that we neglect or deny fundamental moral truths.[3]

The great Protestant theologian Reinhold Niebuhr articulated much the same concern when he warned against the perennial American temptation of appealing to our God "as the sanctifier of whatever we most fervently desire."[4] Consideration of the obligations of Catholic voters will focus on this last group.

PRECEPTS FOR THE EXERCISE OF PRUDENCE IN ELECTORAL DISCERNMENT

There is an ethical tradition that goes back to Aristotle that grounds ethics in the practice of virtue. Building on this tradition, St. Thomas Aquinas gave particular attention to the virtue of prudence and its role in public life. Thomas, following Aristotle, held that prudence was an exercise of practical reason and was oriented toward the search for the good to be found in any practical circumstance.[5] Yet prudence is not only concerned with the *recognition* of the good, for it also guides us toward the right means for accomplishing that good. From a Christian perspective, prudence is concerned with bringing our faith to bear on concrete moral situations. As such, no virtue may be more vital for navigating one's way through our contemporary political terrain. *New York Times* columnist David Brooks offers his own definition of prudence:

> What is prudence? It is the ability to grasp the unique pattern of a specific situation. It is the ability to absorb the vast flow of information and still discern the essential current of events—the things that go together and the things that will never go together. It is the ability to engage in complex deliberations and feel which arguments have the most weight.[6]

The American bishops wrote that "prudence shapes and forms our ability to deliberate over available alternatives, to determine what is most fitting to a specific context, and to act decisively."[7] I contend that the entire process of choosing a candidate for public office is governed by the exercise of prudence. And it is the inevitable complexity of this prudential judgment that prevents us from assuming that all well-informed Catholics will make the same choices. In what follows I will propose four precepts intended to illuminate key features of a faithfully Catholic exercise of prudence in the electoral process.

First Precept: Know Your Religious Tradition

Catholic ethicist Stephen Pope contends that "the most distinctive and important feature of Catholic participation in civic life will be the quality of its moral engagement and the breadth of its moral vision."[8] The cultivation of one's moral vision presupposes, in turn, a fundamental precept: *know your religious tradition.*

The knowledge of a religious tradition certainly includes a firm grasp of the church's formal teaching, particularly as regards Catholic social teaching. For many eager to bring their religious convictions into the public arena, there is an inclination to focus narrowly on a select few issues. Yet Catholicism has a broad and comprehensive body of social teaching that addresses issues of contemporary consequence from family life and immigration, to war, health care, abortion, and the environment. A conscientious Catholic is morally obligated to take into account the full range of Catholic social teaching and not merely those teachings that pertain to a few pet issues. In *Forming Consciences for Faithful Citizenship* the bishops wrote that the "consistent ethic of life provides a moral framework for principled Catholic engagement in political life and, rightly understood, neither treats all issues as morally equivalent nor reduces Catholic teaching to one or two issues."[9] Here the bishops are making a strong case against single-issue voting.

However, the knowledge of one's religious tradition is not limited to a grasp of formal church doctrine. Even more important is the need for a kind of participatory knowledge of the tradition. As helpful as catechisms and creeds are, in the end, knowing one's tradition is not like a chemistry student knowing the periodic table. Genuine knowledge of one's religious tradition can come only from a deep and sustained immersion within that tradition; it cannot be accessed simply by consulting a catechism. This participative knowledge comes by way of doctrine, yes, but perhaps even more by exposure to a tradition's diverse exemplary figures (e.g., its saints and other moral leaders), its narratives, rituals, and ethical practices.

For example, Christians who regularly celebrate the Eucharist are shaped by a ritual practice that has the potential for communicating a deep solidarity with all humanity and particularly the marginalized among us. In the fourth century the bishop and theologian St. John Chrysostom reminded Christians of the connections between gathering at the Lord's Table and their obligations toward the poor and hungry:

He who said: "This is my body" is the same who said: "You saw me hungry and you gave me no food," and "Whatever you did to the least of my brothers you did also to me." . . . What good is it if the Eucharistic table is overloaded with golden chalices when your brother is dying of hunger? Start by satisfying his hunger and then with what is left you may adorn the altar as well.[10]

Faithful eucharistic participation ought to evoke a moral vision oriented toward the common good. Pope Benedict XVI had this in mind when he called for a "eucharistic consistency" in his apostolic exhortation on the Eucharist, *Sacramentum Caritatis*. According to Pope Benedict, authentic Christian worship has "consequences for our relationships with others."[11] A eucharistic community blind to its obligations to the poor and hungry is a community that doesn't fully understand the Eucharist. Of course we are talking about an ideal situation. In practice there are many Christians who are regular church-goers but who do not experience worship in this way for reasons too many to consider in a brief essay.[12] In spite of these impediments, it remains the case that those who are immersed in their tradition are best equipped to interpret adequately that tradition's teaching. This leads me to the second precept.

Second Precept: Identify the Fundamental Moral Principles That Are to Guide Your Electoral Discernment

For some time now a number of Catholic special interest groups have been subtly imposing their own idiosyncratic hierarchy of church teaching on the consciences of Catholic voters. For example, a Catholic organization known as Catholic Answers Action has been producing its own unofficial pamphlet for Catholic voters titled *Voters' Guide for Serious Catholics*. Although this guide has no official standing, it has been very influential among conservative Catholics and therefore merits our consideration.[13] The guide begins by acknowledging the wide range of Catholic social teaching, but it quickly singles out five teachings which it characterizes as "nonnegotiable" teachings to be elevated above all others: abortion, euthanasia, cloning, stem-cell research, and same-sex marriage. But what sets these teachings apart from the others? According to the guide, they are principles that condemn intrinsically evil actions. Yet, as Cathleen Kaveny has observed in a very perceptive article in this collection, there is nothing in Catholic social teaching that declares that the condemnation of intrinsically evil actions is, ipso facto, more authoritative than the condemnation of evils considered in virtue of moral intention and circumstance. She points out that to say that an action is intrinsically evil is simply to say that it is wrong in virtue of its object, regardless of either the motive of the actor or the circumstances. Consequently, intrinsically evil actions are always morally

wrong. To declare an action intrinsically evil is to say nothing about the gravity of the evil. For example, it may be the case that according to Catholic just
war teaching, war is not an intrinsic evil. However, once a moral judgment is
made that an act of war does not fulfill the just war criteria, the evil of that act
of war is not lessened by the fact that it was determined through an analysis of
motive and circumstance. Moreover, if one is going to focus on the opposition
of intrinsic evils as the indispensible moral core of a Catholic voter's electoral
discernment, why not include torture, itself an intrinsic evil, in this moral core?

The above-mentioned voter's guide also suggests that these five nonnegotiables are to be set apart because they regard issues for which there can be but
one legitimate application of church teaching: legal prohibition. Yet this is a
clear case of asserting what needs to be demonstrated. Opposition to an intrinsic evil is an absolute moral obligation for Catholics, but this obligation does
not relieve a Catholic of the prudential judgment regarding how this opposition is to be made socially effective.

To conclude, while granting the need to weigh the relative authority and centrality of Catholic social doctrine, there seems to be something arbitrary about
the identification of these five "nonnegotiables." If this rather idiosyncratic
approach to church teaching is inadequate, what is the alternative? One might
start with a consideration of two overarching moral principles that undergird
virtually the entirety of Catholic social teaching: (1) the unconditional affirmation of the dignity of human life with a special concern for the dignity of the
most vulnerable among us and (2) a commitment to the common good.

For Catholics, the first principle proceeds from the basic Christian conviction that all human life is sacred and that this sacredness bestows upon humans
an inalienable dignity. This dignity requires the preservation of those basic
human rights necessary for human flourishing. The second principle, concern
for the common good, proceeds from the biblical injunction to love one's
neighbor. Love of neighbor, in turn, requires a broad social commitment to
the welfare of others. This second principle holds that the good of each person
is bound up in the good of the larger community. All citizens must resist the
temptation to look after only their own welfare, but must concern themselves
with the welfare of all, even where the common welfare does not accrue benefit to them. Pope Benedict describes this commitment to the common good
quite eloquently in his social encyclical *Caritas in Veritate*:

> Another important consideration is the common good. To love someone
> is to desire that person's good and to take effective steps to secure it.
> Besides the good of the individual, there is a good that is linked to living
> in society: the common good. It is the good of "all of us," made up of

individuals, families, and intermediate groups who together constitute society. It is a good that is sought not for its own sake, but for the people who belong to the social community and who can only really and effectively pursue their good within it. To desire the *common good* and strive towards it *is a requirement of justice and charity*.[14]

These principles ground the "consistent ethic of life" that the American bishops continue to champion and provide a key to electoral discernment. They provide a vital moral framework for the exercise of prudence rather than a simplistic alternative to the complexity of prudential judgment. For having developed a mature moral framework informed by Catholic social teaching and governed by its two most central principles, the Catholic voter must still navigate from the sure ground of binding moral principle to the much more dangerous terrain of concrete moral application. This leads us to a third precept.

Third Precept: Distinguish Matters of Moral Principle from Matters of Prudential Judgment

This precept is concerned with a basic feature of Christian ethics that goes right to the heart of the exercise of prudence. Catholic social teaching certainly possesses a dogmatic foundation grounded in the Decalogue and the teaching of Jesus. Yet an important passage from the Second Vatican Council's *Gaudium et Spes* suggests that the Council was not convinced that *all* moral teaching was divinely revealed:

> The Church guards the heritage of God's word and draws from it moral and religious principles without always having at hand the solution to particular problems. As such she desires to add the light of revealed truth to mankind's store of experience, so that the path which humanity has taken in recent times will not be a dark one. (GS 33)[15]

What is the nature of this distinction between moral principles drawn from God's Word and answers to particular questions which do not necessarily come from divine revelation?

Roman Catholicism has always stressed the importance of human reason in the moral life. Catholicism has insisted that there is an identifiable moral structure to the universe (we can also speak of this as a moral "law" as long as we overlook the rigorist connotations of the word)[16] and that we are capable of discovering it through rational reflection on human experience. Because of human sinfulness, this is not as easy as it might be. For that reason, in addition to the employment of our powers of reason in reflection on our experience, we may also turn to divine revelation. We believe that God's saving Word calls us to moral conversion and a life dedicated to the achievement of virtue and goodness. Therefore, at least some of what we might discover in the natural law through reasoned reflection on human experience is also confirmed in divine revelation. But does this hold for the entirety of the natural law? From the sixteenth through the nineteenth centuries it was not uncommon for theologians to teach that all of the natural law belonged to divine revelation, including the most specific of moral injunctions. Few theologians would hold this position today.

It may be helpful to distinguish between three integrally related categories of moral teachings. Of a more general nature are universal moral teachings regarding the law of love, the dignity of the human person, respect for human life, and an obligation to care for the environment. These affirmations constitute the very foundation of Catholic social teaching, would generally be considered dogmatic in character, and, even though they have never been formally defined, demand of believers an assent of faith.

Most of the more specific contents of what we think of as Catholic social teaching belong, however, to the next two levels: specific moral principles and the concrete application of specific moral principles. Specific moral principles emerge out of the church's ecclesial reflection upon universal moral teachings in the light of theological inquiry, the insights of the human sciences, and rational reflection on human experience. This complex ecclesial inquiry yields such specific moral principles as the affirmation of political, civic, and economic human rights, the restrictive conditions that must exist in order to justify capital punishment, the preferential option for the poor, and the prohibition of the direct taking of innocent life.

These specific moral principles generally fall within the category of church teaching known as authoritative doctrine. These are teachings that possess a provisionally binding status but are not, in principle, irreversible. The main reason for seeing such teachings as nondogmatic lies in the way in which, as these teachings attend more to specific moral issues, they are shaped by changing moral contexts and contingent empirical data. These more specific moral principles can be of great assistance in the moral life, but because they are dependent in part on changing circumstances they can apply only, as the medieval tradition put it, "in the majority of instances" (*ut in pluribus*). This dependence on changing empirical data presents a strong argument against considering such teachings as belonging to divine revelation. Consequently, it is the conclusion of many theologians that, while it is legitimate and necessary for the teaching office of the church to propose specific moral principles for the guidance of the faithful, these teachings are not divinely revealed and cannot be taught as dogma.[17] This means that Catholics must treat these teachings as more than mere opinions or pious exhortations but as normative church teaching that they must strive to integrate into their religious outlook. However, because they are not taught as irreversible, it is possible to imagine a Catholic who might be unable to accept a given teaching as reflective of God's will for humankind and could legitimately withhold giving an internal assent to it. A pacifist's conviction that it is never permissible to engage in an act of war would be an example of withholding assent from a specific moral principle taught authoritatively by the magisterium (but not infallibly).

At an even greater level of specificity are the concrete applications of specific moral principles. Here the dependence on changing contexts and contingent empirical data is even more pronounced than with specific moral principles. It is in this realm that the Second Vatican Council recognized the considerable range of judgment possible for Catholics today. The Council renounced an ecclesiastical paternalism in which the laity passively submitted to the directives of the clergy. The Council bishops boldly proposed a new framework reflected in one of the most remarkable passages of any conciliar document:

> Acknowledging the demands of faith and endowed with its force, they [the laity] will unhesitatingly devise new enterprises, where they are appropriate, and put them into action. Laymen should also know that it is generally the function of their well-formed Christian conscience to see that the divine law is inscribed in the life of the earthly city; from priests they may look for spiritual light and nourishment. Let the layman not imagine that his pastors are always such experts, that to every problem which arises, however complicated, they can readily give him a concrete solution, or even that such is their mission. Rather, enlightened by Christian wisdom and giving close attention to the teaching authority of the Church, let the layman take on his own distinctive role. Often enough the Christian view of things will itself suggest some specific solution in certain circumstances. Yet it happens rather frequently, and legitimately so, that with equal sincerity some of the faithful will disagree with others on a given matter. Even against the intentions of their proponents, however, solutions proposed on one side or another may be easily confused by many people with the Gospel message. Hence it is necessary for people to remember that no one is allowed in the aforementioned situations to appropriate the Church's authority for his opinion. (GS 43)[18]

This passage offers a balanced account of the Catholic Christian's obligations in the world. It is the laity who are to be the experts in applying church teaching to ever-changing social contexts. The clergy provide guidance by their preaching and faithful presentation of Catholic teaching, but it lies with the laity to do the difficult work of bringing that teaching to bear on the problems and challenges of the modern world. Striking in this passage is the bishops' honest admission that Catholics of good faith may differ with one another regarding how best to apply Catholic teaching in a given circumstance.

In the 1980s the American bishops explored this final category in two groundbreaking documents, one on war and peace and the other on economic justice. Both documents acknowledged that while the bishops often make authoritative pronouncements regarding foundational moral principles, the specific policy applications they propose are not binding on the consciences of Catholics. For example, in *The Challenge of Peace* the bishops wrote:

> When making applications of these principles, we realize—and we wish readers to recognize—that prudential judgments are involved based on specific circumstances which can change or which can be interpreted differently by people of good will. . . . However, the moral judgments that we make in specific cases, while not binding in conscience, are to be given serious attention and consideration by Catholics as they determine whether their moral judgments are consistent with the Gospel.[19]

For example, the bishops held that their condemnation of the first use of nuclear weapons constituted a concrete application of specific moral principles in a particular context. Catholics should carefully attend to the bishops' viewpoint, but they were not morally bound by it.

It would be difficult to exaggerate the importance of this distinction. Even Catholics who embrace the full range of church moral teaching may legitimately disagree with one another regarding the concrete implementation of these teachings in society. For example, church social teaching calls Catholics to a preferential option for the poor, a special concern for those who are poor and powerless in the world. No conscientious Catholic is free to dismiss the plight of the poor as somebody else's problem. Yet even as two Catholics may agree that they have a religious and moral obligation toward the poor, they may legitimately disagree on the particular economic policy initiatives that will best alleviate poverty. In like manner, two Catholics might disagree regarding whether the application of Catholic moral teaching on abortion requires a legal remedy in the form of criminalization.

Now, as I noted earlier, many Catholics who accept the distinction between binding moral principle and prudential judgment regarding the concrete application of these principles tend to overlook this distinction when it comes to certain issues. Nowhere is this more evident than in the volatile debates surrounding the question of abortion. The Catholic Church teaches that abortion is a moral evil. But how ought Catholics work toward integrating this moral teaching into their civic obligations in a pluralistic and democratic society? How, in other words, do we move from binding moral principle to societal implementation?

It is commonly assumed that so-called "pro-life" Catholics, by virtue of our acceptance of the church's teaching on abortion, are morally obligated to vote for political candidates who support the appointment of Supreme Court judges intent on reversing *Roe v. Wade*. The pursuit of the reversal of *Roe v. Wade* is, in my view, a legitimate and defensible strategy for implementing Catholic teaching. Although I claim no special expertise in constitutional law, I believe a good argument can be made that *Roe v. Wade* is based on flawed constitutional interpretation. However, we cannot forget that a reversal of *Roe v. Wade* would have as its only direct effect a return of the issue to state legislatures. It is far from clear that even the majority of the fifty state legislatures would vote to criminalize abortions. And this is to say nothing of the practical problems associated with legal enforcement of anti-abortion laws or the fact that illegal and unsafe abortions would almost certainly continue.

My larger point is that, *as a matter of binding moral principle*, what Catholic teaching demands of a conscientious Catholic is a commitment to oppose abortion, not just privately, when faced with such a decision in the life of one's family, but publicly as well. But might conscientious Catholics, precisely *because of* their convictions regarding the evil of abortion, pursue alternate strategies that in their judgment might be *more* effective than criminalization in reducing the number of abortions in our country? To put the matter simply, could not a Catholic decide that it was more fruitful to change the culture than to change the law? I believe the answer is yes. Catholics can quite plausibly and defensibly act on church teaching by committing themselves to the cultivation of societal values that support not only the life and dignity of the unborn, but also the life and dignity of the already born, including the dignity of poor women who, having become pregnant, often find themselves in an impossible situation.

Many Catholics have made the reversal of *Roe v. Wade* bear the full weight of Catholic opposition to abortion. They have also made opposition to *Roe v. Wade* a veritable litmus test for Catholic orthodoxy. This approach, however well meaning, has undermined the exercise of prudence by suggesting that, regarding certain issues, prudence's concern for attending to the particulars of practical circumstances is unnecessary. This brings us to a fourth precept for the exercise of prudential judgment in electoral discernment.

Fourth Precept: Carefully Attend to the Particulars
of Political and Social Contexts

It is considered among the highest compliments to refer to someone as a "person of principle." Yet in the exercise of prudence, principle alone does not suffice. One must attend to the particulars of a given context if the pertinent moral principles are to be appropriately applied. It is legitimate and necessary to consider not only a candidate's stated positions but also the likelihood that the candidate would actually bring about the implementation of some social value embedded in Catholic teaching. Candidates and parties have their own priorities, and just because they take a particular stance on an issue, there is no guarantee that they will make that issue a priority should they be elected. So, for example, a candidate might say all the right things about education reform, but a careful study of his past record and speeches may reveal that this issue is in fact very low on the candidate's list of priorities. One must take into account not only a candidate's stated position, but also the strength and sincerity of the candidate's commitment to a given issue.

Other particulars would include the scope of authority that a candidate for a particular office would possess. As Cochran and Cochran have pointed out, a candidate's position on war and peace will be important in a presidential election but it will be much less so for the election of a state legislator. Someone running for the House of Representatives will have virtually no say on the appointment of Supreme Court Justices. Catholic teaching on the death penalty is important, but presidents have considerably less power over the administration of the death penalty than do governors.[20] A prospective voter must weigh the likelihood that a candidate would have it in her power to actually effect change on an issue of concern to Catholics.

Finally, this attention to particulars means that one must also engage in a reading of the "signs of the times." "In the ebb and flow of politics, issues emerge and recede in relevance."[21] In a period of international calm one might choose not to focus on a candidate's foreign policy positions whereas in a period of international tension a more careful assessment of a candidate's approach to geopolitical conflict will become a priority.

In sum, this final precept encourages a religiously motivated voter to consider the particulars of a given political and social context and to give due attention not only to the principles that are to be brought into play but also the likely outcomes. This concern for the concrete political and social context was admitted by Pope Benedict when, as prefect for the Congregation for the Doctrine of the Faith, he granted that it could be appropriate for a Catholic to vote for a political candidate who was pro-choice if there were proportionate reasons, that is, if one was not voting for the candidate *because of* the candidate's support of abortion rights but rather because, having taken all of the particular factors we have just discussed into account, one had come to the conclusion that support of this candidate would most further the common good.[22]

CONCLUSION

Vatican II understood well the complexities of the exercise of prudence in the public order. In the passage cited above in which the bishops called the laity to take the initiative in applying church teaching to contemporary social questions, they recognized the real possibility of disagreement in Catholics' prudential judgments. How then were Catholics to deal with this disagreement? Sadly today many Catholics respond to these inevitable disagreements with shrill condemnation and recourse to simplistic bumper sticker slogans and thirty-second sound bites. In doing so they are often unwittingly participating in the larger politics of demonization that has become endemic in our American political culture. Whether we are talking about the Rush Limbaughs and Sean Hannitys of the political right or the Michael Moores and Keith Olbermanns of the political left, what both sides share is a determination to demonize their opponents, imputing the worst of intentions upon those with whom they disagree. Too often Catholics have aped this demonizing tendency.

Yet the Council offered a different way. In the passage from *Gaudium et Spes* quoted above, the Council called Catholics, when faced with different prudential judgments regarding the best way to implement Catholic social teaching, to ". . . always try to enlighten one another through honest discussion, preserving mutual charity and caring above all for the common good" (GS 43).[23] This alternative approach requires much of us. It demands that we submit our most precious viewpoints and convictions to the harsh light of the Gospel. It demands that we have the courage to listen to those with whom we disagree, imputing to them the best rather than the worst of intentions. It demands the humility to know that others of equally good faith may disagree with us. It demands that we forsake bumper sticker platitudes and pseudo-Christian sound bites in favor of thoughtful, informed, and yes, prayerful analysis. For anything less demeans the richness and transformative power of our religion and falls short of the faithful citizenship to which all American Catholics are called.

QUESTIONS FOR FURTHER REFLECTION

1. The author cites some literature that divides Catholic voters into three groups: (1) nominal Catholics, (2) ideological Catholics, and (3) faithful or conscientious Catholics. Do you agree with these categories and the description of the factors that influence their votes? Which group would the Catholic bishops prefer Catholics to be in? What could they do to get them there?

2. The author cites a number of different perspectives on what constitutes "prudence." How would you define this term? Would it affect the way you vote?

3. In a broad religious tradition like Catholicism, is it ever prudent to focus on a narrow range of issues in making a political judgment? What if you believe that certain narrow issues are more important than others? Can this be a part of your prudential judgment?

4. The author writes of "participatory knowledge" of one's religious tradition. What does he mean by that? How is Pope Benedict XVI's term "eucharistic consistency" a part of "participatory knowledge"? How does that affect prudential judgment?

5. The author criticizes lists of "nonnegotiables" for Catholic voters. What does he believe is incorrect about such lists? Do you agree with him?

6. What overarching moral principles does he prefer to use in making prudential judgments? How would he apply them to making political decisions? Are these principles more or less helpful than "nonnegotiable" lists?

7. Does the Catholic Church believe that all of its moral teachings are divinely revealed? What is the difference, if any, between moral principles drawn from God's Word and those that are subsequent applications of it? Does one bind Catholics more than the other?

8. The author contends that such moral principles as the affirmation of political, civic, and economic human rights emerge from the Church's reflection on its dogmatic teaching. Are these teachings authoritative? Can they ever change? What is the relationship of these moral principles in their application to changing circumstances?

9. Consider the concrete application of specific moral principles to individual situations. What did the Second Vatican Council say about the framework for the faithful to make such individualized applications of these moral principles?

10. Is there a distinction between binding moral principles and prudential judgment regarding the concrete application of these principles? Could such a distinction ever be made in dealing with the question of how to fight the evil of abortion?

11. The author writes that "in the exercise of prudence, principle alone does not suffice." What does he mean by that? What other factors go into the decision to give political support to candidates who say that they agree with certain principles that we believe are important?

NOTES

1. Clarke E. Cochran and David Carroll Cochran, *The Catholic Vote: A Guide for the Perplexed* (Maryknoll, NY: Orbis Books, 2008), 41.

2. Ibid.

3. USCCB, *Forming Consciences for Faithful Citizenship: A Call to Political Responsibility from the Catholic Bishops of the United States* (Washington, DC: USCCB, 2007), 4 [no. 14]. This document can be accessed at *http://www.usccb.org/faithfulcitizenship/FCStatement.pdf.*

4. The Niebuhr quotation is found in E. J. Dionne, "Religion's Reach and the Tides of Change," *Notre Dame Magazine* 37 (Summer 2008): 48.

5. *Summa Theologiae* II–II, q. 47, a. 2. For a detailed study of the virtue of prudence in Thomistic ethics, see Daniel Mark Nelson, *The Priority of Prudence* (University Park: University of Pennsylvania Press, 1991).

6. David Brooks, "Why Experience Matters," *New York Times,* September 16, 2008.

7. USCCB, *Forming Consciences for Faithful Citizenship*, 7 [no. 19].

8. Stephen J. Pope, "Catholic Social Thought and the American Experience," in *American Catholics and Civic Engagement: A Distinctive Voice,* vol. 1 of *American Catholics in the Public Square*, ed. Margaret O'Brien Steinfels (New York: Sheed & Ward, 2004), 32.

9. USCCB, *Forming Consciences for Faithful Citizenship*, 12 [no. 40].

10. John Chrysostom, *In Evangelium S. Matthaei, hom.* 50:3–4: PG 58, 508–9.

11. No. 83. Text may be accessed on-line at the Vatican website.

12. Pope, "Catholic Social Thought and the American Experience," 36–37.

13. For a careful and balanced analysis of this guide, along with another produced by Catholics in Alliance for the Common Good, see Harold E. Ernst, "How to 'Vote Catholic': Dueling Catholic Voter Guides in the 2006 Midterm Elections," in *Faith in Public Life,* College Theology Society Annual 53 (2007), ed. William J. Collinge (Maryknoll, NY: Orbis Books, 2008), 179–201.

14. Pope Benedict XVI, Encyclical Letter *Caritas in Veritate.* This document was accessed at *www.vatican.va.*

15. This document was accessed at *www.vatican.va.*

16. For a consideration of the ambiguities inherent in speaking of a moral "law," see John Mahoney, "The Language of Law," in *The Making of Moral Theology* (Oxford: Clarendon, 1987), 224–58. See also Jean Porter, *Natural and Divine Law: Reclaiming the Tradition for Christian Ethics* (Grand Rapids: Eerdmans, 1999).

17. See John Boyle, "The Natural Law and the Magisterium," in *Church Teaching Authority: Historical and Theological Studies* (Notre Dame, IN: University of Notre Dame Press, 1995), 43–62; Richard A. McCormick, *Corrective Vision: Explorations in Moral Theology* (Kansas City: Sheed & Ward, 1994), 86–89; Franz Böckle, "Le magistère de l'Église in matière morale," *Revue théologique de Louvain* 19 (1989): 3–16; Francis A. Sullivan, "Some Observations on the New Formula for the Profession of Faith," *Gregorianum* 70 (1989):

552–54; André Naud, *Le magistère incertain* (Montreal: Fides, 1989), 77–121; Karl Rahner, "Basic Observations on the Subject of Changeable and Unchangeable Factors in the Church," *Theological Investigations* 14 (New York: Seabury, 1976), 3–23.

18. This document was accessed at *www.vatican.va*.

19. *The Challenge of Peace* (no. 10). See also *Economic Justice for All*, no. 135.

20. Cochran and Cochran, *The Catholic Vote*, 104.

21. Ibid., 104–5.

22. Congregation for the Doctrine of the Faith, *Doctrinal Note on Some Questions Regarding the Participation of Catholics in Political Life* (2002). This document can be accessed at *www.vatican.va*.

23. This document was accessed at *www.vatican.va*.

SIX

Not a Single-Issue Church: Resurrecting the Catholic Social Justice Tradition

John Gehring

If the 2004 presidential election represented a triumph for cultural conservatives who dominated the political debate over moral issues, Catholic progressives ended that year disillusioned. For centuries, papal encyclicals and the rich history of Catholic social teaching have provided a powerful voice on poverty, health care, labor rights, the death penalty, environmental stewardship, and the essential role of government in serving the common good. How had this Christian witness in public life been reduced to abortion politics and a holy trinity of conservative talking points on taxes, "big government," and free markets? A "values voter," the media pundits told us, was someone focused on just a handful of hot-button issues stoking the flames of America's "culture wars." As for those other pesky challenges like war and poverty, everyone knew we could just leave those to the rabble-rousing secular "lefties" who were of no consequence.

Also fueling the sense of frustration among progressive and moderate Catholics that year was the public pillorying of Senator John Kerry, the Democratic nominee for president, by the Catholic hierarchy. A Catholic inspired by his faith tradition's commitment to social justice, Kerry faced the wrath of Archbishop Raymond Burke of St. Louis. The archbishop said that Kerry could not receive Communion in his archdiocese because of his views on abortion. A few other outspoken bishops gave the same admonition. Media coverage swelled into a sensational frenzy dubbed the "wafer wars." Kerry lost the decisive Catholic swing vote to George W. Bush by five percentage points, 47 percent to 52 percent, and with it the election.

In those days, Catholic progressives articulating the broad spectrum of Catholic social justice values in the media were rare. The most ubiquitous Catholic pundit on television news was William Donohue, the president of the Catholic League for Religious and Civil Rights. The pugnacious commentator made over twenty appearances on television leading up to the election. Along with perpetuating the pernicious stereotype that "Hollywood is controlled by secular Jews who hate Christianity," Donohue used his air time to denounce the "gay death style," and frequently claimed Senator Kerry "never found an abortion he couldn't justify."[1] In the more than 160 press releases Donohue released in 2004 alone, none mentioned as election issues the Iraq war (which the U.S. Catholic bishops opposed), poverty, or other pressing moral and political issues central to Catholic teaching.[2]

But now, both the style and the substance of Catholicism in the public square are dramatically changing. More Catholics are speaking out to advance a broader agenda rooted in our faith's long-standing commitment to peace, social justice, and the common good. Catholic organizations such as Catholics in Alliance for the Common Good, Catholics United, and NETWORK, a National Catholic Social Justice Lobby, are go-to sources for prominent media outlets. This means a greater diversity of Catholic voices in the news, speaking about the moral dimensions of not just abortion, but also of health care reform, economic justice, immigration, and climate change. These groups are cultivating a faith-based movement focused on social justice that doesn't concede the values terrain to the Christian right. Even Catholic conservatives who not too long ago seemed to have a monopoly on the moral values narrative in American politics are taking notice. As the editor of *Crisis* magazine and InsideCatholic.com told Religion News Service, "Progressive Catholics have finally gotten their act together. They are more organized and effective. Certainly they are a force."[3]

WHAT HAPPENED TO THE SEAMLESS GARMENT?

"The Bishops vs. The Bomb"—*Time* magazine featured this intriguing headline on its May 16, 1983, cover. The American Catholic bishops, lead by Cardinal Joseph Bernardin of Chicago, had just released a pastoral letter about nuclear weapons. *The Challenge of Peace: God's Promise and Our Response* offered a pointed critique of U.S. nuclear arms policy, which ruffled the feathers of top military brass and political powerbrokers in Washington. Three years later, the bishops released *Economic Justice for All*, a pastoral letter on Catholic social teaching and the U.S. economy. In an era when income inequality soared and President Ronald Reagan frequently demonized government, the bishops' letter bluntly called poverty in America a "scandal" and rejected "the notion that a free market automatically produces justice."[4] The consistent ethic of life or "seamless garment" vision articulated by Cardinal Bernardin and the U.S. bishops' conference demonstrated that—along with the tragedy of abortion—economic justice, the pursuit of peace, opposition to the death penalty, and stewardship of the environment are all "life issues" bearing on human dignity.

This Catholic vision of the common good has inspired seminal movements in American politics. Franklin D. Roosevelt drew from Catholic social thought in shaping the New Deal, which advanced the minimum wage, Social Security, and fair labor standards. Though Roosevelt himself was a nominal Episcopalian, his ideas were influenced by Monsignor John A. Ryan, a populist Catholic priest from Minnesota, whose writings on economic justice, labor, and social inequality were widely read in the decades following World War I. In 1919, the U.S. Catholic bishops asked Ryan to write their *Program for Social Reconstruction*, a document that Jesuit scholar Joseph M. McShane, SJ, credited with launching "the American Catholic search for social justice" in earnest.[5] The program called for what at the time were dramatic social reforms: a minimum wage, public housing for workers, labor participation in management decisions, and insurance for the elderly, disabled, and unemployed. In 1931, Pope Pius XI released *Quadragesimo Anno*, an encyclical issued on the fortieth anniversary of Pope Leo XIII's landmark "labor encyclical" *Rerum Novarum*. The pontiff offered a stinging critique of unchecked capitalism that resonated far beyond ecclesial corridors of power. That same year, as Lew Daly observed in his 2007 *Boston Review* essay, "In Search of the Common Good: The Catholic Roots of American Liberalism," Roosevelt delivered a speech calling for "social justice through social action," in which he quoted extensively from the encyclical.[6]

From the middle of the 1950s through the 1960s, Catholics joined Jews and Protestants as the civil rights movement awakened the nation's conscience to the social sins of segregation. Appeals to human dignity and the common good were far from abstract principles during a time when religious witness in public life focused primarily on collective responsibility and prophetic justice. In the post–civil rights era, seismic political and cultural shifts coincided with the rise of religious leaders who emphasized personal morality and sexual ethics over structural injustices such as racism and poverty. Growing discontent with the liberalizing influences of birth control and "free love" reached a high-water mark after the 1973 *Roe v. Wade* decision legalizing abortion. Many Catholics who identified as Democrats increasingly felt betrayed by a party they viewed as rejecting traditional values and religious traditions as retrograde holdovers from a bygone era. As the Democratic Party and progressive religious leaders often conceded debates over culture, the family, and bioethics to conservatives, traditional Catholics and evangelicals mobilized around a strategic effort to create what the late Jerry Falwell called a "moral majority."

In recent years, prominent Catholic conservatives like George Weigel of the Ethics and Public Policy Center, Deal Hudson, a former Catholic outreach director for President George W. Bush, the late Father Richard John Neuhaus, and Father Frank Pavone of Priests for Life have pushed for a return to Catholic "orthodoxy." In books, blogs, speeches, television appearances, and through well-funded conservative networks, they have emphasized abortion as the preeminent political issue for Catholics, railed against "dissident" Catholics, and criticized the U.S. Conference of Catholic Bishops for statements on war and economic justice. Along with organizations such as the Cardinal Newman Society, a self-appointed watchdog group for Catholic orthodoxy on college campuses, these "theocons" have demonized Catholic progressives and trumpeted a "traditional" Catholicism suspicious of social justice advocacy or a "preferential option for the poor." Papal biographer and frequent Catholic commentator George Weigel has no qualms connecting this vision of Catholicism with partisan politics. "The Republican Party is a more secure platform from which Catholics can work on the great issues of the day than a party in thrall to abortion 'rights,' gay activism, and a utilitarian approach to the biotech future that is disturbingly reminiscent of 'Brave New World,' " Weigel wrote in his syndicated newspaper column.[7] Despite his criticism of the U.S. Conference of Catholic Bishops' strong opposition to the invasion of Iraq, Weigel is the intellectual darling of many bishops, and his column is featured in diocesan newspapers across the country.

The ideological drift rightward among some members of the Catholic hierarchy and influential Catholic pundits undermines the Church's own teachings about the role of faith in politics. In 2003, the Vatican's Congregation for the Doctrine of the Faith issued its *Doctrinal Note on Some Questions Regarding the Participation of Catholics in Political Life*, which warned against narrowing the broad spectrum of Catholic values to a single issue. "The Christian faith is an integral unity, and thus it is incoherent to isolate some particular element to the detriment of the whole of Catholic doctrine," the statement read. "A political commitment to a single isolated aspect of the Church's social doctrine does not exhaust one's responsibility toward the common good."[8] And this from *Forming Consciences for Faithful Citizenship*, the U.S. bishops' election-year document on political responsibility: "Catholic teaching about the dignity of life calls us to oppose torture, unjust war, and the use of the death penalty; to prevent genocide and attack against noncombatants; to oppose racism; and to overcome poverty and suffering."[9] As Auxiliary Bishop Gabino Zavala of the Archdiocese of Los Angeles told *Washington Post* columnist E. J. Dionne Jr. in October 2008: "We are not a one-issue Church . . . but that's not what always comes out."

A CHOICE FOR CATHOLIC BISHOPS: CONFRONTATION OR ENGAGEMENT?

In late October 2008, parishioners at St. John's Roman Catholic Church in Honesdale, Pennsylvania, gathered for a forum organized a few weeks before the presidential election. A local businessman, a University of Scranton professor, a Catholic sister from Marywood University, and a county commissioner shared a diverse range of views about candidates McCain and Obama. By all accounts, the conversation was civil, politically balanced, and engaging. One panelist made the point that the U.S. bishops' *Forming Consciences for Faithful Citizenship* statement encouraged Catholic voters to weigh a range of moral issues when assessing candidates. The bishop of the diocese, Most Reverend Joseph Martino, arrived as the panelists were making their remarks and angrily protested. "No USCCB document is relevant in this diocese!" Martino thundered. "There is one teacher in this diocese, and these points are not debatable!"[10] Bishop Martino, whose tumultuous tenure in Scranton ended with his retirement in 2009, wanted his Catholic flock to ignore the election-year statement from his own bishops' conference and follow a letter that he had written that insisted that a candidate's position on abortion trumped any other issue. Public officials who "persist in public support for abortion," his letter stated, should not "partake in or be admitted to the sacrament of Holy Communion."[11]

Catholic progressives are not the only faithful worried about the dangers posed by some U.S. church leaders turning away from civil engagement in the public square and embracing a confrontational style when it comes to politics. Just days after the election of Barack Obama, the nation's Catholic bishops gathered in Baltimore for their annual fall meeting. As bishops lined up to criticize the president-elect's position on abortion, Bishop Blase Cupich of South Dakota cautioned his fellow bishops: "Keep in mind a prophecy of denunciation quickly wears thin, and it seems to me what we need is a prophecy of solidarity, with the community we serve and the nation that we live in."[12] But when the University of Notre Dame invited President Obama to give the commencement address six months after the election, the explosive reaction among many Catholic bishops belied that measured tone. Archbishop John C. Nienstedt of St. Paul and Minneapolis called it a "travesty" and described the president as an "anti-Catholic politician."[13] Bishop John D'Arcy of South

Bend, Indiana, boycotted Notre Dame's graduation. Cardinal Francis George of Chicago, president of the U.S. bishops' conference, initially described the invitation as an "extreme embarrassment"[14] to Catholics. Bishop Thomas G. Doran of Rockford, Illinois, called it "truly obscene" and sarcastically suggested renaming the school "Northwestern Indiana Humanist University."[15] The Cardinal Newman Society circulated a petition sent to Notre Dame president Father John Jenkins accusing the university of choosing "prestige over principles, popularity over morality."[16]

Unlike years past when religious progressives were not organized to provide effective media responses, this time a statement signed by over twenty Catholic theologians, which denounced the shrill attacks against Father Jenkins and Notre Dame, ran as a full-page ad in the *South Bend Tribune*.[17] It cautioned "those who seek to disrupt these joyous proceedings or to divide the Church for narrow political advantage that history is not on your side." The theologians noted that Notre Dame has a long tradition of inviting presidents from both political parties to give the commencement address. This list includes former presidents George W. Bush and Ronald Reagan, whose positions on the death penalty, use of military power, torture, and other central life issues did not align with Catholic social teaching. "These former leaders were received as sitting presidents who came to speak about great issues of our time," the statement read.

"The same standard should apply for President Obama, a Christian with deep respect for the role of faith in public life and whose commitment to universal health care, comprehensive immigration reform, environmental stewardship, and an economy that works for all Americans reflect core Catholic values."

While protesters flew a plane over campus with graphic images of an aborted fetus and attempted to demonize the president at every turn, President Obama himself called for "open hearts, open minds, and fair-minded words." In his address, Father Jenkins praised the president as a leader whose commitment to universal health care, compassionate immigration reform, nuclear disarmament, and racial reconciliation reflect Catholic values. He strongly reiterated Catholic opposition to abortion, but also commended the president for coming to Notre Dame in a spirit of respectful dialogue. In doing so, Father Jenkins honored a Catholic intellectual tradition that rejects the slash-and-burn rhetorical extremism so prevalent in a culture where cable news shouting matches reduce complex issues to simplistic sound bites. That may work on Fox News, but it should not work in the Catholic Church.

During his speech, President Obama addressed the moral dimension of abortion, emphasized the need to support pregnant women and reduce unintended pregnancies, called for greater access to adoption, and embraced conscience clauses for health care providers. Unlike some Catholic bishops who decried Notre Dame's invitation as a scandal, an editorial in the Vatican's newspaper, *L'Osservatore Romano*, commended the president's speech for seeking common ground.[18]

The Obama–Notre Dame commencement controversy—along with the toxic tone of our nation's abortion debates—has provoked self-reflection among those bishops who see prudence, reason, and a return to pastoral sensitivity as a more effective model for winning hearts and minds. In a rare public airing of criticism from an active bishop, Archbishop Michael J. Sheehan of Santa Fe, New Mexico, gave an interview with the *National Catholic Reporter* in August 2009 decrying the combative tactics of some bishops as counterproductive to getting a fair hearing for Catholic values. He lamented the fact that a few church leaders even refuse to talk to politicians or deny them Communion based on a single issue, and Sheehan disagreed strongly with his brother bishops who lashed out at Notre Dame for inviting President Obama to give the commencement address. According to the *National Catholic Reporter*, here's what Archbishop Sheehan told his fellow bishops:

> I don't feel so badly about Obama going [to Notre Dame] because he's our president. I said we've gotten more done on the pro-life issue in New Mexico by talking to people that don't agree with us on everything. We got Governor Richardson to sign off on the abolition of the death penalty for New Mexico, which he was in favor of. We talked to him, and we got him on board and got the support in the legislature. But you know, he's pro-abortion. So? It doesn't mean we sit and wait, that we sit on the sides and not talk to him. We've done so much more by consultation and by building bridges in those areas. And then to make a big scene about Obama—I think a lot of the enemies of the church are delighted to see all that. And I said that I think we don't want to isolate ourselves from the rest of America by our strong views on abortion and the other things. We need to be building bridges, not burning them.[19]

While the media highlights the most controversial religious voices—Cardinal James Stafford describing Barack Obama's election as an "apocalyptic" event surely made irresistible headlines—most Catholic leaders recognize the need for thoughtful dialogue. Pope Benedict XVI's cordial meeting with President Obama at the Vatican in July 2009 offered an example of how the global Catholic Church recognizes politics as the art of the possible rather than a zero-sum game. The Holy Father found common ground between the church's broad international agenda and many of the president's priorities: Middle East peace, nuclear deterrence, poverty alleviation, interfaith dialogue, comprehensive immigration reform, and global climate change. Instead of vilifying Obama on the issue of abortion, Pope Benedict gave Obama a signed copy of *Dignitas Personae*, a Vatican document on bioethics. No screaming or spectacle, simply a gracious model of faith and reason at work.

The Catholic Church risks losing credibility in the public square when bishops are perceived to be closely aligned with ideologues pushing narrow agendas. As Archbishop Emeritus of San Francisco John Quinn wrote in *America* magazine:

> The condemnation of President Obama and the wider policy shift that represents signal to many thoughtful persons that the bishops have now come down firmly on the Republican side in American politics. . . . The perception of partisanship on the part of the Church is disturbing to many Catholics given the charge of *Gaudium et Spes* that the Church must transcend every political structure and cannot sacrifice that transcendence, no matter how important the cause.[20]

Catholics in America have journeyed a long way from being a despised immigrant minority in a culture that questioned their commitment to democracy. Today Catholics are leaders in the influential fields of politics, business, and journalism. The Catholic Church is a powerful voice for social justice, peace, and human dignity around the world. But the Church is also at a defining crossroads. The choice between an embattled fundamentalism that hunkers down against hostile threats from a wider culture, and the hope of a vibrant faith engaged in constructive dialogue with those who do not share our values or beliefs could well define the future of Catholicism in America. An engaged Catholicism does not fear the diverse ideas of a pluralistic democracy or slam the door on those we disagree with on polarizing issues. It brings faith and reason to the always imperfect task of touching minds and hearts through principled persuasion guided by love and mutual respect.

CATHOLIC SOCIAL TEACHING
AND FREE-MARKET FUNDAMENTALISM

As the economic crisis deepened and Wall Street titans like Lehman Brothers collapsed, a bookish German theologian best known as Pope Benedict XVI worked on updating a long-anticipated encyclical. The pope had delayed his encyclical for several months to more adequately address the moral context of a spiraling global economy. *Caritas in Veritate* (Charity in Truth) proved a timely reflection on economic justice, labor unions, environmental exploitation, and international development rooted in respect for human dignity.

Most notably, this bold critique of free-market fundamentalism has left some conservative Catholics enthralled with laissez-faire economics scrambling to downplay passages that take a skeptical view of unfettered capitalism. Indeed, Benedict goes where many U.S. politicians fear to tread in his call for equitable distribution of wealth, robust financial regulations, and the essential role government has in promoting the common good. If the pope were running for political office in the United States on this platform, you can imagine the attack ads accusing him of being a "tax-and-spend liberal" or, even worse, a socialist bent on a "government takeover" of our financial system. While Pope Benedict is not stealing lines from Marx and recognizes the importance of private capital, he insists that markets devoid of a moral compass are insufficient instruments of justice.

When the encyclical was released, the American Catholic right balked. George Weigel dismissed the pope's critique of economic liberalism as lacking Benedict's full imprimatur. Weigel claimed that the encyclical could be best understood as having two authors: the pope and the Vatican's Pontifical Council for Justice and Peace. Weigel's essay, dripping with condescension, is entitled "*Caritas in Veritate* in Gold and Red: The Revenge of Justice and Peace (or So They May Think)." As the title implies, Weigel believes those like himself with "advanced degrees in Vaticanology" could mark in red those leftist sections written by the Justice and Peace office and highlight in gold the part Benedict really believes and wrote himself. "The net result is, with respect, an encyclical that resembles a duck-billed platypus," Weigel wrote.[21]

The proposition that the pope's real motivation in his encyclical was to mollify the pinkos in Justice and Peace is absurd. As the Catholic author and *National Catholic Reporter* blogger Michael Sean Winters observed,

> Weigel not only misunderstands the relationship a Christian should have to the poor, he misunderstands the relationship a Catholic should have to a papal encyclical. I had thought that it was the Pope and the bishops who had the task of authoritatively interpreting the doctrine of the Church. Silly me. Mr. Weigel, with his gold and red pens, is the official arbiter of what passes as orthodoxy. . . . Weigel is wrong on the merits, but he is also wrong in his stance. This encyclical—all of it—bears the Pope's signature and the respect due to all statements of the magisterium.[22]

Instead of taking the social justice concerns of Pope Benedict seriously, Weigel instead urges Catholics to recall Pope John Paul II's "pro-capitalist teachings." He seems to conveniently forget these words from John Paul during a speech in Latvia in 1993: "The Church, since Leo XIII's *Rerum Novarum*, has always distanced herself from capitalist ideology, holding it responsible for grave social injustices. . . . I, myself, after the historical failure of communism, did not hesitate to raise serious doubts on the validity of capitalism."[23]

Or this from John Paul II's encyclical *Centesimus Annus*: "The collapse of the communist system in so many countries certainly removes an obstacle to facing these problems in an appropriate and realistic way, but it is not enough to bring about their solution. Indeed, there is the risk that a radical capitalistic ideology could spread which refuses even to consider these problems . . . and which blindly entrusts their solution to the free development of market forces."[24]

And finally, John Paul II's words about neoliberal economic policies from *Ecclesia in America*: "More and more, in many countries of America, a system known as 'neoliberalism' prevails; based on a purely economic conception of man, this system considers profit and the law of the market as its only parameters, to the detriment of the dignity of and the respect due to individuals and peoples. At times this system has become the ideological justification for certain attitudes and behavior in the social and political spheres leading to the neglect of the weaker members of society."[25]

Despite Pope John Paul II's warnings about an "idolatry" of the market, the Catholic right has long offered up full-throated encomiums for economic liberalism and market supremacy. Michael Novak of the American Enterprise Institute, who presumably with a straight face once compared the modern corporation to the Suffering Servant of Isaiah, got out in front before the encyclical was released to assure Catholics that the pope would not be upsetting the free-market status quo. In a commentary for the journal *First Things* titled "Economic Heresies of the Left," Novak argues that in "actual capitalist practice, the love of creativity, invention, and groundbreaking enterprise are far more powerful than motives of greed."[26] Novak's breathless praise continues: "The fundamental systemic motive infusing the spirit of capitalism is the imperative to liberate the world's poor from the premodern ubiquity of grinding poverty."[27] So capitalism is not first and foremost concerned with profit, but liberating the world from poverty. This argument does not pass the laugh test. It sounds like the "Washington Consensus" boilerplate peddled by the World Bank and the International Monetary Fund when those institutions forced developing nations to adopt aggressive privatization, "austerity budgets," and deep cuts to social services with disastrous results.

Father Robert Sirico, president of the Acton Institute, a nonprofit organization dedicated to promoting "a free and virtuous society characterized by individual liberty and sustained by religious principles," is another frequent Catholic commentator who sounds like he is on staff at the libertarian Cato

Institute. Sirico has dismissed as a "biblical fallacy" the belief that government can play a role in Christians' obligation to help the poor. "Jesus never called on public authority to enact welfare programs," Sirico wrote in the Acton Institute's *Religion and Liberty* journal. "He never demanded that his followers form a political movement to tax and spend."[28] The Republican National Committee could have written Sirico's argument. Daniel Finn, a theologian at St. John's University in Collegeville, Minnesota, responded in *Commonweal* magazine with a commentary titled "Libertarian Heresy: The Fundamentalism of Free-Market Theology":

> Catholic biblical scholarship and magisterial teaching have rejected the fundamentalism of "If the Bible doesn't say it, it shouldn't be done." We might further note that Jesus didn't talk about either free markets or democracy, both of which Sirico himself praises as moral expressions of dedicated Christian faith. There is something intellectually dodgy about selectively applying fundamentalism to critique one's opponents' ideas while sparing one's own.[29]

Not long ago, those who demonized government and preached the gospel of free-market salvation with evangelical zeal had few worries. The titans of corporate America were glorified on the cover of *Fortune* and "trickle-down" economics was in vogue. But things fall apart. Decades of deregulation, crass decisions at the highest levels of business and government, and a consumer culture that celebrates materialism are catching up with reality. The financial crisis is also a moral crisis that requires a profound shift in values. Our nation's diverse religious communities have a proud tradition of speaking prophetically about economic justice, and the need to temper the often cruel vagaries of the market with collective responsibility to care for our neighbors. Amid another global economic collapse in 1931, Pope Pius XI affirmed a positive role for government and the obligation to pay workers a living wage. In our own time, Pope Benedict XVI has stressed the need to find "a new synthesis between the common good and the market, between capital and labor."[30] Those who trumpet a holy trinity of tax cuts, unfettered markets, and a savage brand of corporate capitalism serve narrow ideologies hard to square with the teachings of Jesus, who preached "good news to the poor" and kicked the money-changers out of the Temple. While the American ethos of "rugged individualism" and self-reliance often chafes against Judeo-Christian notions of solidarity with the poor, the scope of the economic crisis offers a historic opportunity to rebuild our economy to serve the common good, not simply the privileged few.

HEALTH CARE REFORM:
A MORAL IMPERATIVE OR "SOCIALIZED MEDICINE"?

If you watched enough cable news during the summer and fall of 2009 you would think the fight over health care reform had been reduced to protestors screaming about socialism, "death panels," and the evils of big government. In a sign that religious progressives are becoming a more potent force in the public square, a campaign organized by Christian, Jewish, and Muslim organizations united behind health care reform as a moral imperative offered a stark contrast to the misinformation that distorted this critical debate.

The "40 Days for Health Reform" coalition hosted a national conference call that featured religious leaders and citizens sharing painful stories from the front lines of a broken health care system. One hundred and forty thousand citizens participated. Instead of shouting and demagoguery, there was thoughtful reflection, civil dialogue, and factual analysis. Ministers and rabbis spoke about values that transcend partisan politics or narrow ideologies. A Muslim American neurologist expressed frustration with insurance companies denying coverage to those in desperate need of treatment. A fifteen-year-old Catholic with scoliosis talked about how her family was going without medical care because they lost Medicaid coverage. The faith community refused to concede the debate to right-wing talk-radio pundits, Washington insiders, or special interests defending the status quo.

"40 Days for Health Reform" included more than thirty denominations and religious organizations that represented Americans across race, region, and political affiliation. The campaign included a national TV ad on CNN, prayer vigils, sermon weekends, and lobbying visits with key members of Congress. Again, Catholics on the other side of the issue offered an alternative voice in the media to the fear mongering of the far right, helping to frame health care reform as a moral issue that transcended partisan agendas. At the heart of complicated legislative battles over health care are profound ethical questions. Even if we are satisfied with our own health care, what responsibility do we have as a society to make sure the system works for everyone? How do we balance individual interests with policies that best serve the common good? While specific solutions to a twenty-first-century health care crisis can't be found in the Bible, Koran, or the Torah, our faith traditions offer timeless values about human dignity, compassion, and loving our neighbors as ourselves. People of goodwill can disagree over the most effective ways to ensure reform. But we must not waver from this core principle: health care is a human right, not a privilege.

Not so, argues Rev. Michael Orsi, a Research Fellow in Law and Religion at Ave Maria School of Law. It's not every day you find a commentary penned by a Catholic priest with this jarring headline: "Bishops Wrong: Health Care Not a Right."[31] Writing in *Human Events*, a publication that somewhat conspiratorially describes itself as the "Headquarters of the Conservative Underground," Orsi took issue with a statement from the U.S. Conference of Catholic Bishops sent to Congress that said "health care is not a privilege, but a right and a requirement to protect the life and dignity of each person."[32] Orsi argues that the bishops' advocacy on behalf of comprehensive health care reform implies a "moral imperative which in the case of health care does not exist."[33] It would be interesting to see him float that ivory-tower theory with a desperately ill patient denied coverage by an insurance company or a father who puts off seeing a doctor because he can't afford the expense. Nearly forty-five thousand Americans die every year in large part because they lack health insurance and can't access quality medical care, according to a Harvard Medical School study released in September 2009.[34] If fixing a failed health care system allowing people to die for lack of quality medical care is not a "moral imperative," then what is? The *Compendium of the Social Doctrine on the Church*, compiled by the Vatican's Pontifical Council for Justice and Peace, lists health care as a human right alongside food, housing, and other basic components of a just society.

While the U.S. Conference of Catholic Bishops has long promoted universal health care as a human right, once again a few outspoken bishops sounded like they were reading from right-wing talking points when they warned about a "government socialization of medical services," as Archbishop Joseph F. Naumann of Kansas City, Kansas, and Bishop Robert W. Finn of Kansas City–St. Joseph in Missouri did in a joint pastoral statement.[35] Bishop R. Walker Nickless of Sioux City, Iowa, wrote that the "Catholic Church does not teach that government should directly provide health care" and cautioned that "any legislation that undermines the vitality of the private sector is suspect."[36] This raised serious concerns with prominent theologians and social justice leaders who warned in a public statement that these comments only "embolden opponents of reform and distort Church teaching about the essential role government has in serving the common good."[37] The statement described false claims about "death panels" or a "government takeover" of health care as "gross distortions perpetuated by those who often seem more interested in handing the Obama administration a political defeat than in making sure quality health care is available for all Americans."[38] The theologians and Catholic social justice leaders wrote that "it is troubling to see some bishops sending messages that give spiritual sanction to narrow partisan agendas promoted by these staunch opponents of reform."[39]

In a September 18, 2009, *Wall Street Journal* commentary, Anne Hendershott, the chair of the Politics, Philosophy, and Economics Program at the

King's College in New York, criticized Catholic organizations committed to health care reform in a piece titled "Health-Care Reform and the President's Faithful Helpers."[40] Hendershott writes: "For faithful Catholics, it is discouraging to see that Catholic Charities USA and the Catholic Health Association have both embraced the plan. And it is even more discouraging to learn that some parish priests and bishops are leading the fight for it." This argument would be laughable if it was not another depressing example of the depths to which our polarized health care debate has descended. Centuries of Catholic social teaching recognize access to quality medical care as a fundamental human right. Just days before Hendershott's column, Cardinal Renato Martino of the Vatican's Pontifical Council for Justice and Peace—surely a "faithful Catholic"—applauded health reform efforts in the United States and emphasized the essential role of government in serving the common good.[41] While an intellectually honest critique would have been a welcome contribution to a profound national challenge that requires serious ideas in response, Hendershott's ideological rant purporting to represent the "authentic" Catholic position failed to meet that standard.

Perhaps the low point of the Catholic right's opposition to health care reform came at the death of Senator Ted Kennedy. When Kennedy died in August 2009 after waging a dignified battle against brain cancer, the American Life League—a group that bills itself as a "Catholic pro-life education organization"—fired off a shameless e-mail to supporters asking them to purchase "Bury Obamacare with Kennedy" signs in order to declare their "outrage" over health care reform. American Life League president Judie Brown expressed pride that her signs were featured prominently at an antigovernment rally in Washington hosted by Fox News commentator Glenn Beck. Catholic "media outlets" such as Life Site News and Catholics News Agency (not to be confused with the official Catholic News Service) perpetuated right-wing propaganda about "Obamacare" and stirred fear about "socialized medicine."

One Catholic diocesan newspaper entered the health care debate on the side of the opposition by going after Sr. Carol Keehan, a Daughter of Charity who is president and chief executive officer of the Catholic Health Care Association. Keehan has been a leading advocate for health care reform during her distinguished career. Jack Smith, the editor of *The Catholic Key Blog* of the Diocese of Kansas City–St. Joseph, wrote of Sister Carol: "For her public support of the president's pro-abortion appointees to her campaign to enact health care reform now, she is accused of being at odds with the USCCB and the pro-life cause."[42] This sparked outrage from Catholic priests, sisters, and laity who have worked with Sr. Keehan over the years. *National Catholic Reporter* correspondent John Allen, an internationally respected writer and commentator on church issues, even set aside his usual journalistic detachment to respond in a commentary titled "Incivility Hurts the Pro-Life Cause":

> Sr. Carol enjoys obvious trust in official circles; when Benedict XVI came to America, she was part of the medical team traveling with the pope. Over the years she's emerged as an important spokesperson for Catholic health care, including the church's unambiguously pro-life position. . . . Moving forward, it's important that influential Catholic leaders, particularly those with the greatest credibility in pro-life circles, find ways to call off the rhetorical fireworks. They don't help the pro-life cause, and good people end up as collateral damage.

For many, the Catholic right's opposition to health care reform was dealt with most effectively by *Civiltà Cattolica*, a journal published in Rome by the Society of Jesus, whose contents are reviewed by the Vatican Secretariat of State. In the June 5, 2010, edition, Father Andrea Vicini, SJ, authored an article titled "Health Care Reform in the United States," in which he compared the historic importance of this law to Franklin D. Roosevelt signing the Social Security Act, and Lyndon Johnson's role in passing civil rights, Medicare, and Medicaid legislation. "The health care reform law signed by President Obama continues this story of social reform, introducing measures that aim for a greater justice for all citizens, in particular for the most vulnerable," Father Vicini wrote.[43]

Health care reform is a monumental victory for upholding the sanctity of life, born and unborn. A Harvard Medical School study found that 45,000 Americans die each year because they lack health insurance. Health reform will save lives by providing 32 million citizens with affordable coverage, ending discrimination against those with preexisting conditions and removing lifetime caps on benefits. The law also provides women with the critical help they need to carry pregnancies to term. In particular, reforms incorporate key elements of the Pregnant Women Support Act, including $250 million over ten years to help pregnant and parenting teens.

More than one million abortions are performed in the United States every year. Canada, Germany, Japan, and Britain all have lower abortion rates than the United States, despite having less restrictive abortion laws. Why? In large part because those countries offer comprehensive health care that includes robust prenatal and postnatal care. British Cardinal Basil Hume once told a reporter: "If that frightened, unemployed nineteen-year-old knows that she and her child will have access to medical care whenever it's needed she's more likely to carry the baby to term. Isn't it obvious?"

THE KENNEDY FUNERAL:
CATHOLIC ORTHODOXY POLICE
STRIKE AGAIN

Cardinal Sean O'Malley of Boston could never be accused of being soft on the issue of abortion or afraid to challenge pro-choice politicians. A strong critic of President Obama's support for abortion rights, O'Malley has even said Catholic support for pro-choice officials "borders on scandal."[44] So when O'Malley participated in the funeral Mass of Senator Ted Kennedy at Mission Church, the Redemptorist Basilica of Our Lady of Perpetual Help, most Catholics recognized he was simply acting as a compassionate pastor helping to bury the dead and give comfort to a grieving family. The fundamentalist Catholic right exploded in predictable indignation. Raymond Arroyo, news director at the Eternal Word Television Network (EWTN), the global television outlet founded by Mother Angelica, fired away: "The prayer intercessions at the funeral Mass, the endless eulogies, the image of the cardinal archbishop of Boston reading prayers, and finally Cardinal McCarrick interring the remains sent an uncontested message: One may defy church teaching, publicly lead others astray, deprive innocent lives of their rights, and still be seen a good Catholic, even an exemplary one."[45]

Cardinal O'Malley offered sobering words to those elements of the pro-life movement that believe their cause is served best by shrill attacks. On his blog and in an official statement issued through the Archdiocese of Boston, O'Malley offered this warning: "At times, even in the Church, zeal can lead people to issue harsh judgments and impute the worst motives to one another. These attitudes and practices do irreparable damage to the Communion of the Church. If any cause is motivated by judgment, anger or vindictiveness, it will be doomed to marginalization and failure."[46]

O'Malley was not the only bishop disturbed by the vitriol in some Catholics' response to the Kennedy funeral. Bishop Robert C. Morlino of Madison, Wisconsin, wrote a column for his diocesan newspaper with a similar call to compassion and humility.

> The death of Senator Kennedy has called forth at least an apparent rejection of mercy on the part of not a few Catholics. On the cross of Christ, God's justice came into conflict with God's mercy. God's justice was fully satisfied, but mercy triumphed in the conflict, according to the teaching of Pope Benedict. Without denying any misdeeds on the part of Senator Kennedy, the Church, seeking to reflect the face of Christ, proclaimed God's mercy for the whole world to see in a subdued but unmistakable way. It was more than appropriate. . . . The funeral rites for

Senator Kennedy challenge all of us to question ourselves as to whether we are less eager to grant mercy than God Himself is.[47]

The outrage expressed over Senator Kennedy's funeral and President Barack Obama's visit to Notre Dame highlights a reactionary strain of fundamentalism in the Catholic community that risks undermining our Church's rich tradition of synthesizing faith and reason. It also marginalizes the Catholic Church from being an effective advocate in a contested public square, where the diverse ideas of a pluralistic democracy are hashed out and where thoughtful dialogue, and not hurled anathemas, will accomplish more for the common good. This danger is perhaps most stark when it comes to how Catholic bishops and laity address the polarizing issue of abortion.

"WE ARE AT WAR!" ABORTION POLITICS AND THE CONTESTED SEARCH FOR COMMON GROUND

At the 2009 Gospel of Life Convention held at St. Thomas Aquinas High School in Overland Park, Kansas, Bishop Robert Finn of the Kansas City–St. Joseph diocese took the podium and rallied his audience to take up the fight in defense of human life:

> We are at war! Harsh as this may sound it is true—but it is not new. This war to which I refer did not begin in just the last several months, although new battles are underway—and they bring an intensity and urgency to our efforts that may rival any time in the past. But it is correct to acknowledge that you and I are warriors—members of the Church on earth—often called the Church Militant.[48]

While Finn explained this battle was not violent in nature, the message was clear: ending the evil of abortion means an uncompromising culture war with the enemies of life. A month after Finn's speech, the Kansas late-term abortion doctor George Tiller was shot and killed while serving as an usher at his church. Surely Finn can't be blamed for the death of Tiller, and the doctor was long a target of violence before the bishop's rousing call to spiritual arms. But Mark Silk, director of the Leonard E. Greenberg Center for the Study of Religion and Public Life, made an important point on his well-read blog, *Spiritual Politics*, the day of the murder. Silk, a former religion reporter and respected religion analyst, offered this reflection:

> Is none of Dr. Tiller's blood on Bishop Finn's hands? I wouldn't presume to say so. Will any responsibility be shouldered by Bishop Finn? I'm not holding my breath. But somebody in the pro-life movement should have

the decency at least to entertain the possibility that what happened today in Wichita is a consequence of the heating up of anti-abortion rhetoric since the election of Barack Obama and to urge that it be cooled down.[49]

Abortion has been the most polarizing culture war battle for more than three decades. Liberals and conservatives have long defended rigid ideologies with a righteous zeal that does little to help women and families. But a new consensus is emerging that can help unite Democrats and Republicans behind a comprehensive abortion reduction agenda. The Pregnant Women Support Act, legislation that helps expectant mothers with prenatal health care, nutritional needs, and other critical programs, was fully incorporated into the recently passed national health care reform law. It's more essential than ever that we reject the false divide between "social justice" and "pro-life" advocacy. Policies that help put Americans back to work, ensure families have affordable health care, and strengthen fraying social safety nets also lower the abortion rate, which is more than four times higher for women living in poverty than for women earning 300 percent above the poverty line.

Citizens weary of divisive abortion politics are hungry for a breakthrough. A 2008 post-election poll conducted by Public Religion Research found that most voters—including 81 percent of Catholics and 86 percent of white evangelicals—believe elected officials should work across party lines to increase economic support for vulnerable women, expand adoption opportunities, and prevent unintended pregnancies. While these are positive trends, hard work remains. A chorus of critics across the ideological spectrum has lined up to malign common-ground abortion reduction efforts. Liberal bloggers slam Catholics and evangelicals working on this approach as radical "anti-choice" hard-liners cozying up to the religious right. The National Right to Life Committee, on the other hand, starkly dismisses common ground on abortion as the "burial ground."[50] The Pro-Life Action League mocks it as a "sellout."[51] If politics is the art of the possible, these common-ground naysayers seem more comfortable defending turf and demonizing opponents than seizing a unique political moment when pro-choice and pro-life public officials are finally doing more than exploiting abortion as a "wedge issue" to divide voters and win elections.

Those who view access to abortion as a fundamental right and Americans who believe it is a profound threat to the sanctity of life must still reach across bitter divides with mutual respect and humility. Pro-life citizens can maintain a prophetic spirit that speaks truth to power while at the same time engaging in dialogue and responding pragmatically to social and political realities. Those who make an idol of "choice" as the ultimate virtue can recognize that choice without responsibility is a false freedom. In an instant-gratification culture that often divorces sex from loving relationships, pro-choice advocates can also acknowledge that cultivating greater reverence for the dignity of sexual intimacy is as important as promoting access to contraception. It is also a mistake to caricature all pro-lifers as reactionary fundamentalists, aligned with a conservative political orthodoxy. This only perpetuates unhelpful stereotypes, undermines potential alliances, and alienates the majority of religious Americans who recognize that the wisdom of our different faith traditions defies easy political labels. If those on opposing sides of this polarizing issue were to embrace a spirit of greater humility, compassion, and critical introspection, enemies could become potential allies and old assumptions might slowly fade. Comprehensive efforts to reduce abortions are a cause for hope that the pro-life and the pro-choice communities should embrace. After more than three decades of political paralysis and legal gridlock, the time has come to break new ground—common ground through thoughtful dialogue.

In an effort to uphold a consistent ethic of life that eschews a "single-issue" approach to faith and politics, progressive Catholics have been criticized by pro-choice advocates on the left and some hard-line Catholic bishops. Here is how Archbishop Charles Chaput of Denver put it in a speech that he gave in October 2008:

Democratic-friendly groups like Catholics United and Catholics in Alliance for the Common Good have done a disservice to the Church, confused the natural priorities of Catholic social teaching, undermined the progress pro-lifers have made, and provided an excuse for some Catholics to abandon the abortion issue instead of fighting within their parties and at the ballot box to protect the unborn.[52]

Compare this with the depiction of the same groups in a twenty-page "expose" prepared by Catholics for Choice, a Washington-based abortion rights organization:

Catholics in Alliance is willing to trade the pro-woman, pro-choice heritage of the Democratic Party for the mirage of Catholic voters so cowed by the Catholic hierarchy's position on abortion that they will not vote Democratic. . . . Clearly [Catholics in Alliance] was created by a handful of Democrats who felt that Catholics would be unable to reject the instructions of their bishops.[53]

The archbishop of Denver and a pro-choice Catholic organization certainly make strange bedfellows, but these wildly opposing characterizations of one progressive group reflect the thorny challenges of finding a prudent path through the quagmire of abortion politics. It also reflects the way an all-consuming focus on abortion—as the defining Catholic litmus test—can often distort perspectives. When a lay Catholic social justice organization dedicated to advancing a consistent ethic of life is simply dismissed as doing a "disservice to the Church," something is askew. This is a cause of great sadness for faithful Catholics who believe our bishops have an essential message to share about the sacredness of human life, but who often malign and alienate those dedicated to this important mission because they may on some occasions disagree with bishops regarding the most prudent way to accomplish particular goals given the messy politics of a pluralistic democracy.

WHERE DO WE GO FROM HERE?
CATHOLICS AND EVANGELICALS UNITE! (AGAIN)

The relationship between Catholics and Evangelicals has long been characterized by mistrust and even open hostility. When John F. Kennedy ran for president, suspicion about the senator's Roman Catholicism ran so deep that Billy Graham's *Christianity Today* editorialized that the Vatican "does all in its power to control the governments of nations."[54] The president of the National Association of Evangelicals sent a letter to pastors warning: "Public opinion is changing in favor of the church of Rome. We dare not sit idly by—voiceless and voteless."[55] Kennedy faced such pressure to clarify how his religion would influence his presidency that he addressed the issue directly on September 12, 1960, at a meeting of the Greater Houston Ministerial Association. Kennedy promised he would not take any marching orders from Rome and pledged his belief in "an America where the separation of church and state is absolute."[56]

Just a few decades later, conservative Catholics and Evangelicals began building an alliance that would have significant political and cultural implications. Conversations between the late Rev. Richard John Neuhaus, a leading Catholic intellectual who edited the journal *First Things*, and Charles Colson, the former Nixon aide who became a born-again Christian while serving prison time for his role in Watergate, bonded over a shared concern about the growing secularization of American society. These two men brought together theologians and religious leaders such as Bill Bright, founder of Campus Crusade for Christ, the religious broadcaster Pat Robertson, and the theologian James Packer. Leading Catholics at the table included the late Cardinal John O'Connor of New York and the late theologian Cardinal Avery Dulles. In 1994, the group of evangelical and Catholic leaders released a document called "Evangelicals and Catholics Together." While primarily theological in nature, the document also laid the foundation for a political partnership between conservative Catholics and conservative evangelicals on issues like abortion, government aid for religious schools, and opposition to gay rights. In a 2004 interview with the *New York Times*, Father Neuhaus described the ecumenical alliance as "an extraordinary realignment that if it continues is going to create a very different kind of configuration of Christianity in America."[57]

A year after "Evangelicals and Catholics Together" was released, Pat Robertson's Christian Coalition, at the time the leading conservative political organization, launched a new affiliated group called the Catholic Alliance. Christian Coalition political director Ralph Reed had the goal of recruiting a million conservative Catholics into the Christian Coalition and dramatically impacting electoral politics with this new alliance of pro-life voters.[58] While the Catholic Alliance fizzled and failed to live up to Reed's grand hopes, conservative Catholics and evangelicals continued to find common cause and were decisive in the 2000 election of George W. Bush. As Deal Hudson, the self-described "Catholic gatekeeper" to the Bush administration, writes in his book *Onward, Christian Soldiers: The Growing Political Power of Catholics and Evangelicals*:

> A coalition of Catholic and evangelical voters could successfully elect any national candidate they united to support—in sheer numbers, such a coalition was simply too large and too strategically placed to defeat. Who would have thought in the midst of the late '60s or early '70s that religiously active Catholics and Evangelicals would emerge, thirty years later, with such cultural and political clout?[59]

Unlike Hudson's vision of conservative ascendancy, the future of faith in politics may well be defined by a growing convergence between moderate and progressive Catholics and a new generation of centrist evangelicals. Frustrated with culture war ideology, these Catholics and evangelicals reject the proposition that standing up for "family values" and being "pro-life" only means speaking out on a handful of issues and voting for one political party. Catholics in Alliance for the Common Good, Faith in Public Life, and Sojourners have given greater voice to the "silent majority" of religious voters who have felt alienated by a public Christianity that aligns with narrow political agendas instead of our faith's call to serve the poor, the exploited, and those living at the margins of society. These religious Americans could be described as "Gospel Voters"—faithful citizens who judge themselves and political candidates by Jesus' call to love our neighbors as ourselves and to build God's kingdom by feeding the hungry, clothing the naked, and caring for the sick.

This model of faith in the public square does not seek to replicate the blunt tactics of the religious right, whose leaders became too cozy with one political party and even alienated many Christians with their abrasive style. Instead, an emerging common-good faith movement seeks a just, compassion-centered approach to religion in politics, divorced from any political party. As this nascent coalition evolves, Catholic progressives and moderate evangelicals will pose a formidable religious bloc in the years ahead. Centrist evangelicals like Rev. Jim Wallis of Sojourners, David Gushee of the New Evangelical Partnership for the Common Good, former National Association of Evangelicals vice president Rev. Richard Czick, and Ron Sider of Evangelicals for Social Action all have deep respect for Catholic social justice traditions. Catholics are inspired by evangelicals' spirited commitment to living the Gospel and personal witness of faith. Despite theological and cultural differences, there remains untapped potential to cultivate greater cooperation between young leaders from these different traditions who share a common commitment to social justice in the United States and around the globe. The broadening evangelical agenda that now includes a commitment to environmental stewardship, nuclear deterrence, and global poverty has a natural alignment with Catholic teaching. "The evangelical center is self-consciously and explicitly calling on evangelicals to learn from Catholic social teaching," Robert P. Jones, the president of Public Religion Research Institute and an expert on the emerging evangelical center, told me. Jones recalls teaching a class with David Gushee, a leading moderate evangelical at Mercer University in Atlanta, when Gushee strongly encouraged his evangelical students, who lack a strong social justice theology, to learn from the Catholic tradition. "After nearly two decades of lowering the historical antipathy between these groups and theological cross-fertilization, something new is happening," said Jones. "Evangelicals are discovering Catholic social teaching."

New opportunities to bring Catholics and evangelicals together in thoughtful dialogue outside of Washington should be pursued more strategically. Building a common-good faith movement will take decades. Predicting the death of the religious right has always been a fool's errand. But Catholic progressives and evangelical moderates are now reclaiming faith in public life in ways that will likely have a lasting impact on electoral politics and, more importantly, the most urgent moral challenges of our time.

QUESTIONS FOR FURTHER REFLECTION

1. What effect does the author think that conservative Catholics had in the 2004 presidential election? Do you agree? What changes does the author see with the entrance of progressive Catholics into the political process? Do you agree? Do you accept the distinctions that the author makes between

conservative and progressive Catholics? Do you think that such terms serve a purpose in political discussions?

2. What do you understand by the term "seamless garment"? Do you see any analytical usefulness in such a term? If so, what is it? Do you agree that the term has been missing from much recent political dialogue in the Church?

3. How does the author think that Catholic social justice concepts have impacted American history? How has Catholic cooperation with other religious groups impacted American history?

4. What effect does the author think that the *Roe v. Wade* abortion decision has had on Catholic participation in politics? What have the Vatican and the national bishops' conference said this role should be? Do you agree with the hierarchy's vision of Catholic participation in political life?

5. What difficulties does the author have with confrontational politics? What does he consider to be a more effective alternative? Do you agree? Why or why not? Should Catholics perhaps be confrontational on some issues and less so on others? Who should decide what those issues would be?

6. What does the author think is the effect of the American bishops choosing sides in the political debate? Do you agree with him? What would he have the bishops do instead? How effective do you think this would be?

7. Does the author think that free-market fundamentalism is compatible with Catholic social thought? Why or why not? What connection does the author see between advocates of free-market capitalism and opponents of abortion? Do you agree? Do you think that this is a natural connection? What have the various popes cited by the author had to say about free-market capitalism?

8. What does the author think the Church's role should be in advocating for health care for the poor and underprivileged? Do you agree? What should the American bishops do with a health care law that is not foursquare with Catholic values and beliefs? Is there room for compromise here? On what basis?

9. Do you agree that Catholics are at war on the abortion issue? If you do agree, what do you see as your personal role in this "war"? If you do not agree, why don't you?

10. The author writes that thoughtful dialogue among people of good will might help to resolve thorny political issues like abortion. Do you agree? What kind of good will could you bring to this issue? What would the dialogue sound like between you and a person of good faith on the other side of the abortion issue? Try to write out such a dialogue.

NOTES

1. "Who Is Catholic League President William Donohue?" *Media Matters for America Report,* http://mediamatters.org/research/200412210001.

2. Ibid.

3. "Lay Catholics Push Back on Abortion and Politics," *Religion News Service,* October 16, 2008, *http://pewforum.org/news/rss.php?NewsID=16676.*

4. *Economic Justice for All: Pastoral Letter on Catholic Social Teaching and the U.S. Economy,* National Conference of Catholic Bishops. November 13, 1986, *http://www.usccb.org/sdwp/international/EconomicJusticeforAll.pdf.*

5. "In Search of the Common Good: The Catholic Roots of American Liberalism," *Boston Review,* May 2007, *http://bostonreview.net/BR32.3/daly.php.*

6. Ibid.

7. "I Voted for Obama. Will I Go Straight to . . . ?" *Washington Post,* February 24, 2008.

8. Congregation for the Doctrine of the Faith, *Doctrinal Note on Some Questions Regarding the Participation of Catholics in Political Life, www.vatican.va.*

9. U.S. Conference of Catholic Bishops. *Forming Consciences for Faithful Citizenship,* http://www.faithfulcitizenship.org/.

10. "Bishop Stresses Abortion View at Political Forum," *Wayne Independent,* October 20, 2008, *http://www.wayneindependent.com/news/x270972980/Bishop-stresses-abortion-view-at-political-forum.*

11. *A Pastoral Letter from Bishop Martino,* October 2008, *http://www.dioceseofscranton.org/Bishop's%20Pastoral%20Letters/RespectLifeSundaySeptember30th2008.asp.*

12. "The Bishops and Obama: Absolutism and Democratic Deliberation," *Commonweal,* December 5, 2008.

13. "Archbishop Nienstedt Opposes 'Travesty' of Obama Invite," *Catholic Online,* April 1, 2009, *http://www.catholic.org/politics/story.php?id=32935.*

14. "Notre Dame Invitation to President Obama Embarrasses Catholic Church," *Chicago Sun Times,* April 2, 2009.

15. "Rockford Bishop Rips Notre Dame Over Obama Invite," *Rockford Register Star,* April 10, 2009.

16. "Petition to Fr. Jenkins," *The Cardinal Newman Society,* April 29, 2009.

17. "Catholic Theologians Denounce Attack on Notre Dame," *Catholics in Alliance for the Common Good,* May 14, 2009, *http://www.usnews.com/news/blogs/god-and-country/2009/05/14/catholics-who-back-obamas-visit-raise-voices-with-newspaper-ad.*

18. "Vatican Newspaper Says Obama Sought Common Ground at Notre Dame," *Catholic News Service,* May 18, 2009, *http://www.catholicnews.com/data/stories/cns/0902273.htm.*

19. "Bishop Decries 'Combative Tactics' of a Minority of U.S. Bishops," *National Catholic Reporter,* August 26, 2009.

20. "The Public Duty of Bishops: Lessons from the Storm in South Bend," *America,* August 31, 2009.

21. "Caritas in Veritate in Gold and Red," *National Review Online,* July 7, 2009.

22. "New Heights of Hubris from George Weigel," *America,* July 8, 2009.

23. John Sniegocki , "The Social Ethics of Pope John Paul II: A Critique of Neoconservative Interpretations," *Horizons: The Journal of the College Theology Society* (2006).

24. *Centesimus Annus,* Pope John Paul II, January. 5, 1991, *www.vatican.va.*

25. *Ecclesia in America,* Pope John Paul II, January 22, 1999, *www.vatican.va.*

26. "Economic Heresies of the Left," *First Things,* June 29, 2009, *www.firstthings.com/onthesquare/2009/06/economic-heresies-of-the-left.*

27. Ibid.

28. "Mandated Giving Doesn't Come from the Heart," *Religion and Liberty* (Fall 2007), *http://www.acton.org/publications/randl/rl_174article04.php.*

29. "Libertarian Heresy: The Fundamentalism of Free-Market Theology," *Commonweal,* September 26, 2008.

30. "Pope Says Labor Unions Important in Resolving Financial Crisis," *Catholic News Service,* February 2, 2009, *http://www.catholicnews.com/data/stories/cns/0900492.htm.*

31. "Bishops Wrong: Health Care Not a Right," *Human Events,* July 30, 2009, *http://www.humanevents.com/article.php?id=32911.*

32. U.S. Bishops Letter to Congress, September 30, 2009, *http://www.usccb.org/sdwp/national/2009-09-30-healthcare-letter-senate.pdf.*

33. "Bishops: Wrong Health Care Not a Right."

34. "Study Links 45,000 US Deaths to Lack of Insurance," *Reuters,* September 17, 2009.

35. *Joint Pastoral Statement on Principles of Catholic Social Teaching and Health Care Reform*, September 1, 2009, *http://www.diocese-kcsj.org/news/viewNews.php?nid=60.*

36. "Some Catholic Bishops Assail Health Plan," *New York Times,* August 27, 2009.

37. "Bishops Urged to Speak with United Voice on Health Care Reform," *Catholics in Alliance,* September 14, 2009, *http://www.catholicsinalliance.org/node/21100.*

38. Ibid.

39. Ibid.

40. "Health-Care Reform and the President's Faithful Helpers," *Wall Street Journal,* September 18, 2009.

41. "Cardinal Martino Applauds Universal Health Care Initiative," *Catholic News Service,* September 15, 2009.

42. "Sister Carol Keehan: Catholic Health's $856,093 Nun," *Catholic Key Blog,* August 6, 2009, *http://catholickey.blogspot.com/2009/08/sr-carol-keehan-catholic-healths-856093.html.*

43. Andrea Vicini, SJ, "La Riforma Sanitaria negli Stati Uniti," *La Civiltà Cattolica,* 2010. II 466–78, at p. 467. The Italian reads, "La riforma sanitaria firmata dal presidente Obama continua questa storia di riforme sociali, introducendo misure che mirano a una maggiore giustizia per tutti i cittadini e, in particolare, per i più vulnerabili."

44. "O'Malley Draws Line with Democrats," *Boston Globe,* November 15, 2007.

45. "Ted Kennedy: The Catholic Legacy and the Letters," August 31, 2009, EWTN, *http://origin.ewtn.com/news/blog.asp?blogposts_ID=782&blog_ID=2.*

46. "Boston Cardinal Answers Critics on Kennedy Funeral," *Washington Post,* "On Faith," September 3, 2009.

47. "God's Mercy and Senator Edward Kennedy," *Madison Catholic Herald,* September 3, 2009.

48. "Warriors for the Victory of Life," 2009 Keynote Address, Gospel of Life Convention, *http://catholickey.blogspot.com/2009/04/we-are-at-war-bishop-finns-gospel-of.html.*

49. "Abortion Reduction, Kansas Style," *Spiritual Politics,* May 31, 2009.

50. "Some Abortion Foes Shifting from Ban to Reduction," *Washington Post,* November 18, 2008.

51. Ibid.

52. "Archbishop Criticizes Obama, Catholic Allies," *Associated Press,* October 22, 2008, http://*www.chicagodefender.com/article-2238-archbishop-criticize.html.*

53. "The Trouble with Catholics in Alliance for the Common Good," *Catholics for Choice, http://www.catholicsforchoice.org/documents/TheTroublewithCACG.pdf.*

54. "The 'Hypermodern Foe': How Evangelicals and Catholics Joined Forces," *New York Times,* May 30, 2004.

55. Ibid.

56. John F. Kennedy speech, Greater Houston Ministerial Association, September 12, 1960.

57. "The 'Hypermodern Foe.'"

58. Mark J. Rozell, "Political Marriage of Convenience? The Evolution of the Conservative Catholic–Evangelical Alliance in the Republican Party," *Catholics and Politics: The Dynamic Tension between Faith and Power* (Washington, DC: Georgetown University Press, 2008).

59. Deal W. Hudson, *Onward, Christian Soldiers: The Growing Political Power of Catholics and Evangelicals* (New York: Threshold Editions, 2008).

SEVEN

Conscience and Citizenship: The Primacy of Conscience for Catholics in Public Life

Gregory A. Kalscheur, SJ

In their statement *Forming Consciences for Faithful Citizenship*,[1] the U.S. bishops acknowledge that "the responsibility to make choices in political life rests with each individual in light of a properly formed conscience."[2] The bishops go on to acknowledge, quoting the *Catechism of the Catholic Church*, that in all an individual says and does, he is obliged to follow faithfully what he knows to be just and right.[3] The *Catechism* itself further explains that "a human being must always obey the certain judgment of his conscience. If he were deliberately to act against it, he would condemn himself."[4] Similarly, in his 1993 encyclical *Veritatis Splendor*, John Paul II stated that a human being "must act in accordance with [the judgment of conscience]. If man acts against this judgment or, in a case where he lacks certainty about the rightness and goodness of a determined act, still performs that act, he stands condemned by his own conscience, *the proximate norm of personal morality*."[5] These principles taken together are an expression of the idea known for centuries in the Catholic tradition as the primacy of conscience.[6]

Before going any further, however, it is important to acknowledge that "'conscience' is [a] word . . . often used but little understood."[7] For this reason, I want at the outset to emphasize what conscience and the primacy of conscience do *not* mean in the Catholic tradition. As the bishops note in their *Forming Consciences for Faithful Citizenship* statement, "[c]onscience is not something that allows us to justify doing whatever we want nor is it a mere 'feeling' about what we should or should not do."[8] In a 1991 address titled "Conscience and Truth," Cardinal Joseph Ratzinger (now Pope Benedict XVI) explained that conscience is degraded into a mechanism for rationalization if it is understood simply as one's subjective certainty and lack of doubt about a moral question.[9] Similarly, when we talk about the primacy of conscience, we do *not* mean that people have a right to do whatever they want, or that there are no objective norms of morality.

Any proper understanding of the primacy of conscience needs to be rooted in an authentically Catholic understanding of conscience itself. The Catholic tradition insists that both conscience and the primacy of conscience must be understood in relationship to truth: there is objective moral truth, and the human person is capable of apprehending that truth. As Cardinal Ratzinger explained in his 1991 address, to reduce conscience to subjective certitude is to retreat from truth.[10]

In section 17 of *Forming Consciences for Faithful Citizenship* the bishops give us a brief statement explaining what conscience is. They begin by describing conscience as "the voice of God resounding in the human heart, revealing the truth to us and calling us to do what is good while shunning what is evil." They then go on to explain that "conscience is a judgment of reason whereby the human person recognizes the moral quality of a concrete act that he is going to perform, is in the process of performing, or has already completed."

This summary description shows that conscience is a concept with several different dimensions. Most fundamentally, conscience is a basic characteristic of the Catholic understanding of what it is to be a human person: to be human is to possess a basic orientation to know and to do the true and the good. To be human is to possess a basic capacity to recognize the true and the good and to recognize that one must act in accordance with the true and the good. At the same time, the Catholic understanding of conscience also includes the process of discernment and moral reasoning by which we recognize what acting in accord with the true and the good demands of us in particular concrete situations. Finally, conscience refers to the judgment of what "I must do" in the particular situation.[11] When our conscience determines that a particular action is in accord with the true and the good, which is another way of saying that the action is a response to God's objective call, then this action is morally required of us.[12] In the words of Thomas Aquinas, when a person's reason proposes something as being God's command, slighting the dictate of reason amounts to slighting the law of God.[13]

This understanding of conscience is a central part of the teaching of Vatican II on the dignity of the human person. One of the key texts is section 16 of the Pastoral Constitution on the Church in the Modern World. Here is how that conciliar text describes the dignity of the moral conscience:

> In the depths of his conscience, man detects a law which he does not impose upon himself, but which holds him to obedience. Always

summoning him to love good and avoid evil, the voice of conscience when necessary speaks to his heart: do this, shun that. For man has in his heart a law written by God; to obey it is the very dignity of man; according to it he will be judged.

The Catholic understanding of conscience also plays a decisive role in Vatican II's Declaration on Religious Freedom. The Council there emphasized the relationship between conscience and truth:

It is in accordance with their dignity as persons—that is, beings endowed with reason and free will and therefore privileged to bear personal responsibility—that all men should be at once impelled by nature and also bound by a moral obligation to seek the truth. . . . They are also bound to adhere to the truth, once it is known, and to order their whole lives in accord with the demands of truth.[14] . . . Wherefore every man has the duty, and therefore the right, to seek the truth . . . in order that he may with prudence *form for himself* right and true judgments of conscience, under use of all suitable means. . . . [A]s the truth is discovered, it is by a personal assent that men are to adhere to it.

On his part, man perceives and acknowledges the imperatives of the divine law through the mediation of conscience. *In all his activity a man is bound to follow his conscience in order that he may come to God, the end and purpose of life.* It follows that he is not to be forced to act in a manner contrary to his conscience. Nor, on the other hand, is he to be restrained from acting in accordance with his conscience, especially in matters religious.[15]

I've quoted these documents of Vatican II at some length for two reasons: First, to show how crucial maintaining the connection between conscience and truth is to any authentically Catholic understanding of conscience. Second, to show how prominent a place the tradition gives to primacy of conscience properly understood.

The Declaration on Religious Freedom clearly states that to be a human person is to have a moral obligation to seek the truth. Moreover, to be a human person is to have a duty to seek the truth in order that one can *form for oneself* right and true judgments of conscience. As one seeks the truth, one is bound to adhere to the truth as it is known, and one is bound to order one's life in accord with the demands of truth. In all our activity we are bound to follow our conscience. This is what it means to speak of the primacy of conscience. This affirmation of the primacy of conscience should not be lightly disregarded. Pay attention to these words from Joseph Ratzinger's 1969 commentary on section 16 of Vatican II's Pastoral Constitution on the Church in the Modern World:

> Over the pope as the expression of the binding claim of ecclesiastical authority there still stands one's own conscience, which must be obeyed before all else, if necessary even against the requirement of ecclesiastical authority. [The conscience of the individual] confronts him with a supreme and ultimate tribunal, which in the last resort is beyond the claim of external social groups, even of the official church.[16]

Cardinal John Henry Newman expressed much the same idea in a frequently quoted line from his *Letter to the Duke of Norfolk*: "Certainly, if I am obliged to bring religion into after-dinner toasts . . . I shall drink—to the Pope, if you please,—still to Conscience first, and to the Pope afterwards."[17] For Newman, conscience comes first; conscience has primacy. But, properly understood, the authority of the pope and the primacy of conscience are not in opposition to one another, because both the pope and the individual's conscience are striving to know the truth. We cannot affirm the primacy of conscience apart from this affirmation of the centrality of truth.[18]

Within the tradition, the obligation to follow one's conscience means that one must follow the certain judgment of one's conscience, even though that judgment might turn out objectively to be in error. As I noted earlier, St. Thomas taught that a person who ignores the judgment of his conscience is slighting the judgment of God. Thomas came to that conclusion in the course of answering the following question: Is a mistaken conscience binding? Thomas answered, "Yes," a mistaken conscience is binding, although the person might in fact be culpable for making a mistake as a result of failing properly to have formed his conscience.[19] The Pastoral Constitution on the Church in the Modern World put St. Thomas's idea into these words: "Conscience frequently errs from invincible ignorance without losing its dignity. The same cannot be said of a man who cares but little for truth and goodness, or for a conscience which by degrees grows practically sightless as a result of habitual sin."[20]

This brings us to the question of what proper conscience formation involves. In section 17 of the *Forming Consciences for Faithful Citizenship* statement, the bishops make it clear that "Catholics have a serious and life-long obligation to form their consciences in accord with human reason and the teaching of the church."[21] They then go on in section 18 to explain that the process of conscience formation involves several elements. First, and most fundamentally, we must cultivate a desire to embrace goodness and truth. The bishops state that "for Catholics this [desire to embrace goodness and truth] begins with a willingness and openness to seek the truth and what is right by studying sacred Scripture and the teaching of the church." In addition, the bishops note that it is "important to examine the facts and background information" that are relevant to deciding how we ought to act with respect to the various public policy choices that we face. The bishops also emphasize that "prayerful reflection is essential to discern the will of God." Finally, our process of conscience formation must humbly recognize that the failure to live up to the obligation to form our consciences can lead us to make erroneous judgments. The bishops suggest a number of factors that can lead to errors of judgment about moral conduct, including "ignorance of Christ and his Gospel, bad example given by others, enslavement to one's passions, assertion of a mistaken notion of autonomy of conscience, rejection of the church's authority and her teaching, [and] a lack of conversion and charity."[22]

Notice that the bishops highlight a "mistaken notion of the autonomy of conscience" as a potential source of error. The problem is not the primacy of conscience, but a mistaken notion of the autonomy of conscience. We each have to commit ourselves to forming *for ourselves* right and true judgments of conscience, but we cannot form our consciences *by ourselves*.[23] It is also important to keep in mind that good conscience formation is rooted in questions of character formation before it ever gets to more particular questions about what one should do in a particular situation.[24] The way in which I approach more particular moral questions will flow out of the way in which I answer foundational questions of character: what sort of a person do I really want to be? Do I have a desire to be open to the truth, no matter where the truth might lead me? Am I open to the ways in which all my various relationships of family and friendship shape me? Am I attentive to the ways in which the culture around me shapes me? Is my sense of who I am rooted in my desire to be a faithful disciple of Jesus? To what extent is the core of my identity shaped by my participation in the life of the church? Do I allow my imagination and way of seeing the world to be shaped by the scriptural and liturgical life of the church? Have I thought about why it is important for me to take seriously what the church teaches about various issues? Do I have a genuine desire to be a person of integrity, and do I understand what integrity demands of me?

Formation on this foundational level of conscience is critical. In "Conscience and Truth," Cardinal Ratzinger noted that we can allow the foundational moral sense that lies at the heart of our humanity and our capacity for self-criticism to fall silent, which is a dangerous and dehumanizing "sickness of the soul."[25] Cardinal Ratzinger states that "it is never wrong to follow the convictions one has arrived at—in fact, one must do so." But even though the erroneous conscience is binding, Cardinal Ratzinger explained that "it can very well be wrong to have come to such askew convictions in the first place, by having stifled the protest of [conscience]. The guilt lies then in a [deeper place,] in the neglect of my being which made me deaf to the internal prompt-ings of truth."[26]

Conscience formation also demands that we ask hard questions about what is really going on in a situation that calls for decision, what the consequences in the world might actually be of acting in one way or another, and what the available alternatives for action might really be. Are my eyes open to what is really happening? Am I open to bringing the exercise of reason to bear by ask-ing all the relevant questions about a situation that calls for moral action? "The properly informed conscience sees [reality] rightly. Do we see what is really there? Or do we just see what we want to see?"[27]

The bishops' *Forming Conscience* statement calls Catholics to form their consciences "in accord with human reason and the teaching of the church."[28] Church teaching is thus "a very important, though not exclusive, factor in the formation of conscience and in one's moral judgment."[29] Catholics who take their faith seriously should care deeply about what the church says regarding the moral principles that relate to questions of public policy. We should listen carefully to church teaching, because it is our conviction that Christ will not abandon his church to error in those things that are essential to our salvation. "We believe that the Holy Spirit dwells within the whole church to guide and illumine its actions," and this trust "grounds our expectation that those" given the ministry of authoritative teaching within the church "can discern the Spirit and, when [they are] faithfully following the Spirit, do not lead the church astray."[30]

We also recognize that the Spirit-guided teaching of the church is based on a wealth of moral resources, expertise, and centuries of reflection on human experience which "are too many and too complex for any one person to under-stand and use well in making a decision."[31] We can have more confidence in our judgment when we draw on the moral wisdom of our community rather than trusting in our own limited resources, wisdom, and experience.

At the same time, in thinking about the role that church teaching plays in the formation of conscience, we need to recognize that the church teaches with different levels of definitiveness.[32] Some church teaching is understood to be infallible, definitive, and unchanging. This sort of teaching expresses the fundamentals of Catholic belief and calls for an assent of faith. Examples of this sort of teaching would include the articles of faith expressed in the Creed and foundational moral teachings like the affirmation of God's unconditional love and the command that we love God and love our neighbor.[33] There are also good reasons to think that the teaching of John Paul II in his encyclical

Evangelium Vitae confirming the grave immorality of the direct and voluntary killing of human beings, abortion, and euthanasia was intended to invoke the infallibility attributed to the teaching of the ordinary universal magisterium.[34]

But most of the moral teaching of the Church isn't presented as infallible in this way. How, then, should we think about the role to be played in our formation of conscience by the authoritative but noninfallible teaching of the church? This question was addressed at Vatican II in section 25 of *Lumen Gentium*, the Council's Dogmatic Constitution on the Church:

> In matters of faith and morals, the bishops speak in the name of Christ and the faithful are to accept their teaching and adhere to it with a religious assent. This religious submission of mind and will must be shown in a special way to the authentic magisterium of the Roman Pontiff, even when he is not speaking ex cathedra.[35]

What does the Council mean when it calls us to "religious submission of mind and will" to the authoritative but noninfallible teaching of the church? Francis Sullivan, SJ, an expert in the study of the teaching authority of the church, has explained that "religious submission of mind and will" calls us to renounce any attitude of obstinacy in our own opinions and to adopt an attitude of docility toward the teaching of the church. To renounce obstinacy is to reject any tendency that we might have to close our minds to church teaching by refusing to give it a fair hearing. Obstinacy is an attitude that simply says, "I've made up my own mind, don't bother me."[36]

In contrast to this improper attitude of obstinacy, docility refers to "a willingness to be taught, a willingness to prefer another's judgment to one's own when it is reasonable to do so." Father Sullivan explains that "docility calls for an open attitude toward the official teaching, giving it a fair hearing, doing one's best to appreciate the reasons in its favor, so as to convince oneself of its truth, and thus facilitate one's intellectual assent to it." In sum, "religious submission of mind and will" means making "an honest and sustained effort to overcome any contrary opinion I might have and to achieve a sincere assent of my mind to [the] teaching."[37] In the realm of noninfallible teaching, the church cannot impose on conscience any further obligation than this.[38]

Vatican II also addressed the role of authoritative teaching in conscience formation in section 14 of the Declaration on Religious Freedom. The Declaration explains that "in the formation of their consciences, the Christian faithful *ought carefully to attend* to the sacred and certain doctrine of the Church." The words "ought carefully to attend" are crucial here. During the Council's debate on the Declaration, a proposal was made to change this particular text. Instead of saying, "ought carefully to attend to," the suggestion was made that the text should say that the faithful "ought to form their consciences according to" the teaching of the church. In response, the commission in charge of preparing the text said this: "The proposed formula seems excessively restrictive. The obligation binding on the faithful is sufficiently expressed in the text as it stands."[39] The final text approved by the Council simply calls on the faithful, in the formation of their consciences, to carefully attend to church teaching. Father Sullivan offers this interpretation of the decision of the Council: "It seems to me that this way of expressing the obligation of the faithful in the face of the moral teaching of the magisterium leaves a certain amount of room for them to exercise their personal judgment in the formation of their consciences. This, I take it, is an expression of respect for the moral sense of the faithful."[40]

Read in this way, section 14 of the Declaration on Religious Freedom is a significant affirmation of the primacy of conscience. There are, however, some voices in the church today who assert that we should stop talking about the primacy of conscience. Cardinal George Pell, the archbishop of Sydney, Australia, has repeatedly spoken out against what he describes as "the so-called doctrine of the primacy of conscience." He argues that this idea is incompatible with traditional Catholic teaching.[41] His objection to talk of the primacy of conscience is intended to make two points. First, it is an effort to respond to his sense that invocation of the primacy of conscience increasingly is being used to justify whatever we would like to do, rather than to discern what God wants us to do. Second, it is an attempt to make clear that the truth and God's word have primacy, not conscience. Cardinal Pell argues that the role of conscience is to discern the truth in particular cases, but "individual conscience cannot confer the right to reject or distort New Testament morality as affirmed or developed by the Church."[42]

Cardinal Pell also seems to suggest that conscience formation can be reduced to simply following the teaching of the church:

> We cannot rely on our tastes in moral matters because we are all vulnerable to acquiring the taste for immorality and egoism. . . . While we should follow a well-formed conscience, a well-formed conscience is hard to achieve. And if we suspect—as surely we all sometimes must— that our conscience is under-formed or malformed in some area, then we should follow a reliable authority until such time as we can correct our consciences. And for Catholics, the most reliable authority is the Church.[43]

I agree with Cardinal Pell's insistence that we must understand the primacy of conscience in connection with our obligation to seek the truth and adhere to it. But I think it would be a profound mistake to stop talking about the primacy of conscience. As the central Vatican II texts on conscience indicate, affirming the dignity and primacy of conscience says something of real importance about responsible personhood. If we really expect voters and public officials to make responsible, conscientious decisions about matters of public policy, we should not suggest that proper formation of conscience is simply a matter of falling into line with church teaching. Such an approach will not contribute to the ability of Catholics in public life to make conscientious decisions, because church teaching does not generally speak definitively to the concrete questions that voters and public officials face.

Cardinal Pell's approach also seems to be in significant tension with the discussion of conscience formation set forth in section 14 of the Declaration on Religious Freedom. The sort of reliance on church authority that Cardinal Pell proposes looks more like the approach to conscience formation rejected by the Council in the text it finally adopted. Catholics are obliged to carefully attend to church teaching, not to form their consciences according to church teaching. The method of conscience formation suggested by Cardinal Pell is hard to reconcile with the Declaration on Religious Freedom's insistence that human dignity demands the exercise of responsible freedom: we are called *both* to a respect for the moral order that is appropriately submissive to authority *and* to come to decisions on our own judgment and in the light of truth.[44] We have a duty to seek the truth so that we may with prudence *form for ourselves* right and true judgments of conscience, using all suitable means.[45]

The conscience of Catholic public officials received significant attention in a document issued in November 2002 by the Vatican's Congregation for the Doctrine of the Faith. The C.D.F.'s *Doctrinal Note on Some Questions Regarding the Participation of Catholics in Political Life* reminds Catholics involved in public life "that a well-formed Christian conscience does not permit one to vote for a political program or an individual law which contradicts the fundamental contents of faith and morals."

The C.D.F.'s *Doctrinal Note* attempts to respond to public officials who draw a sharp line between their personal moral beliefs as Catholics and their public policy positions. In the face of the threat to moral integrity presented by this sort of compartmentalization, the *Doctrinal Note* provided a timely reminder that law and politics cannot be separated from morality and truth.

This insistence that moral beliefs inform policy choices is, in the end, a matter of integrity. It is, as the *Doctrinal Note* explains, a question of our "duty to be morally coherent," a duty that is "found within one's conscience, which is one and indivisible."[46] We do not lead parallel moral lives that can be compartmentalized into separate spheres, one spiritual and one secular: "Living and acting in conformity with one's own conscience on questions of politics is . . . the way in which Christians offer their concrete contributions so that, through political life, society will become more just and more consistent with the dignity of the human person."⁴⁷

This understanding of the unity of conscience guides the teaching of the *Doctrinal Note* on the public official's grave and clear obligation to oppose any law that attacks human life. Let's assume that a legislator has reached the conscientious conclusion that abortion is a grave moral evil because it constitutes an attack on the inviolable dignity of human life. This conscientious conclusion is not simply a matter of personal morality with no public import; it is a conviction of conscience that should influence the way in which the legislator thinks about public policy. As an attack on the fundamental right to life, abortion is contrary to justice and the common good. If legislators wish to live a life of integrity and moral coherence, their participation in politics should not be cut off from the conscientious judgment they have made about the morality of abortion. Since a legislator's role is to craft positive law that will best promote the common good, a legislator who holds the conscientious conviction that abortion is a grave moral evil has a corresponding duty to craft laws aimed at reducing the incidence of abortion.

Pope Benedict has identified a broad set of fundamental values as "not negotiable" in making public policy decisions. These values that are "not negotiable" include "respect for human life, its defense from conception to natural death, the family built upon marriage between a man and a woman, the freedom to educate one's children," and, most broadly, "the promotion of the common good in all its forms."⁴⁸ While these fundamental moral values are non-negotiable, translating those values into specific public policy or voting decisions will inevitably involve complex decision making. *How*, for example, a policy maker should go about striving to reduce the incidence of abortion in contemporary American culture, under existing constitutional constraints and in the face of significant social disagreement with regard to the underlying moral issue, is an exceptionally complicated question.

Good lawmaking is never simply a matter of directly transposing moral principles into rules of civil law. Drawing on a jurisprudential tradition rooted in the thought of Thomas Aquinas, the Jesuit theologian John Courtney Murray explained that moral law and civil law are essentially related, but necessarily differentiated:

> Both the science and art of jurisprudence and also the statesman's craft rest on the differential character of law and morals, of legal experience and religious or moral experience, of political unity and religious unity. *The jurist's work proceeds from the axiom that the principles of religion or morality cannot be transgressed, but neither can they be immediately*

translated into civilized human law. There is an intermediate step, the inspection of circumstances and the consideration of . . . the public advantage to be found, or not found, in transforming a moral or religious principle into a compulsory rule for general enforcement upon society.[49]

This intermediate step—the careful inspection of circumstances—is the work of the virtue of prudence. While Catholics must not support policies that compromise or undermine a fundamental ethical value or constitute formal cooperation with evil,[50] the *Doctrinal Note* recognized that there can be "a variety of strategies available for accomplishing or guaranteeing the same fundamental value." Indeed, the note specifically states that the church's efforts to educate the consciences of the faithful do not reflect a desire on the part of the church "to exercise political power or eliminate freedom of opinion of Catholics regarding contingent questions."[51]

Deciding how best to promote fundamental moral values through civil legislation that will truly function as good law promoting the common good in all its forms under the concrete conditions of a given society is always a contingent question that calls upon those in public life to exercise the virtue of prudence.[52] Deciding whom to vote for in an election calls upon all citizens to exercise the virtue of prudence. In section 19 of their *Forming Consciences for Faithful Citizenship* statement, the bishops remind us that prudence "enables us 'to discern our true good in every circumstance and to choose the right means of achieving it.' Prudence shapes and informs our ability to deliberate over available alternatives, to determine what is most fitting to a specific context and to act decisively."[53] "It is prudence that immediately guides the judgment of conscience" and helps us to "apply moral principles to particular cases."[54] The virtue of prudence demands that we ask, *what is the best that is possible to achieve now*, not what is the best that we might hope to achieve in an ideal world that does not exist?[55] Guided by the virtue of prudence, the process of conscience formation is appropriately attentive to the *limits* of what it might be *possible* for the law to accomplish under existing social, political, and constitutional conditions.[56]

As the bishops note in their statement, the process of framing legislation is "subject to prudential judgment and 'the art of the possible.' "[57] John Paul II provided an example of prudence at work in his encyclical *Evangelium Vitae,* where he explained,

when it is not possible to overturn or completely abrogate a pro-abortion law, an elected official, whose absolute personal opposition to procured abortion was well known, could licitly support proposals aimed at limiting the harm done by such a law and at lessening its negative consequences at the level of general opinion and public morality. This does not in fact represent an illicit cooperation with an unjust law, but rather a legitimate and proper attempt to limit its evil aspects.[58]

The work of John Courtney Murray offers a related example of the virtue of prudence at work. Murray explained that the Catholic tradition of jurisprudence recognizes that the law should not be used to prohibit a given moral evil unless that prohibition can be shown to be something that the law is capable of addressing prudently. Following St. Thomas, Murray argued that human law must be framed with a view to the level of virtue that it is actually possible to expect from the people required to comply with the law.

Accordingly, Murray suggested a series of questions that the legislator must consider in assessing the prudence of a proposed law: Will the prohibition be obeyed, at least by most people? Is it enforceable against the disobedient? Is it prudent to enforce this ban, given the possibility of harmful effects in other areas of social life? Is the instrumentality of a coercive law a good means for the eradication of the targeted social evil? And since a law that usually fails is not a good means, what are the lessons of experience with this sort of legal prohibition? If legislation is to be properly crafted from a moral point of view with the goal of promoting the common good of society, these are the questions that a public official exercising the virtue of prudence must answer.[59]

So what does a commitment to the primacy of conscience mean for Catholics striving to be faithful citizens in today's pluralistic, democratic society? A commitment to the primacy of conscience calls us to strive for moral integrity and an undivided conscience. It demands that we dedicate ourselves to a lifelong process of conscience formation, rooted in a commitment to truth, and carefully attending to the teaching of the church and the insights of human reason as we strive to *form for ourselves* right and true judgments of conscience. It recognizes that decisions in public life call for the exercise of the balancing virtue of prudence, always asking what will best promote the common good in all its dimensions through the concrete decision that must be made in the context of the reality that exists right now.[60] It acknowledges that prudence may suggest to different conscientious decision makers a variety of strategies available for accomplishing or guaranteeing the same fundamental value. And in the midst of often deep moral disagreement in our society, respect for the primacy of conscience calls us to engage in the respectful dialogue that is essential if we are to join together with our fellow citizens in an authentic search for truth,[61] forming hearts and minds committed to making choices that will protect human dignity and promote the common good.

QUESTIONS FOR FURTHER REFLECTION

1. What concept of conscience is articulated in the teachings of the Church? Is there a specifically Catholic conception of conscience? How would you define conscience? Do you consult your conscience often or only on important issues? Is your conscience a kind of moral auto-pilot?

2. What does it mean to have a well-formed conscience? What do we need to do to form our consciences properly? How do we know when our consciences are well-formed? How do you understand the relationship between a well-formed conscience and truth? What do you understand by the primacy of the conscience as a Catholic teaching?

3. Are the primacy of the conscience and the need to conform our consciences to objective truth mutually compatible? What do you think that Blessed John Henry Newman meant when he said that he would drink to the pope, but to conscience first? Does the primacy of the conscience elevate it as a moral guide above papal teachings? Above objective truth? Can a well-formed conscience still be in error? If a conscience is in error, is it still a reliable moral guide?

4. Which is worse—to act from an ill-formed conscience or to act in violation of conscience? Why do you think so? How autonomous are our consciences?

5. The author says that the Church teaches with different levels of definitiveness. What are the categories of definitiveness of Church teaching identified by the author? Give some examples of Church teaching that fit into each category.

6. When they were writing the Declaration on Religious Freedom, why do you think the Council Fathers of Vatican II chose to say that "in the formation of their consciences, the Christian faithful ought to carefully attend to the sacred and certain doctrine of the Church" rather than "in the formation of their consciences, the Christian faithful ought to form their consciences according to the teaching of the Church"? Do you see any difference in these standards? If so, what is it?

7. How are we called both to respect proper teaching authority in the Church and come to our own moral decisions in the light of truth? Can conscience formation be reduced to simply following the teachings of the Church? Why or why not? How does the primacy of conscience say something important about responsible personhood?

8. The Congregation for the Doctrine of the Faith has taught that "a well-formed conscience does not permit one to vote for a political program or an individual law which contradicts the fundamental contents of faith and

morals." Is this the same thing as saying that Catholic legislators must adhere to all of the teachings of the Church when they vote in the legislature, or is it saying something different? On what do you base your answer?

9. Which of the following laws would you consider an attack on human life?

> an abortion control law
> an abortion funding law
> a law authorizing the death penalty
> a law adopting a budget that cuts funding for food
> and medical subsidies for the poor
> a law authorizing an unjust war
> a law providing teenage access to contraceptives
> a law removing bans on gun possession
> a law authorizing torture
> a law authorizing same-sex civil marriage

Can you envision a Catholic with a well-formed conscience taking the opposite position from you on any of the above?

10. Can lawmakers simply transport their moral principles into rules of civil law? Can civil law always mirror moral law? What about those members of society who do not perceive the moral law the same way that Catholics do? Do they have any rights that a Catholic legislator needs to be concerned about?

11. The Congregation for the Doctrine of the Faith has said that there is no desire on the part of the Church "to exercise political power or eliminate freedom of opinion of Catholics regarding contingent questions." Is deciding what laws, what phrases in laws, will best promote fundamental moral values a contingent question?

12. What is the role of the virtue of prudence in making political decisions? Can prudence ever support a less than perfect law? A less than perfect political candidate? How? What examples of this does Pope John Paul II give in *Evangelium Vitae*? In the end, what does a commitment to the primacy of conscience mean for Catholics striving to be faithful citizens in America's pluralistic, democratic society?

NOTES

1. *Forming Consciences for Faithful Citizenship: The U.S. Bishops' Reflection on Catholic Teaching and Political Life*, 37 *Origins* 389 (November 29, 2007).

2. Ibid., at 390, no. 7.

3. Ibid., at 392, no. 17 (quoting *Catechism of the Catholic Church*, no. 1778).

4. *Catechism of the Catholic Church*, no. 1790.

5. John Paul II, *Veritatis Splendor*, no. 60.

6. See Brian Lewis, "The Primacy of Conscience in the Roman Catholic Tradition," 13 *Pacifica* 299, at 307 (2000). See also Joseph Koterski, SJ, "Conscience and Catholic Politicians" (Part 1) (Zenit interview, April 11, 2006), available at *http://www.zenit.org/article-15772?l=english* ("The Church has long recognized the primacy of conscience, so long as one understands the term properly. It is not just that one may obey one's conscience, but that one must do so—but, first, one must form one's conscience correctly").

7. Richard M. Gula, SS, *Reason Informed by Faith: Foundations of Catholic Morality* (New York and Mahwah, NJ: Paulist Press, 1989), 123.

8. *Forming Consciences for Faithful Citizenship*, no. 7.

9. Joseph Ratzinger, "Conscience and Truth," in *On Conscience* at 17, 21–22 (National Catholic Bioethics Center, 2007).

10. Ibid., at 22.

11. For a discussion of the various dimensions of conscience, see Gula, *Reason Informed by Faith*, 131–33; Ratzinger, "Conscience and Truth," at 32–37; Anthony Fisher, "Conscience and Authority," *Zenit* ZE07030301, available at *http://www.zenit.org/article-19058?l=english*.

12. Gula, *Reason Informed by Faith,* at 133.

13. Thomas Aquinas, *Summa Theologica* I–II, Q. 19, Art. 5.

14. Documents of Vatican II, Declaration on Religious Freedom, no. 2.

15. Declaration on Religious Freedom, no. 3 (emphasis added).

16. Joseph Ratzinger, "Commentary on the Pastoral Constitution on the Church in the Modern World," in *Commentary on the Documents of Vatican II*, vol. 5, ed. Herbert Vorgrimler (London: Burns & Oates, 1969), 134.

17. Quoted in Ratzinger, "Conscience and Truth," 23.

18. Ibid., at 24; see also Gula, *Reason Informed by Faith*, 153 (both conscience and authority seek the truth).

19. *Summa Theologica,* I–II, Q. 19, Art. 5–6.

20. Pastoral Constitution on the Church in the Modern World, no. 16.

21. *Forming Consciences for Faithful Citizenship*, no. 17, at 392.

22. Ibid., at 400 n. 2 (quoting *Catechism of the Catholic Church*, no. 1792).

23. Gula, *Reason Informed by Faith*, 124 ("A criterion of a mature conscience is the ability to make up one's mind for oneself about what ought to be done. Note: the criterion says *for* oneself, not *by* oneself. The mature conscience is formed and exercised in community in dialogue with other sources of moral wisdom").

24. Ibid., 137.

25. Ratzinger, "Conscience and Truth," 18–19, 20–21.

26. Ibid., 38.

27. Gula, *Reason Informed by Faith*, n. 7, at 147.

28. *Forming Consciences for Faithful Citizenship*, no. 17.

29. Gula, *Reason Informed by Faith ,* n. 7, at 153.

30. Ibid., 158.

31. Ibid.

32. See *Forming Consciences for Faithful Citizenship*, no. 33 ("The judgments and recommendations that we make as bishops on specific issues do not carry the same moral authority as statements of universal moral teachings").

33. Gula, *Reason Informed by Faith*, n. 7, at 158.

34. See Francis A. Sullivan, SJ, *Creative Fidelity: Weighing and Interpreting Documents of the Magisterium* (Milwaukee: Wipf & Stock Publishers, 2003), 159–60. See also John Paul

II, *Evangelium Vitae*, no. 57, 62, 65. Each of these sections of *Evangelium Vitae* includes reference to the teaching of the ordinary and universal magisterium, followed by a footnote citation to *Lumen Gentium*, no. 25. Father Sullivan explains that "it is obvious that the reference is to the following sentence" in *Lumen Gentium*:

> Although individual bishops do not enjoy the prerogative of infallibility, they do nevertheless proclaim Christ's doctrine infallibly even when dispersed around the world, provided that while maintaining the bond of communion among themselves and with Peter's successor, and teaching authoritatively on a matter of faith and morals, they are in agreement that a particular judgment is to be held definitively. Sullivan, *Creative Fidelity,* 155 (quoting *Lumen Gentium*, no. 25).

Father Sullivan concludes that it is too soon to know whether the immorality of murder, abortion, and euthanasia has been infallibly taught:

> A doctrine is not to be understood as infallibly taught, unless this fact is clearly established, and such a fact can hardly be said to be "clearly established" unless there is a consensus of Catholic theologians about it. It is too soon to know whether there will be the consensus that would show that it is "clearly established" that the immorality of murder, abortion, and euthanasia has been infallibly taught. What this would mean is that the church had taken an irreversible stand on these issues. But that would apply only to the three propositions which the encyclical declares are taught by the ordinary universal magisterium. . . . To say that the three principles affirmed in this encyclical have been infallibly taught would not mean that infallible answers had now been given to the many questions that concern their application. Ibid., at 160.

35. Documents of Vatican II, Dogmatic Constitution on the Church, no. 25.

36. Sullivan, *Creative Fidelity,* n. 34, at 164.

37. Ibid.

38. Gula, *Reason Informed by Faith,* n. 7, at 158.

39. See Sullivan, *Creative Fidelity* n. 34, at 169.

40. Ibid., at 170. See also Frank Brennan, SJ, *Acting on Conscience: How Can We Responsibly Mix Law, Religion and Politics?* (Brisbane: University of Queensland Press, 2007), 31 ("Conscientious Catholics would deviate from church teaching on moral issues only with deep regret and after careful attention to the developing and changing situation, and only on condition that they are satisfied that they have a greater command of the facts or of their situation than the church authority issuing universal declarations faithful to a constant tradition").

41. Cardinal George Pell, *God and Caesar: Selected Essays on Religion, Politics and Society* (Washington, DC: Catholic University of America Press, 2007), 160.

42. Ibid.,161.

43. Cardinal George Pell, "The Inconvenient Conscience," *First Things* (May 2005): 24.

44. Declaration on Religious Freedom, no. 8.

45. Ibid., no. 3.

46. Congregation on the Doctrine of the Faith, *Doctrinal Note on Some Questions Regarding the Participation of Catholics in Political Life*, no. 6 (Washington, DC: USCCB Publishing, 2002).

47.   Ibid. For further discussion of the separation of personal conscience from public policy decisions, see Archbishop William J. Levada, "Reflections on Catholics in Political Life and the Reception of Holy Communion," 34 *Origins* 101–22 (July 1, 2004) ("Over the years since the 1973 *Roe v. Wade* Supreme Court decision, the frustration of many Catholics, bishops among them, about Catholic politicians who not only ignore church teaching on abortion but actively espouse a contrary position has continued to grow."). Bryan Massingale describes two frustrations on the part of the bishops. First, the bishops are frustrated by what they see as inconsistency between the expressed personal opposition to abortion by many Catholic politicians and their failure to engage in public advocacy against abortion. The second source of frustration is the assumption of many Catholic politicians (and members of the wider public) that opposition to abortion amounts to the imposition of a sectarian moral code on a pluralistic society. The bishops maintain that the church's opposition to abortion is based on the natural moral law—"a common moral truth that spans religious affiliations"—that can be recognized and embraced "by all reasonable people of good will." For the bishops, it is difficult to understand why a politician would hesitate to act on a conviction that "is an obvious conclusion of common morality," rather than a sectarian position rooted in revelation. See Bryan Massingale, "Catholic Participation in Political Life," 35 *Origins* 469, 472 (2005); see also Laurie Goodstein, "Guiliani's Views on Abortion Upset Catholic Leaders," *New York Times*, June 25, 2007, at A14 ("Church leaders say they are frustrated by prominent Catholic politicians like Mr. Guiliani who argue that while they are personally opposed to abortion, they do not want to impose their beliefs on others."); *id.* ("Archbishop John J. Meyers of Newark said . . . 'To violate human life is always and everywhere wrong. In fact, we don't think it's a matter of church teaching, but a matter of the way God made the world, and it applies to everyone' ").

48.   Benedict XVI, Post-Synodal Apostolic Exhortation, *Sacramentum Caritatis*, no. 83.

49   John Courtney Murray, SJ, "Leo XIII and Pius XII: Government and the Order of Religion," in *Religious Liberty: Catholic Struggles with Pluralism,* ed. Leon Hooper, SJ (Louisville: Westminster/John Knox Press, 1993), 59–60, emphasis added; see Congregation for the Doctrine of the Faith, *Donum Vitae*, Part III ("The intervention of the public authority must be inspired by the rational principles which regulate the relationships between civil law and moral law. [The civil law] must sometimes tolerate, for the sake of public order, things which it cannot forbid without a greater evil resulting."); R. Mary Hayden Lemmons, "Juridical Prudence and the Toleration of Evil: Aquinas and John Paul II," 4 *University of St. Thomas Law Journal* (2006): 24, 28–29 ("A certain degree of harm must be tolerated, otherwise the burden on those not yet virtuous would be so unbearable that they 'would break out into yet greater evils' ") (quoting Thomas Aquinas, *Summa Theologica* I–II, Q. 96 Art. 2, reply to objection 2); Gregory A. Kalscheur, SJ, "John Paul II, John Courtney Murray, and the Relationship between Civil Law and Moral Law: A Constructive Proposal for Contemporary American Pluralism," *Journal of Catholic Social Thought* (2004): 231, 253–58, 263–64, 266–67; M. Cathleen Kaveny, "The Limits of Ordinary Virtue: The Limits of the Criminal Law in Implementing *Evangelium Vitae*," in *Choosing Life: A Dialogue on Evangelium Vitae,* ed. K. Wildes and A. Mitchell (Washington, DC: Georgetown University Press, 1997), 132–49; see also James L. Heft, SM, "Religion and Politics: The Catholic Contribution," 32 *University of Dayton Law Review* (2006): 29, 42 ("It is necessary for all Catholics, and for Catholic legislators, to agree with the Church's moral teaching on abortion. But I also find it not so clear when it comes to how best to translate that moral teaching into civil law in a society where only one-fourth of the population is Catholic, and when Catholics are not all of one mind on how to deal with *Roe v. Wade*. . . . The bishops should be more helpful to legislators by acknowledging the com-

plexities of the decisions they need to make on legislative matters related to moral issues."); John Langan, SJ, "Observations on Abortion and Politics," *America* (October 25, 2004) ("The enactment of any prohibition of abortion is not simply the enunciation of a moral truth; it is a political and legal act which is to be carried out in an arena where there are many conflicting points of view and interests and where there is widespread hostility to the pro-life position").

50. See *Forming Consciences for Faithful Citizenship*, no. 22 and 34; Gregory A. Kalscheur, SJ, "Catholics in Public Life: Judges, Legislators, and Voters" 46 *Journal of Catholic Legal Studies* (2007): 211, 230–38 (discussing cooperation analysis).

51. *Doctrinal Note*, no. 6 (emphasis added).

52. See Gregory A. Kalscheur, SJ, "American Catholics and the State," *America* (August 2–9, 2004): 17. See also Lemmons, "Juridical Prudence and the Toleration of Evil," 49 (discussing the principles of juridical prudence that inform conscientious legislating); Kalscheur, "Relationship between Civil Law and Moral Law," 255–57; John Langan, SJ, "Homily for Father Robert Drinan's Funeral," *Origins* 36 (February 15, 2007): 556, 557 ("The shape of legislation can be a matter for prudential disagreement, not an issue of faithfulness"); Anthony Fisher, OP, "The Duties of a Catholic Politician with Respect to Bio-Lawmaking," *Notre Dame Journal of Law, Ethics, and Public Policy* 89 (2006): 118–19 (discussing the virtue of political prudence); *id.* at 121 ("We must . . . be loathe to judge our confreres who differ from us on prudential matters in the battle against abortion and euthanasia"); Archbishop John Quinn, "The Virtue of Prudence and the Spectrum of Issues Affecting Human Dignity," *Origins* 34 (November 4, 2004): 334, 335 ("It is fitting to bring into our Catholic consciousness the tradition of prudence in the church's teaching, with its probing question, What will make the situation better rather than worse for the protection of life in the full array of its claims? To lose sight of the full spectrum of issues which affect human dignity runs the grave risk of playing into the hands of those who are eager to allege that the pro-life stance is a sectarian issue"). For a helpful discussion of the nuanced, contextual operation of the virtue of prudence, see Robert K. Vischer, "Professional Identity and the Contours of Prudence," 4 *University of St. Thomas Law Journal* (2007): 46, 50–52.

53. *Forming Consciences for Faithful Citizenship*, no. 19 (quoting *Catechism of the Catholic Church*, no. 1806).

54. *Catechism of the Catholic Church*, no. 1806. Prudence is a moral virtue "acquired by human effort. [It is] the fruit and seed of morally good acts" (*Catechism of the Catholic Church*, no. 1804). As the fruit of good acts, its acquisition may in part grow through a process of trial and error which helps us to learn through experience the difference between good and bad acts.

55. Massingale, "Catholic Participation in Political Life" ("Prudence . . . seeks not the absolute best, but the best that can be attained for now").

56. See Lemmons, "Juridical Prudence and the Toleration of Evil," 30–31.

57. *Forming Consciences for Faithful Citizenship*, no. 32.

58. *Evangelium Vitae*, no. 73; see also John Finnis, "Restricting Legalised Abortion Is Not Intrinsically Unjust," in *Cooperation, Complicity and Conscience: Problems in Healthcare, Science, Law and Public Policy,* ed. Helen Watt (London: Linacre Centre, 2005), 109, 209–45 (discussing the meaning of *Evangelim Vitae*, no. 73, and the complexity of determining when a law in fact is an intrinsically unjust law permitting abortion). Finnis argues that a provision is "permissive" of abortion and intrinsically unjust "only if it has the legal meaning and effect of *reducing* the state's legal protection of the unborn." Ibid. 209; see also ibid., 233 (consideration of the legal and legislative context and circumstances that give rise to a law, as well as

a legislator's intent in voting for the law, are relevant to assessing whether the law's meaning and effect are "permissive" as that term is used in *Evangelium Vitae*, no. 73).

59. See John Courtney Murray, SJ, *We Hold These Truths: Catholic Reflections on the American Proposition* (St. Louis: Sheed & Ward, 1960), 166–67; see also Brennan, *Acting on Conscience*, 73: Simply characterizing something as a grave moral disorder does not help us to determine whether there should be a law against it, especially when there is no moral consensus on the issue in the community. "At election time, we all need to distinguish three discrete questions: Is something a grave moral disorder? Should there be a law against it? Is this the best way to work for a change in public understanding and commitment, providing some prospect for legislative change leading to a change in people's thinking and actions?" Prudent policy making will also be attentive to what Mary Ann Glendon characterizes as the priority of culture over law. Law will be of limited usefulness in protecting human dignity if legal norms don't find support in the underlying culture. See Mary Ann Glendon, "Foundations of Human Rights: The Unfinished Business," in *Recovering Self-Evident Truths*, ed. Michael Scaperlanda and Teresa Stanton Collett (Washington, DC: Catholic University of America, 2007). Cultural renewal may need to precede effective lawmaking. Glendon explains that, through centuries of experience, the church has learned the lesson that "personal formation is essential to cultural formation and . . . no program for advancing the common good is secure unless it rests on firm cultural foundations." In the words of John Paul II, "the dignity of the individual must be safeguarded by custom before the law can do so." Mary Ann Glendon, "Catholic Thought and Dilemmas for Human Rights," in *Higher Learning & Catholic Traditions*, ed. Robert E. Sullivan (Notre Dame, IN: University of Notre Dame Press, 2001), 120. Without denying the genuine pedagogic function of law, attentiveness in conscience formation to the need for this bottom-up approach may lead prudence to recognize that we shouldn't expect too much from the law too soon.

60. See Archbishop Quinn, *The Virtue of Prudence*, see above n. 52.

61. Cf. Pastoral Constitution on the Church in the Modern World, no. 16; see also Brennan, *Acting on Conscience,* 223 ("Insistence on the primacy of church authority in the public forum has a chilling effect on any humble and open inquiry into truth when the majority of interlocutors are not subject to that church authority").

EIGHT

Intrinsic Evil and Political Responsibility: Is the Concept of Intrinsic Evil Helpful to the Catholic Voter?

M. Cathleen Kaveny

In any election year we need not delve too deeply into Catholic political discussions to realize the importance of the term "intrinsic evil." The term is used not only in such documents as *Forming Consciences for Faithful Citizenship*, the 2008 Voting Guide for Catholics issued by the U.S. Conference of Catholic Bishops, but also in political skirmishes among American Catholics. But what, exactly, is an "intrinsic evil"? Why should voters give special attention to intrinsic evils in considering the candidates? Almost no Catholic opinion-maker who invokes the term goes on to ask these questions, let alone to answer them.

Perhaps this is because the answers seem obvious. After all, the term "intrinsic evil" seems to connote great and contaminating evil—evil that we take inside ourselves simply by associating with it. The term itself suggests that "intrinsic evil" involves wrongdoing of an entirely different magnitude than ordinary, run-of-the-mill wrongdoing. Consequently, intrinsic evils must pose great moral dangers to both individuals and society at large, and these dangers ought to dwarf all other considerations in casting one's vote.

Forming Consciences for Faithful Citizenship tells us that intrinsically evil actions "must always be rejected and opposed and must never be supported or condoned," because "they are always opposed to the authentic good of persons." At the same time, some Catholic political commentators have complained about Catholics who support candidates who do not, in the commentator's judgment, adequately oppose such intrinsic evils as abortion, euthanasia, and homosexual acts, the last of which are implied by gay marriage.

The foregoing is meant to illustrate how the term "intrinsic evil" is used in the passionate give-and-take that characterizes many Catholic discussions about voting for a pro-choice politician. It is, however, in significant tension with the great weight of the church's long moral tradition. The term "intrinsic evil" does not have its roots in the expansive imagery of the church's prophetic witness, but rather in its tightly focused analysis of moral acts, which was developed in order to assist priests in evaluating the sins confessed to them in the Sacrament of Penance. It is not a rhetorical flourish, but rather a technical term of Catholic moral theology. Ultimately, as Pope John Paul II reminds us in his encyclical *The Splendor of Truth* (*VS, Veritatis Splendor*), it is rooted in the action theory of St. Thomas Aquinas.

THE MEANING OF "INTRINSICALLY EVIL"

In a nutshell, the fact that an act is called an intrinsic evil tells us two and only two things.

First, it tells us *why* an action is wrong: it is wrong because of the "object" of the acting agent's will. What is the object? To identify the object of an action, you have to put yourself in the shoes of the person who is acting, and to describe the action from that person's perspective. The object, then, is *the immediate goal* for which that person is acting; it is "the proximate end of a deliberate decision" (*VS*, no. 78).

Second, the fact that an act is intrinsically evil tells us that it is always wrong to perform that type of act, no matter what the other circumstances are. A good motive cannot make an act with a bad object morally permissible. In other words, we may never do evil so that good may come of it. To echo an example used by both Pope John Paul II and St. Thomas, a modern-day Robin Hood should not hold up a convenience store at gunpoint in order to give the money to a nearby homeless center. Robin Hood's good motive (altruistic giving) does not wash away the bad object or immediate purpose of his action (robbery).

But to say that an act is intrinsically evil does not, by itself, say anything about the comparative gravity (or seriousness) of the act. It may seem counterintuitive, but in the Catholic moral tradition, some acts that are not intrinsically evil can on occasion be worse both objectively and subjectively than acts that are intrinsically evil. For example, driving while intoxicated would not be considered intrinsically evil, while telling a lie would be. And some homicides that are not intrinsically evil are worse than intrinsically evil homicides, as we shall see in an example below. Furthermore, the fact that an act is intrinsically evil does not by itself tell third parties anything at all about their duty to prevent that act from occurring.

The following analyses and reflections may provide some clarity and further issues for reflection as we continue to debate the use and misuse of church teachings in the political realm.

1. "Intrinsically evil" does not mean "gravely evil."

Reflecting Aquinas's framework for analyzing human action, the *Catechism of the Catholic Church* teaches that for an act to be morally good, it needs to be good in every respect. For an act to be morally wrong, however, any single defect will suffice. Such defects can involve motive, circumstances, or object:

> A human act can be performed for the *wrong motive*. (For example, if I give alms solely in order to earn fame, then my act is morally wrong.)

> An act can be performed *under the wrong circumstances*. (It is entirely good for a newly wedded couple to consummate their union, but not in the church vestibule immediately following the ceremony!)

> Most significantly for our discussion, the immediate "object" (the immediate goal) of the acting agent's will can be disordered or defective. Because an act takes its identity primarily from its object, Catholic moralists say that an act with a *defective or disordered object* is "intrinsically" evil.

So this is an essential point: *intrinsically evil acts are acts that are wrong by reason of their object, not by reason of their motive or their circumstance.*

Splendor of Truth (no. 80) states that intrinisically evil acts are " 'incapable of being ordered' to God, because they radically contradict the good of the person made in his image." Consequently, they can never be morally good, no matter what the intended outcomes. What are some examples? It is always wrong to act with the intention of killing an innocent human being, no matter what the context or larger motivation. This prohibition rules out not merely contract killing but also intentional killing of the dying in order to end their suffering, intentional killing of unborn children, and saturation bombing of cities in wartime.

The church has taught, however, that there are other intrinsically evil acts that have nothing to do with violent assault. Not surprisingly, sex, like death, also provides fertile ground for their identification. Masturbation, homosexual acts, and contracepted heterosexual acts are all, according to Catholic moral teaching, intrinsically evil, in part because "they close the sexual act to the gift of life" (*Catechism of the Catholic Church*, no. 2357). It is never licit for a married couple to use contraception, even if a pregnancy would threaten the life of the woman and the baby she carried. The church teaches that if natural family planning does not provide sufficiently reliable protection, the couple must refrain from sex until menopause rather than use contraception even once.

One might argue, in response, that contraception in this case is acceptable because of the serious threat to the mother and child. Pope John Paul II, however, rejected that form of argument in *Splendor of Truth*. No virtuous motive and no other feature of an intrinsically evil act can make it a good act, although it can mitigate the wrongdoing substantially. To hold otherwise, according to the pope, is to be a "proportionalist" and thereby to place oneself outside the Catholic moral tradition. Needless to say, there are Catholic moralists who disagree with the tradition, and who argue for its revision on a number of grounds. But this is official Catholic teaching.

Over the centuries, Catholic moralists have also identified other acts as intrinsically evil. For example, lying (defined as making a false assertion with the intent of deceiving) has often been identified as an intrinsically evil act. Consequently, it too is always wrong. So it is wrong to lie to the FBI; it is also wrong to tell your Aunt Edna that you think her purple sunflower hat is fabulous if you think it is hideous. While such a lie would be intrinsically evil, it would not be a serious evil. *To recognize that an act is intrinsically evil does not necessarily mean that it is a grave evil, either objectively or subjectively.* While the church has long taught that all sexual misdeeds are objectively serious, it has also recognized that subjective culpability can vary from case to case. Objectively speaking, lying is not always seriously wrong. And few moralists would deny that contraception is less seriously wrong than abortion, which involves the taking of human life.

Furthermore, not all intrinsically evil acts involve a significant violation of justice, the precondition for making an act illegal. No serious candidate for national office could maintain that masturbation, homosexual acts, or contraception should be outlawed in the United States today; and most Catholic legal theorists, whether conservative or liberal, would agree with them.

2. An intrinsically evil homicide is not always worse than every other wrongful homicide.

At this point, someone might object: "What you have just said in the paragraphs above may be true about intrinsically evil acts in general, but not about intrinsically evil acts involving the taking of life—particularly innocent life. Surely these must be the worst acts of all and the greatest acts of injustice, and therefore are the acts that the law needs to condemn most harshly." But even this claim does not hold up under closer scrutiny. Intrinsically evil acts do not necessarily make for the worst form of homicide, with respect either to the subjective culpability of the killer or to the objective wrong done to the innocent victim. The following two examples ought to make that clear.

Consider first a man who burns down his own building one night for the insurance money, foreseeing but not intending that a single mother at work there will die in the blaze. He does not want her to die; her death forms no part of his purpose or plan. He simply does not care whether she dies or not. Now this is a heinous act, revealing great depravity on the part of the perpetrator and causing great harm to the victim. It is not, however, intrinsically evil. The object of his act, to burn down his own building, is not wrong in and of itself. The act is wrong because of its *motive* (theft by insurance fraud) and because of its *circumstances* (the likelihood that an innocent woman would lose her life in the course of it).

Contrast this with a situation involving an elderly man suffering from Lou Gehrig's disease. Fearful of undergoing a protracted and difficult death, he begs his wife to kill him. Finally, she acquiesces to his pleas and kills him painlessly with an overdose of barbiturates. The wife has committed an intrinsically evil act. She has intentionally killed a helpless, innocent person. Her act is seriously wrong, yet her personal blameworthiness is mitigated by her motive of alleviating suffering. Moreover, the objective injustice is mitigated by the fact that her husband not only consented to the act, but begged her to do it.

The law ought to prohibit both acts, because both harm the common good. At the same time, however, the legal system ought to recognize that *the first act, which is not intrinsically evil, is morally worse, both subjectively and objectively, than the second act, which is intrinsically evil.* District attorneys would be eager to prosecute the death-dealing defrauder to the full extent of the law, but many of them would decline to press a murder case against the wife, whose love and loyalty to her suffering husband took a deeply misguided form.

3. Preventing intrinsically evil acts is not always our top moral priority.

Some commentators have suggested that voters ought to prioritize opposition to gay marriage and abortion because third parties have an overriding duty to prevent intrinsically evil acts and to protect their potential victims. But this argument is incorrect. It is not always most important for third parties to intervene to prevent harm caused by intrinsically evil acts. Sometimes preventing harm caused by other kinds of wrongdoing, or even harm caused by natural disasters, can take priority.

Let us return to the examples above, the insurance fraud arsonist and the wife of the man with Lou Gehrig's disease. If a third party were unable to help both, he or she could legitimately choose to save the woman about to die as a result of her boss's fire-setting (an evil act, but not an intrinsically evil one) rather than to protect the man with Lou Gehrig's disease who is about to be voluntarily euthanized by his wife (an intrinsically evil act). Furthermore, under some circumstances one might legitimately choose to protect a person endangered by a natural disaster before coming to the rescue of a victim of human wrongdoing. One might choose, for example, to save a toddler about to drown in a flash flood rather than prevent that act of euthanasia, although the toddler's death would not be due to any human wrongdoing at all.

More generally, one's obligation to intervene to prevent harm to others, whether or not it is directly caused by an intrinsically evil act, depends upon a number of factors. Is one in any way responsible for the harm about to occur? Does one have a special responsibility for either the perpetrator (if there is one) or the victim? What is the likelihood that one's efforts to intervene will succeed? Will those efforts make matters worse if they do not succeed? What good will one fail to do, what evil will one fail to prevent, if one devotes oneself to this particular rescue effort rather than to another? Is intervening in this situation incompatible with performing other duties?

4. The motive and circumstances of particular actions also deserve moral scrutiny.

Some Catholic commentators have claimed that the certainty we have about the wrongfulness of intrinsically evil acts means that we should give their prevention priority over other acts, which may or may not be wrong, depending upon the circumstances. Their argument seems to run like this: the church teaches that abortion, euthanasia, and homosexual acts are always wrong, but not that war or capital punishment is always wrong. Therefore, good Catholics ought to focus their political efforts on preventing acts they know to be wrong, and remain nonjudgmental and politically quiescent about the rest. One commentator has suggested that the church gives us "wiggle room" on issues that do not involve intrinsically evil acts.

This way of understanding a Catholic approach to the morality of human action is deeply mistaken. The church teaches that acts can be wrong because of their object, motive, or circumstances. If a particular act is not wrong by reason of its object, we have a duty to consider motive and circumstances before performing it or endorsing it, particularly if the consequences might bring great harm to other people (as, for example, collateral damage in war).

It is true, for example, that some wars are just and some wars are unjust. Yet this does not mean we can be agnostic about the justice of a particular war being waged by our own government here and now. We have a duty to evaluate that particular war according to the criteria set forth in just war theory. In order to justify the decision to go to war (*jus ad bellum*), seven criteria must be met: just cause, competent authority, comparative justice, right intention, last resort, probability of success, and proportionality of means to ends. We cannot justify indifference to or agnosticism about a particular war on the grounds that war in general is not "intrinsically evil." If we judge a war to be just using these criteria (e.g., World War II), we ought to support it. If we judge a war to be unjust (e.g., the Vietnam War), we ought to oppose it. We cannot hide behind a veil of culpable ignorance. There is no "wiggle room" on such questions for morally serious citizens.

5. In the political process, "intrinsic evil" is not the only useful category in deciding how to vote.

Given the preceding analysis, how much help does the category of "intrinsic evil" offer us in deciding whom to vote for in an important national election? In my view, not much help at all.

A defender of the category's usefulness might say that the fact that a candidate does not disapprove of an intrinsic evil reveals an unworthy character. That may be the case. But so does callousness toward the foreseen (but unintended) consequences of an unjust war, particularly toward the children who are orphaned, maimed, or killed. So does indifference toward starving children in this country and in the world as a whole, many of whom are done an injustice not by individual Americans, but by American policy as a whole. In this fallen world, moral character alone is not enough. Political competence and other practical skills are also required. The person with the best moral character may not be the best president.

Second, a defender of the usefulness of the category "intrinsic evil" might say that it helps us prioritize our actions, and that politicians have an obligation to oppose intrinsic evils, particularly those occurring within our borders, before addressing other sorts of evils occurring elsewhere. After all, we cannot police the world. The trouble with this argument is that in a democracy, we do need to police ourselves. If our policies, including our military policies, are unjustly harming the inhabitants of other countries, we have a duty to stop causing harm outside our borders that is at least as urgent as our duty to prevent harm within them. We Americans justly impose the same duty on other countries, including those harboring terrorists.

"INTRINSIC EVIL" AS PROPHETIC LANGUAGE

Finally, someone who defends the use of the category "intrinsic evil" in thinking about how to vote might admit that there is one issue of overriding importance: abortion. For more than three decades, the regime of legalized abortion has taken the lives of well over a million unborn children a year. The Supreme Court of the United States has conferred constitutional protection upon a woman's right to choose abortion. In this situation, the term "intrinsic evil" helps evoke why abortion deserves prime consideration in voting. Abortion happens inside a woman's womb, inside what should be the safest relationship of all: that between mother and child. Abortion happens deep inside our society, permeating big cities and small towns alike.

But note that this use of the term "intrinsic evil" has moved far beyond the technical use normally employed in Catholic moral theology: it is evocative, not analytical. Its prophetic tone echoes Vatican II's Pastoral Constitution on the Church in the Modern World (*Gaudium et Spes*, no. 27):

> Whatever is opposed to life itself, such as any type of murder, genocide, abortion, euthanasia or willful self-destruction, whatever violates the integrity of the human person, such as mutilation, torments inflicted on body or mind, attempts to coerce the will itself; whatever insults human dignity, such as subhuman living conditions, arbitrary imprisonment, deportation, slavery, prostitution, the selling of women and children; as well as disgraceful working conditions, where men are treated as mere tools for profit, rather than as free and responsible persons; all these things and others of their like are infamies indeed. They poison human society, but they do more harm to those who practice them than those who suffer from the injury.

Moreover, they are a supreme dishonor to the Creator.

Pope John Paul II used this passage to illustrate the incompatibility of intrinsic evil with human flourishing in *Splendor of Truth* (no. 80). Like the use of the clearly prophetic word "infamies" in the Pastoral Constitution on the Church in the Modern World, the prophetic use of the term "intrinsic evil" is meant to start an urgent discussion among people of good will about grave injustices in the world. It does not provide a detailed blueprint for action. Identifying infamies is one thing. Deciding upon a strategy to deal with them is something else again. For many pro-life Catholics, the issue of voting and abortion comes down to this: what does one do if one thinks that the candidate more likely to reduce the actual incidence of abortion is also the one more committed to keeping it legal? The language of intrinsic evil does not help us here. Only the virtue of practical wisdom, enlightened by charity, can take us further.

QUESTIONS FOR FURTHER REFLECTION

1. How does the author indicate that the term "intrinsic evil" has come to be used in American political discourse?

2. What does calling an act "intrinsically evil" tells us about that act? Does calling an act "intrinsically evil" tell us anything about the moral gravity of the act? Can an act that is "intrinsically evil" be less grave, and less immoral, than an act that is not "intrinsically evil"?

3. What kinds of acts has Church teaching considered to be intrinsically evil in the past? Does an act have to be violent to qualify as intrinsically evil? Do you agree that all of these acts should qualify as "intrinsically evil"?

4. Is an act involving the taking of a human life always intrinsically evil?

5. If you have the choice either to prevent an intrinsically evil act or to prevent an act, not intrinsically evil, that will cause great harm to others, what would your choice be? Does the Church teach which choice you must make here?

6. What factors does the author say you should consider in deciding whether you have a moral obligation to intervene to prevent harm to others, whether that harm is caused by an intrinsically evil act or not?

7. Must Catholics give priority to preventing acts that are intrinsically evil over preventing other acts which may or may not be wrong, depending on the circumstances? Is the intrinsically evil act always the most morally grave act that requires prevention?

8. Is waging an unjust war an "intrinsically evil" act? What factors should be weighed in deciding the morality of waging a war? What obligation does a Catholic have in the face of an unjust war?

9. How useful an analytical tool is it to consider whether a political candidate supports acts that are intrinsically evil?

10. What does the author mean by the "prophetic use" of the term "intrinsically evil"? How helpful is this characterization to explain the use of this term by the Church? Does the term's prophetic use have any political utility?

NINE

A Moral Compass for Cooperation with Wrongdoing

Gerard Magill

When fog suddenly surrounds hikers, their compass guides them reliably to safety as they traverse the many crannies, creeks, and crevices. Having that compass provides a justified sense of security as they put themselves at risk on challenging terrain in their quest for joy and fulfillment. The Catholic faithful might be considered as such a band of sojourners navigating the unpredictable landscape of tough moral dilemmas in the quest for holiness and salvation. But what compass do these pilgrims have to guide them through the swirling mists that typify many moral dilemmas in our democratic, pluralistic society?

Debates in morality are associated with arguing about what is right and wrong. That discernment is intricately connected with the quest for holiness. Our moral actions shape our character, and in doing so we can become sanctified sojourners in a life pilgrimage that seeks salvation before God. Holiness matters—our salvation depends on it—and morality can be our pilgrim guide, our reliable compass. Of course, intentionally doing what is wrong is a clear-cut compromise of morality and holiness. However, complicated circumstances can arise that lead to close encounters with serious wrongdoing—involving cooperation with morally wrong actions of another person.

This discussion considers the implications for morality and holiness of close encounters with evil when individuals find themselves cooperating with serious wrongdoing in the voting process, whether as a Catholic politician or as a Catholic voter. In our pluralistic democracy, a profoundly worrying issue in the voting process looms before us like a dense fog that threatens our sense of direction and our moral purpose: how Catholic voters can protect the dignity of human life when items of legislation contain elements connected with legalized abortion. This dilemma over respect for human life may extend to euthanasia if that worrisome debate obtains further legislative traction across the nation. In this quandary over voting, with the sanctity of human life at stake, we can easily lose our way and become complicit with wrongdoing as we seek to participate in democratic elections. Without doubt, moral complicity with such a basic issue can compromise our holiness and threaten our salvation. Thankfully, the Catholic moral tradition, in addressing these dilemmas over the centuries, has developed a moral compass to guide us: the moral principle of cooperation.

The principle of cooperation is perhaps the most widely adopted practical moral principle in our daily lives, though as this discussion explains it can be at times difficult to apply. Simply stated, the principle means that if we *intend* to cooperate in the wrong action of another we are morally culpable. But if we are unavoidably connected with the wrong action of another *without intending* to do so, we may not be morally culpable.

Let's consider the example of a bank robbery. A getaway driver in a bank robbery clearly intends to cooperate with the crime of robbing the bank, even though the driver does not actually enter the bank with a gun and force the bank employees to stuff cash into a bag. That sort of culpable participation is called *illicit formal* cooperation. This means that an individual (in this case, the getaway driver) truly intends to assist in the wrongdoing of another person by participating in a crime (in this case bank robbery). He may not have been the one who pulled the gun on the employees of the bank, but he still assisted the gunman to escape with the cash. On the other hand, if a bank robber uses a gun to stop a passing car and forces the owner of the car to drive him away from the scene of the crime, the driver cannot be said to have *intended* to help out the bank robber. Nonetheless the driver is evidently cooperating by driving the car, albeit under stress of being shot. That sort of participation or cooperation in the crime is not culpable because the driver is under duress and does not intend the morally wrong action—despite the physical participation in the event. This second scenario constitutes *licit material* cooperation. This means that the driver participates in the wrongdoing by being physically ("materially") involved, but there is no illicit formal cooperation insofar as the driver never intended to actually commit bank robbery.

The principle of cooperation provides a moral compass to navigate these close encounters with serious wrongdoing. Specifically, the discussion considers how the principle of cooperation can shed light on the moral quandary facing Catholic politicians and Catholic voters as they engage in democratic processes of voting that are connected with abortion legislation. Three points will be addressed:

First, how the principle of cooperation is a crucial part of the mission of the Catholic Church;

Second, what the distinctions within the principle mean;

Third, how the principle can be applied to the voting quandary today.

THE MISSION OF THE CATHOLIC CHURCH

The U.S. bishops in *Forming Consciences for Faithful Citizenship* explained that the mission of the Church seeks to shape society, transform the world, and promote the common good as a requirement of living our faith.[1] The mission of the Church seeks to provide a transformative influence in the world (fostering holiness) while recognizing the future or eschatological dimension of salvation. It is in this context that the principle of cooperation addresses practical moral dilemmas in which both right and wrong are intertwined. Underlying the moral principle is a commitment to have a transformative influence (fostering holiness) upon a world that is immersed in sin. Yet that transformative influence needs to be realistic because the reign of God will be fully realized only in its eschatological future. In this regard, the moral principle celebrates the metaphor of the Church being a leaven in the world.

The emphasis upon this transformative influence of the Church as leaven in the world is evident in Vatican II and in the pastoral letters of the U.S. bishops such as in their 1986 pastoral letter, *Economic Justice for All*.[2] Vatican II described the mission of the church as a "sacrament of unity" (*Sacrosanctum Concilium*, no. 26) and the "universal sacrament of salvation" (*Lumen Gentium*, no. 48). There are two points here: first to indicate that the physical presence of the church symbolizes its spiritual presence "in which by the grace of God we acquire holiness" (*Lumen Gentium*, no. 48) and become a "holy people" (*Sacrosanctum Concilium*, no. 26); and second, to emphasize that the church "will receive its perfection only in the glory of heaven" (*Lumen Gentium*, no. 48) as the fulfillment of the promise of God's reign.

This tension between acquiring holiness now and future perfection means that the transformative influence of the Church upon the world has two aspects: a saving and an eschatological dimension. As Vatican II explained, "the Church has a saving and eschatological purpose which can be fully attained only in the next life"; and so, as "a visible organization and a spiritual community . . . it is to be a leaven and, as it were, the soul of human society in its renewal by Christ and transformation into the family of God" (*Gaudium et Spes*, no. 40). On the one hand, we must recognize the historical limitations of concrete circumstances as we await the fullness of God's presence: we cannot attain perfection all at once. On the other hand, we must embrace the practical opportunities that are present with God's grace: we can have a transformative influence to foster holiness now. This tension embodies the sacramental nature of the Church's mission.

The U.S. bishops adopted a similar approach in their renowned pastoral letter on the economy. They explained that fulfilling the biblical vision of social justice requires combining hope and realism: "the quest for economic and social justice will always combine hope and realism" *Economic Justice for All*, no. 55). Their point is that applying faith-inspired principles to establish justice "in very different historical and cultural contexts" (*Economic Justice for All*, no. 56) requires "prudential judgments" (*Economic Justice for All*, introduction, no. 20). Prudence is necessary not only because of the diversity of concrete circumstances but more especially because "the world is wounded by sin and injustice" and therefore "in need of conversion and . . . transformation" (*Economic Justice for All*, no. 60). Hence, the bishops emphasized that as "a community of hope" we must live "under the tension between promise and fulfillment" while we are "summoned to shape history" (*Economic Justice for All*, no. 53) by our prudential judgments.

The principle of cooperation helps to make concrete the Church's commitment to transform the world while recognizing the need to be practical. Because of the reality of sin in the world, good and evil are intertwined. It was in recognition of this fact that the principle of cooperation came to prominence historically in the Catholic tradition. So the Church's mission provides the context for understanding and applying the principle of cooperation today. In this context of the Church's mission, it would be mistaken to seek an illusory moral purity that ignores the messy relationship we have in this murky world.[3] Cardinal John Henry Newman was highly attuned to this complex calling of the Church's religious mission in a secular and skeptical world. He trusted God's grace to lead us on through the encircling gloom in his memorable poem "Lead, Kindly Light."[4]

Like Newman's kindly light (God's providential grace), the principle of cooperation seeks to guide us as a compass when the fog of moral uncertainty envelops. Scholars across disciplines agree on the importance of this moral principle. For example, the legal scholar M. Cathleen Kaveny explains that for the earthly pilgrim to respond to suffering and sin at times requires some cooperation with the perpetuation of wrongdoing by individuals and institutions.[5] And the moral theologian James F. Keenan explores the historical genesis and contemporary significance of this nuanced principle for resolving moral dilemmas across contemporary global perspectives.[6] Now the discussion explains how the principle distinguishes between moral and immoral complicity.

THE MORAL PRINCIPLE OF COOPERATION

The principle of cooperation seeks to address the moral problem of complicity with wrongdoing by others. This discussion of the principle indicates its development in the Catholic moral tradition, often referred to as the manualist tradition, to present several important distinctions for today. The purpose of the principle is to clarify how good moral decisions can be made even when there is complicity with wrongdoing.[7] The principle of cooperation is quite different from the principle of toleration that can be traced back to St. Augustine and St. Thomas Aquinas. They argued that when faced with some serious evils, even though we have the effective means to overcome them, accomplishing a greater good or impeding a more serious evil may justify nothing being done.[8] This means tolerating the evil action, but not being involved in its occurrence. Pope John Paul II recognized this principle of toleration in his 1995 encyclical *Gospel of Life*, while clarifying it could not apply to abortion or euthanasia.[9]

The principle of cooperation has a different purpose and is credited usually to St. Alphonsus of Liguori (1696–1787).[10] Unlike the principle of toleration, the principle of cooperation implies concurrence with another in an evil action.[11] This means cooperation in evil,[12] even serious evil like abortion, which the subsequent discussion addresses as being taught by Pope John Paul II. This concurrence can be either moral (as in illicit formal cooperation) or physical (as in licit material cooperation).[13] The principle of cooperation can be applied legitimately only insofar as the action of the cooperator is either morally good or indifferent, but not evil.[14] To comprehend the principle, we need to briefly explore how the Catholic tradition understands the meaning of moral action.

Meaning of Moral Action

The meaning of a moral action is determined by a technical term: the object of moral action. This term clarifies when an action is an intrinsic evil. The importance of this rather erudite concept (the object of moral action) appears in Pope John Paul II's encyclical on morality, *Veritatis Splendor* (1993). The encyclical explains that intrinsic evil refers to the meaning of the moral action and not to the intention of the individual or to the circumstances of the action. That is, there are "acts which, in the church's moral tradition, have been termed 'intrinsically evil' (*intrinsice malum*): they are such always and per se, in other words, on account of their very object and quite apart from the ulterior intentions of the one acting and the circumstances" (*Veritatis Splendor*, no. 80).[15]

From this technical use of vocabulary in Catholic morality two points are significant for the use of the principle of cooperation. First, the principle is designed to address actions that are deemed to be wrong in all circumstances (intrinsic evil). Second, for cooperation to be justified, the action of the person cooperating must never be wrong in itself. For example, when a passerby is forced to drive a getaway car, driving the car is not a morally wrong action.[16] The main purpose of the principle of cooperation is to identify the meaning of a moral action in order to avoid moral culpability, as is determined by the distinction between illicit formal and licit material cooperation.

Illicit Formal Cooperation

Illicit formal cooperation involves the cooperator's consent of will to the evil by intending explicitly or implicitly the evil act of the principal agent,[17] that is, by intending and assisting in the evil act.[18] The critical factor is intention or voluntariness.[19] Here, the cooperator directly intends the evil act and therefore shares moral responsibility for it.[20] This occurs, for example, when a husband approves and pays for his wife's abortion,[21] or to use our previous example, when a getaway driver intentionally participates in a bank robbery with another. Such intentional complicity in the sinful action of another is morally culpable and can never be justified. To further grasp the distinction between illicit formal and licit material cooperation, the U.S. bishops provided a helpful explanation in their 1995 edition of the *Ethical and Religious Directives* (*ERDs*) *for Catholic Health Care Services*:

> The principles governing cooperation differentiate the action of the wrongdoer from the action of the cooperator through two major distinctions. The first is between formal and material cooperation. If the cooperator intends the object of the wrongdoer's activity, then the cooperation is formal and, therefore, morally wrong.[22]

Illicit formal cooperation means that an individual intends a wrong act undertaken by someone else and cooperates with it, that is, participates in it. This type of cooperation is always morally culpable. This formal cooperation is explicit when the person who cooperates (such as a getaway driver in a bank robbery) clearly intends the wrongdoing. However, illicit formal cooperation can also be implicit. This category of implicit formal cooperation elicits much debate, but it is typically associated with cooperation that is immediately associated with wrongdoing.[23] There is a complex debate about what is meant by immediate cooperation,[24] especially when there is implicit consent to participate in another's wrongdoing.[25] But for our purposes, it is sufficient to mention that illicit formal cooperation can be explicit or implicit: explicit when the wrongdoing is clearly intended or implicit when there is immediate cooperation with wrongdoing.

In contrast to illicit formal cooperation there is licit material cooperation that occurs when individuals find themselves cooperating with the wrongdoing of another without intending it in any manner whatsoever. When cooperation is justified (such as when an innocent passerby is forced to be a getaway driver), participation in the wrong action does not involve moral culpability: it is licit material cooperation.

Licit Material Cooperation

In licit material cooperation there is a reluctant cooperation with an immoral act that is perpetrated by another. The cooperator neither agrees with the other individual's intention nor desires the immoral action.[26] This licit form of the principle is referred to as mediate material cooperation. However, this form of the principle can be difficult to apply and always requires prudence.[27] Mediate material cooperation occurs when the cooperator is sufficiently removed from the other individual's evil action.[28] However, as mentioned previously, the action undertaken by the cooperator should not be morally wrong. That is, the person involved in cooperation typically has the right to perform the act, such as an act of preparing surgical instruments in a surgical theater (even if they may be used in some cases for abortions),[29] or the act of driving a car (even if being forced to be a getaway driver). The cooperator should not participate in the sinful act of the other person and should be involved only with acts that may precede or follow the sinful act.[30]

In other words, mediate material cooperation involves the cooperator only with the physical action (e.g., driving a getaway car under duress) and not with the will or intention of the person doing what is wrong (e.g., robbing a bank). The cooperator neither approves nor desires the evil action. So the cooperator is reluctantly involved with the wrongdoing. Another classic example of legitimate or mediate material cooperation is staff reluctantly admitting a woman in a general hospital though the woman is being admitted to have an abortion.[31] Moreover, mediate material cooperation can be sub-divided by considering how closely related the act of cooperation is to the wrongdoing or how indispensable the cooperator's involvement is in the performance of the evil act.[32] Hence, the more closely an individual is involved in cooperating with wrongdoing, the more serious the justification must be,[33] with different levels of justification in varying cases.[34] To justify licit cooperation there needs to be sufficient separation from the wrongdoing as well as sufficient or proportionate reason to justify being involved with the wrongdoing. The U.S. bishops describe these two categories in the 1995 revision of the *ERDs*:

If the cooperator does not intend the object of the wrongdoer's activity, the cooperation is material and can be morally licit. . . . When the object of the cooperator's action remains distinguishable from that of the wrongdoer's, material cooperation is mediate and can be morally licit. . . . The object of material cooperation should be as distant as possible from the wrongdoer's act. . . . Any act of material cooperation requires a proportionately grave reason.[35]

To implement these distinctions, such as distance, requires prudence as a function of a well-formed conscience. The U.S. bishops make this point in the same document:

Prudence guides those involved in cooperation to estimate questions of intention, duress, distance, necessity, and gravity. In making a judgment about cooperation, it is essential that the possibility of scandal should be eliminated.[36]

Other aspects of prudence deal with the issue of the gravity of the wrongdoing, as widely discussed in the manualist tradition,[37] the issue of duress,[38] and the issue of sufficient cause.[39] Moreover, prudence also requires sensitivity to scandal. In a reply from the Vatican to questions from the U.S. bishops on the legitimate use of this principle of cooperation, the Vatican explained:

In the application of the principle of material cooperation, if the case warrants, great care must be taken against scandal and the danger of any misunderstanding by an appropriate explanation of what is really being done.[40]

Some scholars describe scandal as furnishing the occasion for another to sin,[41] or the temptation of another to sin.[42] For other scholars, scandal may arise because of an appearance of evil that is an occasion of spiritual harm to others.[43] Hence, scandal refers not merely to an intention to cause harm; scandal also can refer to providing an occasion of confusion on the part of the faithful about what is morally permissible.

To conclude, although there are many distinctions to be honored when applying the principle of cooperation, two basic points can guide its use. First, *illicit formal* cooperation is always wrong because the individual who cooperates intends the wrongdoing of the other person. Second, *licit mediate material* cooperation can be justified insofar as the individual who cooperates does not intend the wrong deed of the other person despite being under duress to physically participate in it. Now we can apply the principle to the moral quandary of voting when connected with abortion legislation.

COOPERATION WITH WRONGDOING
WHEN VOTING

The principle of cooperation can be a much-needed moral compass to guide Catholic politicians and voters through the fog-like quandary of being connected with the wrongdoing of abortion. Insofar as abortion is an intrinsic evil, the Catholic faithful run the risk of being culpably contaminated by involvement with it during the voting process of democratic elections. Conscience, morality, and holiness can be placed in jeopardy by such a serious issue: moral complicity with such serious wrongdoing can threaten salvation. So the principle of cooperation on this matter deals with high stakes.

Catholic Politicians Connected with Abortion Legislation

The discussion now applies the principle of licit material cooperation to the moral dilemma of protecting the dignity of human life when Catholic politicians and voters may be connected with abortion legislation. The goal here is to explain how the principle of cooperation can help us to address this dilemma in a manner that safeguards the morality and holiness of the faithful. First, let us consider the quandary facing Catholic politicians.

Abortion is condemned in Catholic teaching. Catholic politicians must not formally cooperate: they may not intend, will, or directly participate in the intrinsic evil of directly supporting abortion. Formal cooperation is forbidden outright and always. Pope John Paul II, in his 1995 encyclical *The Gospel of Life*, teaches clearly that "it is necessary to recall the general principles concerning *cooperation in evil actions*" (*Gospel of Life*, no. 73). The pope explains lucidly that we are called upon "not to cooperate formally in practices" that are intrinsically evil:

> Indeed, from the moral standpoint, it is never licit to cooperate formally in evil. Such cooperation occurs when an action, either by its very nature or by the form it takes in a concrete situation, can be defined as a direct participation in an act against innocent human life or a sharing in the immoral intention of the person committing it. (*Gospel of Life*, no. 74)

Despite abortion being an intrinsic evil, official Catholic teaching permits the application of the principle of cooperation to justify licit mediate material cooperation by the Catholic politician. Pope John Paul II in *The Gospel of Life* applies the principle of material cooperation to the problem of Catholic politicians regarding abortion legislation in this way:

> A particular problem of conscience can arise in cases where a legislative vote would be decisive for the passage of a more restrictive law, aimed

at limiting the number of authorized abortions, in place of a more permissive law already passed or ready to be voted on. Such cases are not infrequent. . . . In a case like the one just mentioned, when it is not possible to overturn or completely abrogate a pro-abortion law, an elected official, whose absolute personal opposition to procured abortion was well known, could licitly support proposals aimed at *limiting the harm* done by such a law and at lessening its negative consequences at the level of general opinion and public morality. This does not in fact represent an illicit cooperation with an unjust law, but rather a legitimate and proper attempt to limit its evil aspects. (*Gospel of Life*, no. 73)

What is crucial to note here is that in papal teaching the principle of cooperation can permit "a legitimate and proper attempt to limit" the wrongfulness of laws that permit intrinsic evil, with abortion being specifically identified. This means that a Catholic politician who is evidently pro-life may support laws that, while continuing to permit abortion, in fact limit those abortions such as by addressing their underlying causes. The renowned legal scholar John Finnis argues that "*even if* there is cooperation of pro-life legislators with unjust legislators in enacting just restrictive legislation, this cooperation does not involve the pro-life legislator in the wrongdoing of the unjust legislator, or any other wrongdoing."[44] Moreover, the U.S. bishops recognize this nuance in their 2007 pastoral letter, *Forming Consciences for Faithful Citizenship*:[45]

Decisions about political life are complex and require the exercise of a well-formed conscience aided by prudence. . . . Sometimes morally flawed laws already exist. In this situation, the process of framing legislation to protect life is subject to prudential judgment and "the art of the possible." At times this process may restore justice only partially or gradually. For example, Pope John Paul II taught that when a government official who fully opposes abortion cannot succeed in completely overturning a pro-abortion law, he or she may work to improve protection for unborn human life, "limiting the harm done by such a law" and lessening its negative impact as much as possible. Such incremental improvements in the law are acceptable as steps toward the full restoration of justice. (*Forming Consciences for Faithful Citizenship*, no. 31–32)

These clarifications by the pope and the U.S. bishops explicitly employ the principle of cooperation to explain that Catholic politicians may justifiably support legislation that may continue to permit abortion, provided their stance lessens the harm, such as by alleviating the underlying causes of abortion. This stance may appear bold in contemporary U.S. politics, either secular or ecclesial. Yet the pope and bishops are simply continuing the centuries-long tradition of using the principle of licit cooperation to realize the Church's mission of combining hope and realism to maximize good in the midst of evil and sin. The legitimacy of this stance refers unambiguously to Catholic politicians in the United States who are evidently pro-life—yet remain aligned with their political party platform (which permits abortion) in order to effectively limit or diminish abortions, such as by legislative action on its underlying causes.

The justification of this stance using the principle of licit material cooperation is this: Catholic politicians must not intend the evil of abortion (that would be formal cooperation and always illicit). But they may justify their material cooperation with abortion legislation to support other legislative actions that on balance effectively diminish the evil of abortion. This approach appears to apply both to the legislative branch and the executive branch of government (such as a governor or U.S. president) in voting down or vetoing legislation that *prima facie* restricts abortions—provided they do so to avoid worsening the evil of abortion, such as by avoiding an extensive backlash to the pro-life agenda or by avoiding the loss of an expensive court challenge to the proposed legislation that might repress future efforts for more effective abortion reduction legislation.

Catholic Voters for Politicians Connected with Abortion Legislation

This principle of licit cooperation deals not only with Catholic politicians when connected with abortion legislation but also with Catholic voters who may elect politicians associated with abortion legislation. Of course, the principle of cooperation that permits Catholic politicians to be connected with abortion legislation as explained above similarly applies to Catholic voters. Catholic voters can elect such a politician by appealing to licit material cooperation if they meet the conditions described above. However, the more difficult question for Catholic voters is whether they may vote for a pro-abortion politician who directly supports abortion rights, a stance that constitutes formal cooperation with abortion. Of course, a Catholic voter may not directly support abortion legislation by intending it for its own sake—that would be formal cooperation and thereby immoral. The U.S. bishops make this clear in their 2007 pastoral letter:

A Catholic cannot vote for a candidate who takes a position in favor of an intrinsic evil, such as abortion or racism, if the voter's intent is to support that position. In such cases a Catholic would be guilty of formal cooperation in a grave evil. (*Forming Consciences for Faithful Citizenship*, no. 34)[46]

However, the more nuanced question here is whether a Catholic voter may appeal to the principle of licit cooperation to elect a pro-abortion politician because of the politician's stance on other important issues? The response appears to be in the affirmative. The U.S. bishops explain that Catholic voters may evaluate the issue of abortion within a broader political landscape akin to the process described for politicians:

As Catholics we are not single-issue voters. A candidate's position on a single issue is not sufficient to guarantee a voter's support. Yet a candidate's position on a single issue that involves an intrinsic evil, such as support for legal abortion . . . may legitimately lead a voter to disqualify a candidate from receiving support. (*Forming Consciences for Faithful Citizenship*, no. 42)[47]

There is a subtle point being made here by the bishops. A single issue dealing with an intrinsic evil like abortion "may legitimately lead a voter" to withdraw support. The single issue "may" but does not necessarily require a voter to withdraw support insofar as other issues can legitimately be considered in the deliberative process of voting. The legitimacy of voting for a pro-abortion politician based on other relevant issues is made by Cardinal Joseph Ratzinger as prefect of the Congregation for the Doctrine of the Faith when he applied the principle of licit material cooperation:

When a Catholic does not share a candidate's stand in favor of abortion and/or euthanasia, but votes for that candidate for other reasons, it is considered remote material cooperation, which can be permitted in the presence of proportionate reasons.[48]

Catholic Politicians and Voters: Worthiness of Receiving the Eucharist

If Catholic politicians and Catholic voters may licitly cooperate with wrongdoing that is an intrinsic evil, such as with pro-abortion legislation, the principle of cooperation also can clarify whether they are worthy to receive the Eucharist. Here is where the connection between morality and holiness is abundantly clear. Insofar as the principle clarifies the meaning of moral action when right and wrong are closely aligned, the principle functions as a moral compass to guide Catholics about their worthiness to receive the Eucharist. This issue has been disputed in U.S. national elections. In 2004 the U.S. bishops assigned this issue to the prudential judgment of each diocesan bishop:

> Given the wide range of circumstances involved in arriving at a prudential judgment on a matter of this seriousness, we recognize that such decisions rest with the individual bishop in accord with the established canonical and pastoral principles. Bishops can legitimately make different judgments on the most prudent course of pastoral action. . . . The polarizing tendencies of election-year politics can lead to circumstances in which Catholic teaching and sacramental practice can be misused for political ends. Respect for the Holy Eucharist, in particular, demands that it be received worthily.[49]

This stance elicited a response from a prominent U.S. bishop canonist who argued that Canon 915 assigns this responsibility of refusing the Eucharist to the minister of Holy Communion rather than the diocesan bishop.[50] Irrespective of the canonical debate about who is the appropriate person to deny the Eucharist, the discussion helpfully highlights the basic issue in the principle of cooperation—the nature of the moral action that makes an individual unworthy of receiving the Eucharist. The discussion sheds light on the importance of the distinction between formal and material cooperation when dealing with Catholic politicians and voters connected with abortion legislation.

The relevant clause in Canon 915 makes clear that denial of the Eucharist pertains to those who obstinately persevere in manifest grave sin, making them unworthy to receive the sacrament. This teaching is not in dispute. Rather, the article claims that given the seriousness of procured abortion as an intrinsic evil and insofar as Catholic politicians "continue to support legislation favoring procured abortion," it appears that the Catholic politicians might fit within the category of those who "obstinately persevere in manifest grave sin."[51] In other words, the discussion is a helpful reminder that Catholic politicians, and indeed their voters, may indeed be connected with abortion legislation for immoral reasons—because they may support abortion and if so they are guilty of formal cooperation and thereby they are morally complicit with serious wrongdoing. If that is the case and they intentionally and knowingly persist despite pastoral advice to desist, then because they are perpetrating serious wrongdoing, incurring grave sin, or giving scandal, they make themselves unworthy to receive the Eucharist.[52] This discussion provides a valuable opportunity to summarize how the principle of cooperation can be a moral compass for Catholic politicians and voters connected with abortion legislation.

First, because abortion is an intrinsic evil, Catholic politicians or voters who intentionally support abortion or abortion legislation are morally complicit with serious wrongdoing as a function of formal cooperation. Because of the meaning of this moral action, *illicit formal* cooperation, these individuals are culpable of serious wrongdoing, and if they persist in their unworthiness they make themselves unworthy to receive the Eucharist.[53] The unambiguous immorality of formal cooperation is consistent with papal teaching, teaching from the Congregation for the Doctrine of the Faith, and U.S. bishops' teaching, as described above. For example, Cardinal Joseph Ratzinger emphasized in his 2004 Instruction to the U.S. bishops on election matters that there is a "grave obligation of conscience not to cooperate formally in practices which, even if permitted by civil legislation, are contrary to God's law. Indeed, from the moral standpoint, it is never licit to cooperate formally in evil."[54]

Second, Pope John Paul II, in his encyclical *The Gospel of Life*, explained that Catholic politicians can be connected with abortion legislation in a legitimate manner as a function of *licit mediate material* cooperation, and the encyclical indicates that "such cases are not infrequent . . ." (*Gospel of Life*, no. 73). The pope explains unambiguously: "This does not in fact represent an illicit cooperation with an unjust law, but rather a legitimate and proper attempt to limit its evil aspects" (*Gospel of Life*, no. 73). There is a bold example of this use of licit material cooperation in Cardinal Ratzinger's memorandum on election matters when he justifies the possibility of Catholics voting for a pro-abortion politician for reasons other than abortion. Cardinal Ratzinger refers to "the applicable moral principles" governing a Catholic's vote in such circumstances that he describes as "remote material cooperation."[55]

In sum, the principle of cooperation provides a moral compass to guide Catholic politicians and voters who find themselves to be connected with abortion legislation. On the one hand, they can be involved in *illicit formal* cooperation if they intend the wrongdoing. Even though they do not actually engage in an abortion, their cooperation with it is freely undertaken and intentional in the legislative and voting process. If this occurs, they are morally complicit with wrongdoing. This is always wrong. On the other hand, Catholic politicians and voters may be connected with abortion legislation by *licit material* cooperation provided they do not intend to support abortion. Rather, in circumstances that they cannot alter they may be aligned legitimately with abortion legislation to effectively diminish abortion such as by alleviating its underlying causes. In this case their material cooperation with abortion legislation does not intend or support abortion but is a morally legitimate endeavor to diminish the evil of abortion. When Catholic politicians and voters find themselves in these circumstances there appears to be a duty to justify their stance, typically undertaken publicly for politicians and privately for voters.

EPILOGUE: COOPERATION WITH WRONGDOING WHEN VOTING FOR HEALTH CARE REFORM

In early 2010 Catholic politicians in the U.S. Congress engaged in a fascinating legislative event upon which the principle of cooperation can shed light: health care reform.[56] Historically, the U.S. Catholic bishops provided prominent leadership and dynamic advocacy for health care reform, emphasizing that the "ecclesial mission of health care" and the "Catholic health care ministry" support the "Church's vision of health care," which includes "the right of each person to basic health care."[57] Hence, it was surprising when the U.S. bishops opposed the reform legislation that eventually passed, despite the extension of health care to over thirty million U.S. citizens who previously had no health insurance. Importantly, their disagreement was not about ending the legality of abortion in the nation. They were willing to preserve the legal status quo with regard to abortion remaining legal (recognizing the impossible task in the reform legislation of reversing the 1973 Supreme Court ruling of *Roe v. Wade*[58]) and continuing the 1976 Hyde Amendment that restricted (though permitting some) federal funding for abortion in an annual appropriation bill in the U.S. Congress. This stance can be justified as *licit material cooperation*—supporting health reform while preserving the legal status quo that connected the reform legislation with previous abortion law. Specifically, the bishops supported reform legislation that upheld the status quo as articulated in the Stupak-Pitts Amendment in the U.S. House of Representatives.[59] The reason the bishops opposed passage of the final bill (which adopted the U.S. Senate version) was because it did not adopt the Stupak Amendment. The bishops feared that the final bill could increase federal funding for abortion and not sufficiently provide conscience protection[60]—even though Congressman Stupak eventually supported the bill after a presidential executive order confirmed that the bill would uphold the status quo.[61] Moreover, the Catholic Health Association supported the final bill.[62]

Two inferences about the principle of cooperation result from this legislative event. First, the bishops were willing originally to preserve the legal status quo, which constituted *licit material* cooperation with current abortion law. Yet their pastoral prudence was averse to the potential risk of increased abortion funding and decreased conscience protection that they construed the final bill to entail. Second, this discernment of the bishops was not shared by many Catholic politicians including Congressman Stupak, whose amendment the bishops had originally supported. Although the bishops disagreed as a matter of pastoral prudence and preference, they did not appear in a public manner to morally condemn the legislative decision of these Catholic politicians—suggesting that the legislative decision of the Catholic politicians can be justified as *licit material* cooperation with current abortion legislation.

In sum, the principle of cooperation provides a moral compass to distinguish immoral complicity from an honorable commitment to diminish evil by combining hope and realism in a world of compromised values and sinful actions. In today's increasingly complex and pluralistic democracies, during the process of voting a fog of uncertainty can surround us, confusing our moral direction and threatening our spiritual bearings. As we struggle with intricate moral dilemmas in the holy pilgrimage of faith, the principle of cooperation can provide a reliable moral compass. The principle enables us to honor the sacramental mission of the Church, to nurture morality, to foster holiness, and to have a transformative influence in the world while recognizing the eschatological dimension of salvation. *Lead, kindly light.*

QUESTIONS FOR FURTHER REFLECTION

1. How does the author explain the principle of cooperation with evil-doing? What is the difference between illicit formal cooperation and licit material cooperation with evil-doing? Is it ever permissible to cooperate with evil?

2. What does it mean for the Church to be a "leaven" in the world? How does being a leaven combine hope and realism? What does this concept of the Church as leaven mean for the Church's ability to change the world, including the world of politics?

3. How does the principle of toleration of evil differ from the principle of cooperation with evil? Where do these principles come from in the Catholic moral tradition?

4. Why does the author hold that cooperation with evil applies only to acts that are wrong in all circumstances, i.e., "intrinsically evil"?

5. How can a person cooperate with intrinsic evil and yet avoid moral complicity in the evil of that act? How does the concept of "mediate material cooperation" help to answer that question?

6. What is the role of prudence in making judgments regarding cooperation with evil? What moral principles should guide our prudential judgments in such situations?

7. How did Pope John Paul II in his encyclical *The Gospel of Life* (*Evangelium Vitae*) deal with the issue of material cooperation by a Catholic legislator in abortion legislation? Did Pope John Paul II condemn the Catholic

politician's role in passing a bill that allowed abortions to occur? How is what the pope wrote an example of licit material cooperation?

8. What about when Catholic voters vote for politicians who are pro-choice? Is this vote a form of cooperation (either illicit formal or licit material) in the evil of abortion? If so, which is it?

9. Does the politician's stand on other issues enter into the Catholic's consideration of the morality of this vote? Do the American bishops deal with this question in their pastoral letter *Forming Consciences for Faithful Citizenship*? If so, how?

10. How do principles of formal and material cooperation with evil enter into the application of canon 915, on the denial of Communion to Catholic politicians? Are the same standards applicable to the denial of Communion to Catholic voters?

11. Do you agree with the author that the principle of cooperation provides a moral compass to distinguish immoral complicity with evil from a commitment to diminish evil while still enduring it?

NOTES

1. NCCB, *Forming Consciences for Faithful Citizenship: A Call to Political Responsibility from the Catholic Bishops of the United States* (Washington, DC: USCCB, 2009), no. 9 and no. 14. Also see *Catechism of the Catholic Church*, 2nd ed. (Washington, DC: Libreria Editrice Vaticana, 2000), no. 1913–15.

2. Austin Flannery, OP, ed., *Vatican Council II: The Conciliar and Post Conciliar Documents* (Dublin: Dominican Publications, 1977), and NCCB, *Economic Justice for All: Pastoral Letter on Catholic Social Teaching and the U.S. Economy* (Washington, DC: USCC, 1986).

3. Bishop Donal Murray describes this illusory purity in "Cooperation, Complicity, and Conscience," chapter 1, in Helen Watt, *Cooperation, Complicity, and Conscience* (London: Linacre Centre, 2005), 3.

4. John Henry Newman wrote the poem "The Pillar of the Cloud" in 1833 while stranded off the Straits of Boniface on a boat bound for Marseilles as he returned to England; "Lead, kindly light" is the first line of the poem.

5. M. Cathleen Kaveny, "Tax Lawyers, Prophets, and Pilgrims," chapter 4, in Helen Watt, *Cooperation, Complicity, and Conscience*, 75. For an analysis of the relation between cooperation and appropriation with regard to this principle, see M. Cathleen Kaveny, "Appropriation of Evil: Cooperation's Mirror Image," *Theological Studies* 61 (2000): 280–313. Also see M. Cathleen Kaveny and James F. Keenan, "Ethical Issues in Health-Care Restructuring," *Theological Studies* 56, no. 1 (1995): 136–50. For similar points, also see Luke Gormally, "Why Not Dirty Your Hands?" in Helen Watt, *Cooperation, Complicity, and Conscience*, chapter 2; Michael Bayles, "A Problem of Clean Hands," *Social Theory and Practice* 5 (1979): 165–81, and Leslie C. Griffin, "The Problem of Dirty Hands," *Journal of Religious Ethics* 17 (1980): 31–61

6. See James F. Keenan, "Prophylactics, Toleration, and Cooperation: Contemporary Problems and Traditional Principles," *International Philosophy Quarterly* 29, no. 2 (1989):

205–20; "Institutional Cooperation and the Ethical and Religious Directives," *Linacre Quarterly* 64 (1997): 53–76; "Applying the Seventeenth-century Casuistry of Accommodation to HIV Prevention," *Theological Studies*, 60 (1999): 419–512; "Collaboration and Cooperation in Catholic Health Care," *Australian Catholic Record* 77 (2000): 164. Also see James F. Keenan and Thomas R. Kopfensteiner, "The Principle of Cooperation," *Health Progress* (April 1995): 23–27.

    7.   Sidney Callahan, "Cooperating with Evil," *Health Progress* (May 1989): 12–14.

    8.   St. Augustine considered whether to eliminate or tolerate evils in his own society by weighing the good to be achieved with the negative impact on the public order by doing so. He explained that sometimes, despite being able to eliminate some evil, a greater social good (for example, public order) can require that nothing be done (*De Ordine*, II, 4.12). Similarly, St. Thomas Aquinas, citing Augustine's text, argued that "those who govern correctly ought to tolerate some evils, lest certain goods be impeded or even greater evils obtain" (*ST*, II–II, q. 10, a. 11). For other examples of the discussion of cooperation in Aquinas, see *ST*, II–II, q. 62, a. 2, and q. 169, a. 2, ad. 4, discussed by Charles E. Curran, "Cooperation: Toward a Revision of the Concept and Its Application," *Linacre Quarterly* 41, no. 3 (August 1974): 155.

    9.   "While public authority can sometimes choose not to put a stop to something which— were it prohibited—would cause more harm, it can never presume to legitimize as a right of individuals . . . the legal toleration of abortion or of euthanasia" (*The Gospel of Life*, 1995, no. 71).

    10.   For rules on material cooperation, see St. Alphonsus, *Theologia Moralis*, ed. Leonardus Gaude (Rome, 1905), II, no. 59. For an explanation of St. Alphonsus on material cooperation (referring to *Theol. Mor.*, I, n. 63), see Dominicus M. Prümmer, OP, *Manuale Theologiae Moralis*, I (Freiburg: Herder, 1935), 448; also see Dominic M. Prümmer, *Handbook of Moral Theology*, trans. G. W. Shelton (London: Collins, 1957). There are many explanations of Alphonsus on material cooperation, for example, H. Noldin, SJ, *De Praeceptis*, II (Rome: Oeniponte, 1934), 121; J. A. McHugh, OP, *The Casuist: A Collection of Cases in Moral and Pastoral Theology* (New York: Joseph F. Wagner, 1917), 7.

    11.   Curran, "Cooperation," 153. See especially his section on the "history of the concept" of material cooperation, 155–57. Also see Henry Davis, *Moral and Pastoral Theology: A Summary* (New York: Sheed & Ward, 1952), 36.

    12.   Gerald Kelly, SJ, *Medico-Moral Problems* (St. Louis: Catholic Health Association, 1958), 332.

    13.   P. Marcellino Zalba, SJ, *Theologiae Moralis Summa* (Madrid: Biblioteca de Autores Cristianos, 1957), 1:346. The stricter understanding of cooperation pertains to the physical act: "Cooperatio latiore sensu accepta significat concursum cum alio operante, strictiore autem sensu significat concursum physicam ad pravam actionem alterius principaliter agentis" (H. Noldin, SJ, *De Praeceptis*, II, 116, also see 400).

    14.   A. Konings, CSSR, *Theologia Moralis* I (Chicago: Benziger, n.d.), 138. Also see H. Noldin, *De Praeceptis*, II, 119–21; Edwin F. Healy, SJ, *Moral Guidance* (Chicago: Loyola University Press, [1942] 1960), 47; John A. McHugh, OP, and Charles J. Callan, OP, *Moral Theology: A Complete Course*, vol. II (New York: Joseph F. Wagner, 1929), 608; Bernard Häring, *The Law of Christ*, II (Cork, Ireland: Mercier Press, 1965), 496, 499; Pope John Center, *Observations on Material Cooperation*, pamphlet (Braintree, MA: Pope John Center, 1993), 2, no. 1, second set of subdivisions, 3.

    15.   John Paul II, *Veritatis Splendor*. See especially the section on the object of moral action (no. 71–83).

16. Curran, "Cooperation," 156, citing St. Alphonsus, *Theologia Moralis*), 1.2, t.3, c.2, d.5, a.3, nn.61ff, and Orville N. Griese, chapter 10, "The Principle of Material Cooperation," 389, in Orville N. Griese, *Catholic Identity in Health Care* (Braintree, MA: Pope John Center, 1987). Also see Charles J. McFadden, *Medical Ethics* (Philadelphia: Davis Co., 1961), 330.

17. Curran, "Cooperation," 154. See Augustino Lehmkuhl, *Theologia Moralis*, I (Freiburg: Herder, 1910), 443.

18. Edwin F. Healy, SJ, *Moral Guidance* (Chicago: Loyola University Press, [1942] 1960), 46.

19. Germain Grisez and Russell Shaw, *Fulfillment in Christ. A Summary of Christian Moral Principles* (Notre Dame, IN: University of Notre Dame Press, 1991), 147. Also see Germain Grisez, *The Way of the Lord Jesus*, vol. 1, *Christian Moral Principles* (Chicago: Franciscan Herald Press, 1983), chapters 9 and 12.

20. Benedict M. Ashley, OP, and Kevin D. O'Rourke, OP, *Health Care Ethics: A Theological Analysis* (St. Louis: Catholic Health Association, 1989), 191, and Benedict M. Ashley and Kevin D. O'Rourke, *Ethics of Health Care* (Washington, DC: Georgetown University Press, 1994), 41. Also see Häring, *The Law of Christ*, II, 496–97.

21. Pope John Center, *Observations on Material Cooperation*, 1, no. 1.

22. NCCB, *Ethical and Religious Directives for Catholic Health Care Services* (USCC, Washington, DC: 1995). Referred to as *ERD*. Two subsequent editions have been published, the fourth edition in 2001 and the fifth in 2009, neither including the Appendix of the 1995 edition due to the complexity of the debate over the principle of cooperation.

23. The cooperator is deemed to be so close to the evil as to be tantamount to joining in the act. See Petrus Lumbreras, OP, *Casus Conscientiae*, II (Rome: Athenaeum Angelicum, 1960), 290. See also McFadden, *Medical Ethics*, 330, and *Medical Ethics for Nurses*, 257, and Orville Griese, "The Principle of Material Cooperation," 388. Also see Russell E. Smith, "Formal and Material Cooperation," *Ethics and Medics* 20, no. 6 (June 1995): 1–2, and "Immediate Material Cooperation," *Ethics and Medics* 23, no. 1 (January 1998): 1–2.

24. See, for example, A. Bonnar, *The Catholic Doctor* (New York: P. J. Kenedy & Sons, 1939), 39; Smith, "Immediate Material Cooperation," 23, no. 1: 1–2.

25. "Cooperatio materialis dicitur: a) immediata, si concursus praestatur in ipsa actione physica, etiam sine cooperatione formali" (P. Marcellino Zalba, *Theologiae Moralis Summa*, I, 195). The U.S. bishops explained the closeness with wrongdoing in this way: "Implicit formal cooperation is attributed when, even though the cooperator denies intending the wrongdoer's object, no other explanation can distinguish the cooperator's object from the wrongdoer's object" (NCCB, *Ethical and Religious Directives for Catholic Health Care Services*, 1995, Appendix). Also see Curran, "Cooperation," 154, referring to Benedictus Merkelback, *Summa Theologiae Moralis*, vol. 1: *De Principiis*, 10th ed. (Bruges: Desclée de Brouwer, 1959), 401–2.

26. Charles McFadden, *Medical Ethics*, 329–30. Also see Charles McFadden, *Medical Ethics for Nurses* (Philadelphia: Davis Co., 1946), 256–57, and "Assistance at Immoral Procedures," *Linacre Quarterly* (November 1970): 244.

27. Prümmer, *Manuale Theologiae Moralis*, I, 448. For a list of the roles of prudence in material cooperation, see Arthur Vermeersch, SJ, *Theologiae Moralis*, II (Rome: Universitas Gregoriana, 1945), 89.

28. Griese, "The Principle of Material Cooperation," 388.

29. McFadden, *Medical Ethics*, 329–30. See also John A. McHugh, *Moral Theology*, 603.

30. "Cooperatio materialis dicitur: . . . B) mediata, si concursus praestatur ad actus qui ipsam actionem praecedunt ut praeparatorii vel consequuntur ut completorii" (P. Marcellino Zalba, *Theologiae Moralis Summa*, I, 195, and also 784–85). See also McHugh, *Moral Theology*, 604;. J. A. McHugh, *The Casuist: A Collection of Cases in Moral and Pastoral Theology* (New York: J. F. Wagner, 1906–17); E. Genicot, SJ, and I. Salsmans, SJ, *Theologiae Moralis*, I (Brussels: Uitgeverij, 1946), 182; Pope John Center, *Observations on Material Cooperation*, 1, no. 1, subdivision 2. Merkelbach used the Latin word *subministrat* to convey this explanation of cooperation as supporting the evil action: ". . . mediata quando cooperans aliquid subministrat (materiam, facultatem, media) quod principali agenti inservit ad opus malum exequendum vel facilius exequendum" (Benedictus Henricus Merkelbach, OP, *Summa Theologiae Moralis*, vol. 1: *De Principiis*, 10th ed. [Bruges: Desclée de Brouwer, 1959], 400).

31. Pope John Center, *Observations on Material Cooperation*, 1, no. 1.

32. See, for example, McFadden, *Medical Ethics*, 329, and McFadden, "Assistance at Immoral Operations," 244; Pope John Center, *Observations on Material Cooperation*, 2, no. 1, subdivision 3. See also Griese, "The Principle of Material Cooperation," 399.

33. Gerald Kelly, *Medico-Moral Problems* (St. Louis: Catholic Hospital Association, 1958), 334.

34. McFadden, *Medical Ethics*, 331; see also the section "De gravitate causae excusantis" in H. Noldin, *De Praeceptis*, II, 121–22.

35. ERD, "Appendix."

36. Ibid.

37. "etiam si constat, actionem non esse intrinsecus malam, num adsit causa excusans sufficienter gravis" (Prümmer, OP, *Manuale Theologiae Moralis*, I, 448); "quando causa proportionate gravis existit" (Lehmkuhl, *Theologia Moralis*, I, 444–45); H. Noldin, *De Praeceptis*, II, 121–22; Merkelbach, *Summa Theologiae Moralis*, I, 26 (citing Aquinas, *ST* I, Q.D. de Malo 13, a.4, ad 19: "Pro aliquo incommodo vitando, potest homo licite uti materia alterius vel materiam ei non subtrahere sed praebere").

38. See, for example, Thomas R. Kopfensteiner, "The Meaning and Role of Duress in the Cooperation with Wrongdoing," *Linacre Quarterly* 70, no. 2 (2003). See also James F. Keenan and Thomas R. Kopfensteiner, "The Principle of Cooperation," *Health Progress* (April 1995): 23–27.

39. "hoc pendet ex prudentium aestimatione" (Prümmer, OP, *Manuale Theologiae Moralis*, I, 449). Also see A. Vermeersch, *Theologiae Moralis*, II, 88–89.

40. *Reply of the Sacred Congregation for the Doctrine of the Faith on Sterilization in Catholic Hospitals* (March 13, 1975), no. 3. The document has the Latin title "Quaecumque sterilizatio," published in *Origins* 10 (1976): 33–35. See also the *Commentary on the Reply of the Sacred Congregation for the Doctrine of the Faith on Sterilization in Catholic Hospitals* (September 15, 1977), published in *Origins* 11 (1977): 399–400; the "Statement on Tubal Ligation" from the National Conference of Catholic Bishops (July 3, 1980). These three documents are published together in a pamphlet, *Commentary on the Reply of the Sacred Congregation for the Doctrine of the Faith on Sterilization in Catholic Hospitals* (Washington, DC: USCC, 1983).

41. Häring, *The Law of Christ*, II, 495.

42. Healy, *Moral Guidance*, 49.

43. Griese, "The Principle of Material Cooperation," 410–16.

44. John Finnis, "Restricting Legalized Abortion Is Not Intrinsically Unjust," chapter 12, in Helen Watt, *Cooperation, Complicity and Conscience*, 243; also see John Finnis, "Helping

Enact Unjust Laws without Complicity in Injustice," *American Journal of Jurisprudence* 49 (2004): 11–42.

45. NCCB, *Forming Consciences for Faithful Citizenship: A Call to Political Responsibility from the Catholic Bishops of the United States* (Washington, DC: USCCB, 2009).

46. Cardinal Joseph Ratzinger made a similar point in 2004: "A Catholic would be guilty of formal cooperation in evil . . . if he were to deliberately vote for a candidate precisely because of the candidate's permissive stand on abortion and/or euthanasia" ("Worthiness to Receive Holy Communion," *Wanderer Press* 137, no. 29 [July 15, 2004], final note). This Instruction was sent by Cardinal Ratzinger as prefect of the Congregation for the Doctrine of the Faith to Cardinal Theodore McCarrick to assist him as leader of the Conference of Bishops on domestic policy.

47. The U.S. bishops also quote a Vatican doctrinal note: "It must be noted that a well-formed Christian conscience does not permit one to vote for a political program or an individual law which contradicts the fundamental contents of faith and morals" (Congregation for the Doctrine of the Faith, *Doctrinal Note on Some Questions Regarding the Participation of Catholics in Political Life*, no. 4), in NCCB, *Readings on Catholics in Political Life* (Washington, DC: USCCB, 2006).

48. Cardinal Joseph Ratzinger, "Worthiness," final note.

49. NCCB, *Catholics in Political Life* (Washington, DC: USCCB, 2004).

50. R. L. Burke, "The Discipline Regarding the Denial of Holy Communion to Those Obstinately Persevering in Manifest Grave Sin," *Periodica de re Canonica* 96 (2007): 3–58, discussion at notes 1, 56, and 75.

51. Ibid., Introduction.

52. Ibid., discussion at note 11, and notes 28–30.

53. Ibid., Introduction.

54. Cardinal Joseph Ratzinger, "Worthiness," no. 2.

55. Ibid., "Worthiness," items no. 2, no. 5, and the note at the end of the memorandum.

56. The Patient Protection and Affordable Care Act (H.R. 3590). This is a federal statute signed into law on March 23, 2010, by President Obama along with the Health Care and Education Reconciliation Act of 2010 (Pub.L. 111–52) signed on March 30, 2010, both constituting the health care reform accomplishment of the Democratic 111th Congress.

57. NCCB, *Ethical and Religious Directives for Catholic Health Care Services*, 5th ed. (Washington, DC: USCCB, 2009), preamble and part 1, introduction. See also NCCB, *Health and Health Care: A Pastoral Letter of the American Catholic Bishops* (Washington, DC: USCCB, 1981).

58. *Roe v. Wade*, 410 U.S. 113 (1973).

59. An amendment to the Affordable Health Care for America Act (H.R. 3962) in November 2009.

60. Statements by Cardinal Francis George as president of the United States Conference of Catholic Bishops, March 15, 2010, and March 23, 2010.

61. "Executive Order. Ensuring Enforcement and Implementation of Abortion Restrictions in the Patient Protection and Affordable Care Act," The White House, March 24, 2010.

62. Letter from Sr. Carol Keehan, president and CEO, Catholic Health Association, to the U.S. House of Representatives, March 11, 2010.

BIBLIOGRAPHY

Alphonsus, St. *Theologia Moralis.* Ee. Leonardus Gaude. Roma, 1905.

Aquinas, St. *Summa Theologica (ST)*, II–II, q. 10, a. 11.

Augustine, St. *De Ordine*, II, 4.12.

Ashley, Benedict M., OP, and Kevin D. O'Rourke, OP. *Health Care Ethics: A Theological Analysis.* St. Louis: Catholic Health Association, 1989.

——. *Ethics of Health Care.* Washington, DC: Georgetown University Press, 1994.

Bayles, Michael. "A Problem of Clean Hands." *Social Theory and Practice* 5 (1979): 165–81.

Bonnar, A. *The Catholic Doctor.* New York: P. J. Kenedy and Sons, 1939.

Burke, R. L. "The Discipline Regarding the Denial of Holy Communion to Those Obstinately Persevering in Manifest Grave Sin." *Periodica de re Canonica* 96 (2007): 3–58.

Callahan, Sidney. "Cooperating with Evil." *Health Progress* (May 1989): 12–14.

Curran, Charles E. "Cooperation: Toward a Revision of the Concept and Its Application." *Linacre Quarterly* 41, no. 3 (August 1974): 152–65.

Davis, Henry. *Moral and Pastoral Theology: A Summary.* New York: Sheed & Ward, 1952.

Finnis, John. "Helping Enact Unjust Laws without Complicity in Injustice." *American Journal of Jurisprudence* 49 (2004): 11–42.

Genicot, E., SJ, and I. Salsmans, SJ. *Theologiae Moralis.* I. Brussels: Uitgeverij, 1946.

Grisez, Germain. *The Way of the Lord Jesus.* Vol. 1, *Christian Moral Principles.* Chicago: Franciscan Herald Press, 1983.

——, and Russell Shaw. *Fulfillment in Christ. A Summary of Christian Moral Principles.* Notre Dame, IN: University of Notre Dame Press, 1991.

Griese, Orville N. "The Principle of Material Cooperation." In *Catholic Identity in Healthcare: Principles and Practices.* Braintree, MA: Pope John Center, 1987, 373–419.

Griffin, Leslie C. "The Problem of Dirty Hands." *Journal of Religious Ethics* 17 (1980): 31–61.

Häring, Bernard. *The Law of Christ.* II. Cork, Ireland: Mercier Press, 1965.

Healy, Edwin F., SJ. *Moral Guidance.* Chicago: Loyola University Press, (1942) 1960.

Kaveny, M. Cathleen. "Appropriation of Evil: Cooperation's Mirror Image." *Theological Studies* 61 (2000): 280–313.

——, and James F. Keenan. "Ethical Issues in Health-Care Restructuring." *Theological Studies* 56, no. 1 (1995): 136–50.

Keenan, James F. "Prophylactics, Toleration and Cooperation: Contemporary Problems and Traditional Principles." *International Philosophy Quarterly* 29, no. 2 (1989): 205–20.

——. "Institutional Cooperation and the Ethical and Religious Directives." *Linacre Quarterly* 64 (1997): 53–76.

——. "Applying the Seventeenth-century Casuistry of Accommodation to HIV Prevention." *Theological Studies* 60 (1999): 419–512.

——. "Collaboration and Cooperation in Catholic Health Care." *Australian Catholic Record* 77 (2000): 164.

——, and Thomas R. Kopfensteiner. "The Principle of Cooperation." *Health Progress* (April 1995): 23–27.

Kelly, Gerald, SJ. *Medico-Moral Problems.* St. Louis: Catholic Health Association, 1958.

Konings, A., CSSR. *Theologia Moralis.* I. Chicago: Benziger, n.d.

Kopfensteiner, Thomas R. "The Meaning and Role of Duress in the Cooperation with Wrongdoing." *Linacre Quarterly* 70, no. 2 (2003): 150–58.

Lehmkuhl, Augustino. *Theologia Moralis.* I. Freiburg: Herder, 1910.

Lumbreras, Petrus, OP. *Casus Conscientiae.* II. Rome: Athenaeum Angelicum, 1960.

McFadden, Charles J. *Medical Ethics for Nurses.* Philadelphia: Davis Co., 1946.

———. *Medical Ethics.* Philadelphia: Davis Co., 1961.

———. "Assistance at Immoral Procedures." *Linacre Quarterly* (November 1970): 243–51.

McHugh, John A., OP. *The Casuist: A Collection of Cases in Moral and Pastoral Theology.* New York: Joseph F. Wagner, 1917.

———, and Charles J. Callan, OP. *Moral Theology: A Complete Course.* Vol. 1. New York: Joseph F. Wagner, 1929.

Merkelbach, Benedictus Henricus, OP. *Summa Theologiae Moralis.* Vol. 1: *De Principiis.* 10th ed. Bruges: Desclée de Brouwer, 1959.

Noldin, H., SJ. *De Praeceptis.* II. Rome: Oeniponte, 1934.

Pope John Center. *Observations on Material Cooperation.* Pamphlet. Braintree, MA: Pope John Center, 1993.

Prümmer, Dominicus M., OP. *Manuale Theologiae Moralis.* I. Freiburg: Herder, 1935.

———. *Handbook of Moral Theology.* Trans. G. W. Shelton. London: Collins, 1957.

Sanders, Mark. *Complicities: The Intellectual and Apartheid.* London: Duke University Press, 2002.

Smith, Russell E. "Formal and Material Cooperation." *Ethics and Medics* 20, no. 6 (June 1995): 1–2, and "Immediate Material Cooperation." *Ethics and Medics* 23, no. 1 (January 1998): 1–2.

Vermeersch, Russell E., SJ. *Theologiae Moralis.* II. Rome: Universitas Gregoriana, 1945.

Watt, Helen. *Cooperation, Complicity, and Conscience.* London: Linacre Centre, 2005.

Zalba, P. Marcellino, SJ. *Theologiae Moralis Summa.* I. Madrid: Biblioteca de Autores Cristianos, 1957.

CHURCH DOCUMENTS

Catechism of the Catholic Church. 2nd ed. Washington, DC: Libreria Editrice Vaticana, 2000.

Commentary on the Reply of the Sacred Congregation for the Doctrine of the Faith on Sterilization in Catholic Hospitals (September 15, 1977), *Origins* 11 (1977): 399–400.

Congregation for the Doctrine of the Faith. *Doctrinal Note on Some Questions Regarding the Participation of Catholics in Political Life,* no. 4, in NCCB, *Readings on Catholics in Political Life.* Washington, DC: USCCB, 2006.

Flannery, Austin, OP, ed. *Vatican Council II: The Conciliar and Post Conciliar Documents.* Dublin: Dominican Publications, 1977).

John Paul II. *The Gospel of Life [Evangelium Vitae]* (1995).

John Paul II. *The Splendor of Truth [Veritatis Splendor]* (1993).

NCCB. *Economic Justice for All: Pastoral Letter on Catholic Social Teaching and the U.S. Economy.* Washington, DC: USCC, 1986.

NCCB. *Ethical and Religious Directives for Catholic Health Care Services.* Washington, DC: USCC, 1995).

NCCB. *Forming Consciences for Faithful Citizenship: A Call to Political Responsibility from the Catholic Bishops of the United States.* Washington, DC: USCCB, 2009.

NCCB. *Readings on Catholics in Political Life.* Washington, DC: USCCB, 2006.

Ratzinger, Joseph. "Worthiness to Receive Holy Communion." *The Wanderer* 137, no. 29 (July 15, 2004).

Reply of the Sacred Congregation for the Doctrine of the Faith on Sterilization in Catholic Hospitals (March 13, 1975), no. 3. "Quaecumque sterilizatio," *Origins* 10 (1976): 33–35.

A Parallel That Limps: The Rhetoric of Slavery in the Pro-Life Discourse of U.S. Bishops

Bryan N. Massingale

A survey of the U.S. bishops' statements on the Church's pro-life stance and the struggle against abortion reveals a tendency to draw comparisons with and make parallels between the evil of African slavery in the United States and the practice of terminating fetal life. Thus a national Catholic newspaper reports, "Senior church officials are increasingly comparing the defense of unborn life today . . . to the struggle against racism and slavery in earlier historical periods."[1]

Such comparisons, however, are not a recent phenomenon. As early as 1976, in the aftermath of the 1973 *Roe v. Wade* U.S. Supreme Court decision legalizing the procuring of an abortion, leaders in the U.S. hierarchy noted what they considered to be parallels with the American experience of slavery. In his testimony before Congress on behalf of a constitutional amendment protecting unborn human life, Cardinal Terence Cooke, then archbishop of New York, connected *Roe v. Wade* with the 1857 *Dred Scott* Supreme Court decision concerning slavery. He called both decisions "mistaken and ill-considered" and further declared that each manifested "an equal disregard for human life."[2]

This essay explores and critiques the parallels drawn between the struggles against slavery and abortion in the pro-life discourse of the U.S. Catholic hierarchy. In doing so, my intent is neither to undermine nor challenge the justified concern of the Church's leadership for human dignity and the protection of life. I do not believe, however, that this cause is helped by mistaken, imprecise, misleading, or even offensive lines of argument. Such argumentation, in fact, weakens the case that the bishops seek to make on behalf of our faith. I fear that this is the inevitable outcome of attempting to bolster the argument against abortion by invoking our national and ecclesial experience in the struggles against slavery and racism. To demonstrate the problems with this approach, I will first present the parallels made in certain forms of episcopal pro-life discourse and then examine the difficulties present in such rhetorical appeals.[3]

SLAVERY IN PRO-LIFE DISCOURSE

Upon examining the bishops' appeals to the U.S. experience of slavery in the struggle against abortion, one observes three parallels drawn or usages made: (1) the claim that just as Christians were at the forefront of the abolition of slavery, they are now to be at the vanguard of the campaign against abortion; (2) the equivalence drawn between slavery and abortion through the denial of personhood to a class of human beings; and (3) a refutation of the claim that one can be personally opposed to a moral evil and yet support its legality.

A. Grounding a "New Abolitionism"

In some recent pro-life discourses, one finds explicit comparisons between the struggle against legalized abortion and the movement to abolish slavery. Robert Baker, then bishop of Charleston, South Carolina, provides a detailed exposition of this kind of appeal:

> Without violence of any kind, we join a growing abolition movement in the tradition of the great abolition of slavery movement of the 19th century. . . . During the past two hundred years the Catholic Church has joined forces with major abolition movements. In the 19th century it was with the movement to abolish slavery. In the 20th century the church has taken the lead in helping society put an end to capital punishment and abortion as government-sponsored institutions.[4]

Baker continues this line of thought by declaring, "[W]hile the institution of slavery existed unchecked in society for many centuries, Christian concepts of individual worth and human dignity helped bring the institution down. Slavery is an untenable institution. It is an affront to moral decency. The same is being said by people inside and outside the church today about capital punishment and abortion." The argument, then, is that just as Christian faith recognized the evil of slavery and led Catholic believers to campaign to abolish slavery in the past, these same faith tenets compel and ground Catholic action against abortion in the present.

Cardinal Justin Rigali of Philadelphia offers a similar analysis. Addressing the annual March for Life participants at a mass in 2009, he also drew a parallel between earlier efforts to abolish slavery and the current campaign against abortion. Indeed, he declared that the present effort is the completion of the drive to recognize the equal dignity of all human beings:

> The rejection of slavery and racism has signified an enormous change for the benefit of our civilization. Today, as people called to witness to the Gospel of life, we must constantly proclaim the need for a new change, one that will complete this march toward human equality.[5]

Like Baker, Rigali also invoked the argument of Catholic action in previous justice campaigns in order to ground action in the current anti-abortion cause: "As it did in the past in response to other significant threats to human life, the bishops' conference has authorized us to move forward with a massive post-card campaign to Congress." Thus this prelate argues that just as Christians acted to protect life in the abolition of slavery (and other causes), so too should they be proactive in the abolition of legal abortion.

What this parallel suggests, then, is just as Christians—indeed, Catholics—in the past recognized, struggled against, and eventually overcame the evil of African enslavement in the nation, so too are Catholic Christians summoned to participate in a new abolition movement to overturn the reality of abortion. These prelates summon Catholic believers to become twenty-first-century abolitionists just as their forebears were of old. As one Internet author notes, reflecting the spirit of the just-cited bishops: "If abolitionists could succeed against a moral evil with such deep roots in law, custom, and culture as slavery, [pro-lifers] should have some hope of overturning the abortion regime. . . ."[6]

B. An Equivalent Denial of Personhood

Another way in which slavery is invoked in Catholic and episcopal pro-life discourse is by stating that it, like abortion, reflects a denial of the very person-hood of a class of human beings. We see this comparison reflected in Cardinal Cooke's remarks at this essay's beginning when he opined that both slavery and abortion are practices that express an "equal disregard for human life."

This equivalence is often made by drawing parallels between the Supreme Court's 1857 *Dred Scott* decision on the constitutionality of African slavery and its 1973 verdict in *Roe v. Wade* establishing constitutional protection of a woman's right to procure an abortion. A brief resume of the *Dred Scott* decision helps to appreciate the force of this appeal.

Writing for the six-justice majority in *Dred Scott*, Chief Justice Roger B. Taney argued that persons of African descent in the United States did not enjoy legal freedoms, rights, and protections under our Constitution since the authors of the document—being products of the prevailing social consensus—could not have deemed them to be full and equal members of the human race. Thus the Court held:

[Negroes] were at that time considered as *a subordinate and inferior class of beings*, who had been subjugated by the dominant race and, whether emancipated or not, yet remained subject to their authority, and *had no rights or privileges but such as those who held the power and the Government might choose to grant them.*

They had for more than a century before been regarded as being of an inferior order, and altogether unfit to associate with the white race, either in social or political relations; *and so far inferior that they had no rights which the white man was bound to respect*; and that the Negro might justly and lawfully be reduced to slavery for his benefit. He was bought and sold, and treated as an ordinary article of merchandise and traffic, whenever a profit could be made by it. *This opinion was at that time fixed and universal in the civilized portion of the white race.* It was an axiom in morals as well as in politics, which no one thought of disputing, or supposed to be open to dispute.

[Commenting on the meaning of the words of the Declaration of Independence, "all men are created equal," the Court continued:] But it is too clear for dispute that the enslaved African race were not intended to be included and formed no part of the people who framed and adopted this Declaration; for if the language, as understood in that day, would embrace them, the conduct of the distinguished men who framed the Declaration of Independence would have been utterly and flagrantly inconsistent with the principles they asserted; and instead of the sympathy of mankind, to which they confidently appealed, they would have deserved and received universal rebuke and reprobation. Yet the men who framed this Declaration . . . knew that it would not in any part of the civilized world be supposed to embrace the Negro race, which, by common consent, had been excluded from civilized governments and the family of nations and doomed to slavery. . . . The unhappy black race were [*sic*] separated from the white by indelible marks, and laws long before established, and *were never thought of or spoken of except as property and when the claims of the owner or the profit of the trader were supposed to need protection.*[7]

The argument made by certain pro-life advocates, then, is that just as the *Dred Scott* decision was an official rejection of the personhood of African slaves—now rightly considered a profoundly tragic mistake—so the *Roe* decision likewise tragically and wrongly denies the personhood of unborn human beings. As the Illinois Right to Life Committee declares, both decisions are "an *equivalent* denial of personhood for two different categories of human beings, slaves and unborn children."[8]

This equivalence argument is forthrightly made by leading Catholic prelates. Archbishop Timothy Dolan of New York provides a notable example, rooted in an explicit comparison with *Dred Scott*:

> Tragically, in 1973, in *Roe v. Wade*, the Supreme Court also strangely found in the constitution the right to abortion, thus declaring an entire class of human beings—now, not African Americans, but pre-born infants—to be slaves, whose futures, whose destinies, whose very right to life—can be decided by another "master." These fragile, frail babies have no civil rights at all.[9]

Cardinal Francis George of Chicago, a former president of the U.S. Conference of Catholic Bishops, also appeals to *Dred Scott* by noting the irony that Barack Obama, a person of African descent, would advocate public policies on abortion opposed by the Catholic hierarchy:

> The common good can never be adequately incarnated in any society when those waiting to be born can be legally killed at choice. If the Supreme Court's Dred Scott decision that African Americans were other people's property and somehow less than persons were still settled constitutional law, Mr. Obama would not be president of the United States.[10]

Thus the parallel drawn between slavery and abortion is that both were/are legal practices that rest upon the denial of the human status of a class of human beings. These pro-life advocates, therefore, claim an equivalence between how African Americans were viewed in the past with how unborn infants are considered in the present. To put it succinctly, the claim is that neither blacks in the past nor pre-born human lives in the present are "people."[11]

C. A Rebuttal of Those Who Personally Oppose Abortion Yet Support Its Legality

A final use of the slavery comparison in pro-life discourse lies in how it bolsters rebuttals to those Catholic legislators who state that while they are personally opposed to the practice of abortion, they do not favor efforts to legally proscribe it. Here the appeal to the nation's experience of African enslavement is used to demonstrate the incoherence of being both opposed to a moral evil and yet unwilling to eradicate it. Bishop Joseph Galante, the now retired Ordinary of Camden, New Jersey, provides an illustration of this kind of appeal:

> Yet to say, "I will address those factors that might have the benefit of reducing abortion, but will not oppose the very laws that permit it," is not only unpersuasive, it is also an illogical and unsustainable position.

Substitute the word "racism" or "slavery" for abortion in the above sentence to see how the argument crumbles under the weight of incoherence.[12]

Galante suggests that just as it is unreasonable to say that one desires to reduce practices of racism or enslavement and be unwilling to oppose the laws that sanction these evils, it is also unreasonable to say one is opposed to abortion and yet be unwilling to legally proscribe it. In agreement with this line of argument, J. C. Watts, an African American pro-life activist, bluntly states, "That's the same as saying, I'm personally opposed to slavery, but if somebody else wants to own slaves, it's OK."[13]

The strength of this appeal rests upon the present-day pervasive moral consensus of human slavery's evil and the resulting incredulity of suggesting that one would not be opposed to legally eradicating it. Indeed, because of slavery's contemporary repugnance and the parallel drawn between race-based legal disenfranchisement and the treatment of the unborn, some noted Catholic pro-life advocates have declared that Catholics in public life who argue for the acceptance of abortion do not deserve a civil hearing. They ask rhetorically, "If Catholic politicians advocated segregation or—even worse—slavery, would there be a call for civility toward them?"[14]

These, then, are the various ways in which appeals to slavery are present in the pro-life discourse of leading Catholic prelates and other pro-life activists. I now turn to an examination of the flaws, weaknesses, and limitations of such comparisons and lines of argument. I argue that the use of slavery in Catholic and Christian pro-life rhetoric is not only misplaced and mistaken; it borders on being offensive to those who bear the pain of slavery's legacy.

SLAVERY AND ABORTION: A FALSE AND INEXACT COMPARISON

A. The Danger of Historical Revisionism: Catholics and Slavery's Abolition

We have seen how one of the major, if not the chief, usages of the slavery comparison in the abortion debate is via the call for a "new abolitionism." The appeal here is to what ought to be a common moral outrage at both social evils, rooted in the past abolitionist witness and practices of nineteenth-century Catholic believers. Yet this usage suffers from a major, even fatal flaw: the moral outage at African human enslavement was a consensus established not *because of* the actions and policies of U.S. Catholic leaders and believers, but *in spite of* them.

To be fair, at least one Catholic prelate recognizes the dilemma caused by the Church's inglorious historical engagement with slavery. Archbishop Dolan, as indicated above, believes that the "comparison of abortion to slavery is an apt one." Yet he acknowledges the difficulty of rooting this comparison in past Catholic practices. He admits, "With very few exceptions . . . Catholics in the United States did little or nothing to condemn the dramatically moral evil of slavery and demand its end. And that is our shame to this day."[15]

Dolan's admission is simply a frank acknowledgment of the historical record. Rather than being active participants in slavery's abolition, the vast majority of Catholic leaders were implacably opposed to the abolitionist movement. Indeed, historian Kenneth Zanca aptly titles one section of his study of U.S. Catholics and slavery with the damning assessment, "Abolition and Abolitionists: Uniquely a Minority Protestant View."[16] A similar conclusion is reached by historical theologian Beverly Mitchell, who notes that the percentage of abolitionists in the North was never more than 1 percent of the population.[17]

The movement to abolish slavery in this nation was a Protestant undertaking, and even then only on the part of a decided few. Indeed, leading Southern newspapers of the time praised Catholic noninterference in the debates over slavery, as opposed to the stances adopted by some Protestant authorities. One noted with admiration the fact that Catholic pulpits "are not desecrated every Sabbath with anathemas against slavery."[18] Another offered the following glowing endorsement:

A tribute of warm commendation is due to the Catholic Church throughout the United States for the entire abstinence of its clergy from all intermeddling . . . with national troubles. Protestants as we are, we feel bound to acknowledge and commend the manner in which they have held entirely aloof from the anti-slavery agitation . . . but confined themselves to the appropriate duties of a kingdom which is not of this world.[19]

Thus, contrary to the rhetoric of Baker, Rigali, and other church prelates, Christians generally—and Catholics especially—were not at the vanguard of slavery's abolition; they were, at best, "passive bystanders in this moral crusade."

Note that I said "at best." This is not an idle observation. While Dolan's admission of Catholic silence over slavery is somewhat accurate, it also woefully understates U.S. Catholicism's role and complicity in African enslavement. Catholics were not merely silent or permissive in the face of this moral evil; rather, they were active defenders of and participants in American slavery.

Traders and Owners. Catholics, including many members of the hierarchy, were slave buyers, sellers, and masters. The Jesuits, the Vincentians, the Sulpicians, and the Capuchins were among the religious orders of men who bought, owned, and sold African slaves; similarly the Ursulines, the Carmelites, the Dominicans, the Sisters of Loretto, and the Sisters of Charity among the women religious.[20] Moreover, there exist testimonies from the formerly enslaved that testify to the cruelty they suffered at the hands of so-called "Christian masters." The noted black abolitionist Frederick Douglass even declared, "Were I again to be reduced to the chains of slavery, next to that enslavement, I should regard being the slave of a religious master the greatest calamity that could befall me. For of all the slaveholders with whom I have ever met, religious slaveholders were the worst."[21]

Catholic slave masters and mistresses were not exempt from such indictments. A fugitive slave named Edward gave this account of his owner, a Catholic woman called "Betsy Brown": "She was a very bad woman; would go to church every Sunday, come home and go to fighting amongst the colored people; was never satisfied; she treated my mother very hard; would beat her with a walking stick. . . . Over her slaves she kept an overseer, who was a very wicked man." Orlando Hunt, another escaped slave, also testified to the harsh treatment he endured from a Catholic master: "I was owned by High Holser, a hide sorter, a man said to be rich, a good Catholic, though very disagreeable; he was not cruel, but was very driving and abusive in his language towards colored people. I have been held in bondage about 18 years by Holser, but have failed, so far, to find any good traits in his character."[22]

The historical record, then, does not support the claims that Catholics either "joined forces" with the abolitionist movement or were merely silent bystanders. Catholic believers and leaders were the direct beneficiaries of exploited African labor; "unjust enrichment" is the inescapable companion of human enslavement.[23]

Partisan Defenders. Catholic involvement and complicity is further evidenced in the spirited defenses of African enslavement offered by U.S. Catholic bishops. John England of Charleston was among the most ambitious and prolific, defending slavery in a series of public letters in which he justified the institution on the basis of Scripture, natural law, and church teaching, squarely putting "the Church on the side of Southern slave interests."[24] Augustin Verot of St. Augustine was often called "the Rebel Bishop" because of his forthright defense of the Confederate cause. He pointed out that the Church, while enjoining decent treatment for slaves, never condemned the practice of human ownership itself.[25] Finally, Auguste Martin of Natchitoches (now Alexandria, Louisiana) defended slavery as a "disguised blessing" for the Africans, for it offered these "children of the race of Canaan" the gift of spiritual grace rooted in the knowledge and practice of the true faith. Thus, he concluded, slavery was not an evil but rather "a betterment both material and moral for a degraded class."[26]

These Catholic leaders, then, did not merely keep a permissive silence or offer discreet counsel to the slaveholders in their care. Rather, they publicly embraced and forthrightly defended the practice of African enslavement and sought to show its congruence with Christian faith. Historians also note that no Catholic prelate ever corrected or offered alternative readings of the Catholic teaching.[27]

In view of this damning historical record, using the slavery comparison to ground a "new abolitionism" must be judged as naive and uninformed, at best. At worst, it is difficult to escape concluding that it is a kind of "self-righteous conceit."[28] Catholics were far from active participants in, much less the leaders of, a campaign against African enslavement. They were slave traders and owners, proponents and defenders, and fierce opponents of the major social movement to end this moral evil. The continued use of this comparison in pro-life discourse not only invites dismissal, ridicule, and derision; it risks the hostility and estrangement of the many believers who are descendants of slaves and who still endure the legacy of slavery's brutal past.[29]

B. Citizenship Not Personhood:
A Misleading and Inexact Parallel

The second use of the slavery appeal in certain pro-life discourses is to state that slavery and abortion reflect an equivalent denial of personhood to a class of human beings. The claim is that both African slaves and unborn lives are subject to legal decisions and folk practices that deny their full human status. "Equivalence" is the key term in this appeal. The success of the appeal turns upon an "equivalent" loss or denial of personhood. The argument is that just as we now reject the monstrosity of denying the personhood of black people, so we should now be filled with a similar revulsion at legal denials of personal status for the unborn.

Yet the claim to equivalence is the weakness of this appeal. For the essence of slavery lies not in a denial of personhood, but in the ownership of persons. American slavery was the state- and religious-sanctioned ownership of human beings, maintained through coercion and other brutal practices, for the purpose of exploited labor and unjust enrichment.[30] The acknowledgment of the enslaved community's "personhood" is evidenced both in common social practices and in the *Dred Scott* legal decision so often cited to support this supposed equivalence.

The Enslaved as Persons in Common Practice. Slave owners indisputably recognized that the enslaved were persons possessing sentience and independent volition. Why else would slave insurrections be feared, unsupervised gatherings be forbidden, harsh punishments be meted out, fugitive laws be passed, or armed posses be necessary if the enslaved did not possess a freedom and will that could be—and often was—at odds with that of their masters?[31] In addition, the enslaved were baptized and catechized. These practices demonstrate not only an acknowledgment of personhood, but also an admission that the enslaved possessed a human "soul" destined for eternal salvation.[32]

Moreover, slave masters had sexual relationships with their slaves, though such intercourse was often exploitative for the gratification of carnal pleasure or the increase of the master's slave population.[33] Such couplings, however, acknowledge—albeit in abusive ways—a common, shared humanity. This personhood is further conceded through the practice of enslaved women being charged with rearing and even nursing the white children of a plantation household. Infrequently, slave masters also entered into marriage-like relationships with an enslaved woman.[34] Even where such unions were legally and socially proscribed, the very prohibition acknowledged that the enslaved could freely choose to love—an unquestionable quality of personhood. Finally, slaves were at times emancipated by their owners. The very concept of manumission demonstrates that the underlying personhood of the slave was never seriously in question; slavery was a legal "fiction," not a metaphysical claim or theological status.

Thus historical theologian Beverly Mitchell rightly concludes: "Societies could not escape the reality that the slave was a conscious being and that attempts to bend the will of the slave to that of the master inevitably led to conflict."[35]

In fact, it is precisely because of the moral unease that attended the ownership of *persons* that slavery's justification and defense became so paramount—and problematic. Indeed, the historical record shows that American society developed no consistent rationalization for the practice of African enslavement or ownership.[36] These justifications ranged from the effects of God's curse upon some of Noah's descendants, to the alleged intellectual inferiority of Africans established by so-called "scientific" evidence, to the argument that slavery was part of God's plan for the redemption of pagan Africa.[37] What made such rationalizations necessary, however, were the moral quagmires occasioned by the undeniable personhood of one's property. The implacable reality of the enslaved's consciousness and independent volition is what made slavery so ethically challenging and legally problematic.

While one can be opposed to abortion for many reasons, one has to concede that the personhood of the enslaved was commonly acknowledged and accepted in social practice. This differential treatment of enslaved and preborn life undermines the argument that slavery and abortion both rest upon an equivalent denial of personhood. At the least, those who assert such an equivalence have to demonstrate that embryonic human life, from the "moment of conception," possesses the same degree of free volition, independent judgment, and sentient consciousness as did the enslaved Africans. Absent this, the equivalence argument fails.

The Legal Argument of Dred Scott: A Matter of Citizenship. It is true that the infamous Supreme Court *Dred Scott* decision stated that the enslaved were of a "subordinate and inferior class of beings." Such language would seem to give some support for those who claim a kind of equivalent denial of the personhood for both enslaved Africans and unborn lives.

However, a careful examination of *Dred Scott* leads to a more complex understanding of the intent of this ruling. The legal question involved the right of a fugitive slave, Dred Scott, to challenge his return to his master after being captured in a free state. In other words, did this runaway slave have the legal standing to pursue a case in the judicial system? In deciding this question, the Court specifically declared that the constitutional question before it was not one of personhood, but rather, citizenship:

> The only matter in issue before the court, therefore, is whether the descendants of such slaves, when they shall be emancipated, or who are born of parents who had become free before their birth, are citizens of a state, in the sense in which the word "citizen" is used in the Constitution of the United States. And this being the only matter in dispute in these pleadings.[38]

The Court's decision turned upon its decisive finding that persons of African descent could neither be considered as "citizens" nor as possessing the "rights and privileges" of citizenship because the authors of the nation's Constitution could not have considered them equal "members of the political community" that constituted the United States. It is in this connection that the Justices made their tragic reference to Africans being of "an inferior class of beings." The relevant citation follows, responding to the question of whether Africans or their descendants were "citizens":

> We think they are not, and that they are not included, and were not intended to be included, under the word "citizens" in the Constitution, and can,

therefore, claim none of the rights and privileges which that instrument provides for and secures to citizens of the United States. On the contrary, they were at that time considered as a subordinate and inferior class of beings, who had been subjugated by the dominant race, and whether emancipated or not, yet remained subject to their authority, and had no rights but such as those who held the power and the Government might choose to grant them. . . .

In the opinion of the court, the legislation and histories of the times, and the language used in the Declaration of Independence, show, that *neither the class of persons* who had been imported as slaves, nor their descendants, whether they had become free or not, were then acknowledged as a part of the people, nor intended to be included in the general words used in that memorable instrument.[39]

My intent in rehearsing this history is neither to defend nor excuse this abominable decision. Honesty compels us to admit, however, that while *Dred Scott*'s understanding of the enslaved's personhood is muddled and convoluted, the decision did not entail a denial of "personhood" or the human status of the enslaved, but the denial of the rights and status of citizenship. This is an important distinction, which makes the parallel or comparison with abortion inexact, to say the least. Indeed, the Court acknowledged that the enslaved and their descendants, whether emancipated or not, do constitute a "class of persons." Yet the Court held that such "persons" were not "citizens," and that therefore they were not entitled to petition the courts for a redress of grievances. My point is that the record seriously challenges the claims (1) that this decision turned upon a denial of personhood; and (2) that an equivalent denial is at play in the moral debate over legalized abortion.

Those who would argue for such an equivalence have to demonstrate that the current judicial system posits the personhood of unborn life "from the moment of conception," and yet denies the unborn fetus the rights of citizenship. Absent this, the equivalence argument fails.

In conclusion, one cannot state that a parallel exists between slavery and abortion based upon an equivalent denial of the personhood of the enslaved and the unborn. Both widespread social practices and legal history evidence an acknowledgment of the status of the enslaved as persons that is not matched by a similar consensus concerning embryonic life "from the moment of its conception."[40] At best, the case for equivalence has not yet been adequately made. At worst, this claim of equivalence is a merely a rhetorical assertion and an emotional appeal that rests upon a dubious factual foundation.

C. Personal Opposition vis-à-vis Social Approbation or Indifference

The final use of the slavery parallel in the abortion debate is to undermine the view that one can be personally opposed to a social evil and yet not support public policies that would curb or eliminate it. Such a position, Galante and others argue, is incoherent and unsustainable. Just as it is unthinkable to state that one is opposed to slavery and racism and not be committed to their eradication, so those who believe that abortion is morally wrong cannot make its resolution solely dependent upon the private choices of individual consciences.

Such a position does have strong merits. However, the case for it is undermined by the Church's own unacknowledged engagement with the evils of slavery and racial segregation. In both cases, Church leaders by teaching and example tolerated these social evils and in some cases even counseled against being proactive in their abolition or elimination.

Slavery. We saw above how bishops and other church officials actively defended and sanctioned slave ownership. However, even in situations where there was a reservation articulated concerning its morality, the dominant counsel was to ameliorate, but not overturn, the social status quo.

This teaching is reflected in the views of Francis Kendrick, a bishop of Philadelphia and later the archbishop of Baltimore, who was also a leading Catholic theologian of the time. In an influential volume for the training of future priests, he considered the morality of African enslavement, what he called "the domestic servitude . . . of the posterity of those who were brought from Africa." He held that such enslavement—and the laws forbidding their literacy and free movement—were "to be regretted." Yet, despite this moral reservation (and perhaps, "personal opposition"), the future minister was enjoined not to interfere in social policies:

> Nevertheless, since such is the state of things, nothing should be attempted against the laws nor anything done or said that would make them [the enslaved] bear their yoke unwillingly. But the prudence and charity of the sacred ministers should appear in their effecting that the slaves, imbued with Christian morals, render service to their masters, venerating God, the Supreme Master of all; and that the masters be just and kind, and by their humanity and care for their salvation, endeavor to mitigate the condition of their slaves.

Kendrick concluded by cautioning against being led by a "feeling of humanity" for the enslaved that would "overturn the entire established order."[41]

Note the stance of deference, acquiescence, and even support for the social order and its laws, despite one's personal reservations, hesitations, or "feeling of humanity." Such personal opposition could not lead one to question or challenge—much less change—laws or policies considered unjust or "regrettable." Such deference to the "regrettable" social practice of enslavement is why Catholics were praised for their stance of "noninterference" in the greatest social and moral crisis that faced the nation at the time.

Segregation. A similar stance of acquiescence, capitulation, and acceptance of unjust social mores is also evidenced in the Catholic Church's response to legalized segregation. In a survey of ecclesial engagement with racial injustice, moral theologian Joseph Leonard noted: "Historically, it is impossible to deny that from the end of the Civil War until modern times, an almost universal silence regarding the moral issues involved in segregation blanketed the ecclesiastical scene. The American hierarchy and theologians remained mute."[42]

Notwithstanding the heroic witness of some, too frequently Catholics—rather than being agents of social change and cultural transformation—conformed to the racial mores of our society and engaged in practices of racial denigration. Catholic Christians shared in, and even abetted, the racial fears and prejudices of American society by permissive silence during the horrors of African American lynchings; by a refusal and/or hesitancy to welcome people of color into the priesthood, religious life, and positions of lay leadership; through a hesitant or belated embrace of the movement for civil rights; by the exclusion of or hostility toward persons of color when they sought membership in Catholic parishes; and by ostracizing those who spoke and acted in prophetic ways for racial justice. In these and many other ways, Catholics and their bishops have acted in complicity with the endemic racism of a segregated society.[43]

Moreover, just as with slavery, Catholics were counseled against letting a personal moral opposition to legal segregation become an advocacy for proactive social change. In discussing the morality of the civil rights movement, the noted U.S. moralist John Ford agreed that segregation was morally unjust. However, he maintained that the proper solution lay in encouraging whites to "give rights due to Negroes, rather than to urge the Negroes to press for the rights that are their due."[44] Indeed, the common exhortation of Catholic prelates and leaders of the time was for the faithful to reject both the extremes of the segregationist and "the agitator" (meaning the advocates of civil rights protests such as Martin Luther King Jr.).[45] Instead, they summoned their flocks to extend personal courtesies and respect to African Americans, but not to become active participants in overturning unjust laws.[46]

Some might say that this sad history proves the pro-life advocates' point. There is an incoherence that results from a too-sharp divorce between one's personal opposition to a social evil and one's vacillation or opposition in the face of laws and policies that would curb or eliminate it. I wholeheartedly agree, though the exact relationship between one's personal moral vision and the public policies forged in a religiously pluralistic public square is a complex question.[47] My point, however, is that a church leader's appeal to slavery or segregation to bolster arguments over the incoherence of personal opposition to a moral evil with social acquiescence before it, without being honest about and genuinely repentant over the institution's own tragic history and current implication in racial injustice, undermines one's case.[48] This makes the Catholic Church and its leaders appear to be self-serving and self-righteous. Such attitudes cannot facilitate either the hearing or adoption of their moral views.

CONCLUSION

In view of the above examination, I believe that it is best that Catholic bishops and other pro-life advocates abandon the comparison of slavery with the evil of abortion. I concede that such rhetoric has an emotional resonance, given the repugnance that human enslavement engenders. It also potentially shields church officials from the appearance of being concerned about only a single social issue. It further provides Catholic leaders with an entry into the African American community and a hearing for its pro-life views, . . . a community who might otherwise be suspicious of the Catholic Church, given its tragic complicity in this nation's "original sin" of racism.

Yet it is precisely this tragic history—that the Catholic Church has never fully or adequately acknowledged—and its ongoing legacy which compromises this appeal. The comparison fatally flounders in the face of the Church's historical record and in view of the major factual differences in the social status and recognition of the enslaved vis-à-vis unborn fetal life. To put it bluntly, the pro-life advocacy of the Church's bishops is ill-served by false, misleading, and self-serving forms of argument. The comparison of slavery to the evil of abortion is such an argument.

QUESTIONS FOR FURTHER REFLECTION

1. Why have American bishops used the slavery-abortion comparison in their pro-life discourse? How would you characterize the point that they are trying to make?

2. According to the author, there are three components in the abortion-slavery comparison that the U.S. bishops make. What are those three components?

Do you agree or not? Do you think there are more or fewer components of the comparison? If more, what would they be? If fewer, which components of the author do you disagree with? Why?

3. Is it true that Christians were at the forefront of the fight to abolish slavery? What do today's bishops say about the Church's role in this nineteenth-century movement in American politics? Are they all saying the same thing? What is the historical evidence of the Church's role in fighting slavery?

4. How are the U.S. Supreme Court's decisions in *Dred Scott* and in *Roe* comparable? How are they different? What does each say about the person-hood of the unborn child/enslaved person?

5. Is the comparison of those who do not favor criminalizing abortion with those who supported slavery a fair comparison? If so, how? If not, why not?

6. Were American Catholics owners and traders of slaves? Were American priests and bishops? Did the Church condemn these people? What action did the Church take? Did anyone condemn these activities by Catholics?

7. Why does the author think that the nineteenth-century activities of the Church make today's comparison of abortion to slavery by the bishops a "self-righteous conceit"? Do you agree or disagree? Why? Can an institution's history limit the moral arguments that it can credibly make in the present?

8. Did slaveholders consider their slaves to be fellow human beings equivalent in law and social practices? Do those who favor abortion consider the unborn to be human beings equivalent in law and social practices? Does this make a difference in the moral equivalence of slavery and abortion? Why or why not? What does it mean to say that those who hold that abortion and slavery both rest upon an equivalent denial of personhood must demonstrate that, from the moment of conception, embryonic life possesses the same degree of free volition, independent judgment, and sentient consciousness as did the enslaved? Do you agree or disagree? Why?

9. Does the proposition hold true that you can be personally opposed to a social evil yet not support public policies that would curb or eliminate it in light of the Church's historic tolerance of slavery? How about in light of the Church's historic silence, until the second half of the twentieth century, on segregation?

10. Is there an incoherence that results from too sharp a divorce between one's personal opposition to social evil and one's vacillation or opposition in the face of laws that would curb or eliminate it? Does the bishops' appeal to the moral equivalence of slavery and abortion support this characterization or not?

NOTES

1. John Allen, "Slavery Comparisons on the Rise in Pro-life Rhetoric," *National Catholic Reporter* (December 26, 2008), 7.

2. "Statement of Terence Cardinal Cooke before the Subcommittee on Civil and Constitutional Rights of the House Committee on the Judiciary" (March 24, 1976). Available online at *http://www.usccb.org/prolife/issues/abortion/roevwade/CookeTestimony76. pdf.*

3. I am aware that other groups identified with the pro-life movement also make analogies and comparisons between slavery and abortion. This essay focuses upon the use of such comparisons by U.S. Catholic bishops. I will note the usage by other parties only to further illustrate the implications of such discourse by official church leaders.

4. Bishop Robert Baker, "Abolition Movements of Two Centuries: Slavery, Capital Punishment and Abortion," *Origins* 30, no. 19 (October 19, 2000). Available online at *www.originsonline.com.*

5. Cardinal Justin Rigali, "March for Life," *Origins* 38, no. 34 (February 5, 2009). Available online at *www.originsonline.com.*

6. "Slavery versus Abortion," at *www.prowomanprolife.org/2009/03/31/slavery-versus-abortion/.* A similar appeal grounded in the claim that Christians were at the forefront of the abolition movement against slavery is made on another pro-life website: "It was only by tenacity and sticking to what they *knew* was true in the face of any other arguments that Christians got the ball rolling for stopping slavery. We can do the same" ("Happy Catholic: Christians, Slavery, and Abortion," at *http://catholic.blogspot. com/2008/10/christians-slavery-and-abortion.htm*l. Emphasis in the original.

7. This decision is substantially reproduced in *The Annals of America,* vol. 8 (New York: Encyclopaedia Britannica, 1968), 440–49; emphases added.

8. Illinois Right to Life Committee, "Slavery Compared to Abortion." Online at *www.illinoisrighttolife.org/SlaveryAbortion.htm,* emphasis added.

9. Archbishop Timothy M. Dolan, "On the Front Lines for Life" (October 22, 2009). Available online at *www.cny.org/archive/tdcolumn/tmd102209.htm.*

10. Cardinal Francis George, November 10, 2008, presidential address at the annual Fall meeting of the USCCB, available online at *http://whispersintheloggia.blogspot. com/2008/11/from-chief.html.*

11. See the following statement of a pro-life activist: "You can't ignore the obvious parallels between the way the unborn are treated today, and the way Americans of African lineage were treated 150 years ago. . . . Precisely the same language [is] used to describe the unborn as racists used to describe blacks—they're not people" ("Happy Catholic: Christians, Slavery, and Abortion," at *http://catholic.blogspot.com/2008/10/christians-slavery-and-abortion.html*).

12. Bishop Joseph A. Galante, "Faithful Citizenship: Living in a Way Worthy of the Gospel," *Origins* 38, no. 20 (October 23, 2008). Available online at *www.originsonline. com.*

13. "J. C. Watts Compares Abortion to Slavery." Available online at *http://think-progress.org/2007/05.10/jc-watts-compares-abortion-to-slavery/.*

14. Catholics, "A Catholic Response to the 'Call for Civility,'" *Origins* 37, no. 34 (February 7, 2008). Available online at *www.originsonline.com.*

15. Dolan, "On the Front Lines of Life." Dolan notes that he is citing the words of the "legendary" professor of Church history John Tracy Ellis, from a lecture on the Church and slavery.

16. Kenneth J. Zanca, ed., *American Catholics and Slavery, 1789–1866: An Anthology of Primary Documents* (Lanham, MD: University Press of America, 1994), vii. The author notes several reasons for the Church's absence from the abolitionist cause, among which are the limitations of numbers, its minority status in the country, Protestant hostility, and the view that abolitionism was an "anti-Catholic movement" (111). He also cites additional factors, namely, the widespread view among Catholics that Africans were racially "inferior creatures" and Catholics' "minimal degree of sensitivity to the oppressed" (111, 112). While he documents the involvement of Catholics in slave ownership, he does not directly address this (i.e., economic expediency) as a factor in the Church's stance against slavery's abolition.

17. Beverly Eileen Mitchell, *Black Abolitionism: A Quest for Human Dignity* (Maryknoll, NY: Orbis Books, 2005), 147.

18. *Southern Standard* (New Orleans), 1855, cited in Zanca, *American Catholics and Slavery,* 105.

19. *Richmond Dispatch,* March 8, 1861, cited in Zanca, *American Catholics and Slavery,* 106.

20. Cyprian Davis, *The History of Black Catholics in the United States* (New York: Crossroad, 1990), 35–39.

21. *Narrative of the Life of Frederick Douglass, An American Slave: Written by Himself* (New York: Barnes and Noble Classics, [1845] 2003), 72.

22. Accounts excerpted from Zanca, *American Catholics and Slavery,* 166.

23. On the role of "unjust enrichment" in U.S. slavery and racism, see Joe R. Feagin, *Systemic Racism: A Theory of Oppression* (New York: Routledge, 2006), 16–20.

24. Zanca, *American Catholics and Slavery,* 191.

25. Ibid., 201; Davis, *The History of Black Catholics in the United States*, 53–56.

26. Davis, *The History of Black Catholics in the United States,* 50–52.

27. Zanca, *American Catholics and Slavery,* 191.

28. Ibid., 81; citing Horace Greeley's indictment of New York Archbishop John Hughes's inaction on Catholic anti-black prejudice and violence (1863).

29. The black Catholic historian Cyprian Davis notes that recounting Catholic involvement in slavery is not simply a concern about a tragic and embarrassing past. Slavery set the tone for the U.S. Catholic community's subsequent and enduring relationships with African Americans, both Catholic and Protestant. He writes: "Slavery has cast a long shadow over the history of the United States. It has led to civil strife, racial violence, and ethnic resentments that still fester. American Catholic history is covered by that same shadow. . . . Not only laypersons but religious and priests availed themselves of slave labor. . . . The Catholic church in the United States found itself incapable of taking any decisive action or of enunciating clearly thought-out principles regarding slavery. This factor unfortunately prevented the American church from playing any serious role until the middle of the twentieth century in the most tragic debate that this nation had to face" (Davis, *The History of Black Catholics in the United States,* 65–66).

30. This definition is my summary derived from the studies of Feagin, *Systemic Racism,* 19, and Mitchell, *Black Abolitionism,* 19.

31. For a comprehensive study of the fear of slave insurrections and rebellions, see John Hope Franklin and Loren Schweninger, *Runaway Slaves: Rebels on the Plantation* (New York: Oxford University Press, 1999).

32. Such admissions were common among Catholic prelates during the nineteenth century. See, for example, the letter of Bishop William Elder (Natchez, Mississippi), which speaks of the "high degree of sanctity" among properly catechized slaves (Zanca, *American Catholics and Slavery,* 237).

33. The sexual exploitation of female slaves by a plantation's master and teen-aged sons is a staple feature of the testimonies of freed slaves. See, for example, Douglass's indictment of the compromise of the enslaved sexual virtue (Douglass, *Narrative of the Life of Frederick Douglass,* 100). Other testimonies to this can be gleaned from the masterful study of John W. Blassingame, *Slave Testimony: Two Centuries of Letters, Speeches, Interviews, and Autobiographies* (Baton Rouge: Louisiana State University Press, 1977).

34. Cyprian Davis details one such relationship between Michael Healy and a slave woman named Mary Eliza. Though they could not be legally married, they lived in a monogamous and apparently loving union. Among their children were three priests, who would play prominent roles in Catholic life: James, Patrick, and Alexander Healy. See Davis, *The History of Black Catholics in the United States,* 146–52.

35. Mitchell, *Black Abolitionism,* 19.

36. Ibid., 108.

37. Source documents for the justifications and defenses offered for African enslavement are found in Zanca, *American Catholics and Slavery,* 1–9; 191–216.

38. Excerpts of the *Dred Scott* decision cited in this section are taken from ibid., 54–56.

39. Emphasis added.

40. See, for example, the following observation offered by Notre Dame ethicist Jean Porter: "We have not convinced our fellow citizens that embryonic stem-cell research is morally wrong because we have not convinced them that the embryo, from the first moment of its existence, is a human person in the fullest sense, with the same right to life as anyone else" (Jean Porter, "Is the Embryo a Person? Arguing with the Catholic Traditions," *Commonweal,* February 8, 2002, 8).

41. Francis Kendrick, *Theologia Moralis* on the Morality of Slavery (1843); cited in Zanca, *American Catholics and Slavery,* 200.

42. Joseph T. Leonard, "Current Theological Questions in Race Relations," *Catholic Theological Society of America Proceedings* 19 (1964): 82.

43. The record of Catholic complicity in U.S. racism can be found in the following studies: Davis, *The History of Black Catholics in the United States*; Stephen J. Ochs, *Desegregating the Altar: The Josephites and the Struggle for Black Priests 1871–1960* (Baton Rouge: Louisiana State University Press, 1990); and John T. McGreevy, *Parish Boundaries: The Catholic Encounter with the Twentieth Century Urban North* (Chicago: University of Chicago Press, 1996).

44. Cited in C. Luke Salm, "Moral Aspects of Segregation in Education—Digest of the Discussion," *Catholic Theological Society of America Proceedings* 13 (1958), 61.

45. This was the counsel given in the document of the U.S. Bishops "Discrimination and the Christian Conscience" (1958). King's response to the charge of being an "outside agitator" on the part of so-called Christian "moderate" church leaders, including the local Catholic bishop of Birmingham, is found in his landmark essay, "Letter from Birmingham City Jail" (1963).

46. John J. Lynch, "Notes on Moral Theology," *Theological Studies* 18 (1957): 222.

47.   I examine some of the questions concerning the relationship between a public servant's personal beliefs and public policy in my essay, "Catholic Participation in Political Life,"
Origins 35, no. 28 (December 22, 2005): 469–74.

48.   The current disconnect between the personal morality and public stances of Catholics
in racial matters is documented in a recent study commissioned by the U.S. bishops on the
implementation of their 1979 pastoral letter on racism, *Brothers and Sisters to Us*. This study
concluded that white Catholics are now less likely than they were a quarter century ago to
support policies aimed at redressing the endemic and structured exclusion of persons of color
from public life. See *We Walk by Faith and Not by Sight*: The Church's Response to Racism
in the Years Following *Brothers and Sisters to Us*: A Research Report Commemorating the
25th Anniversary of *Brothers and Sisters to Us* (Washington, DC: United States Conference of
Catholic Bishops, 2004). An executive summary of this report is available at the Conference's
Committee on African American Catholics website, *www.usccb.org/saac*.

ELEVEN

The Disappearing Common Good as a Challenge to Catholic Participation in Public Life: The Need for Catholicity and Prudence

Vincent J. Miller

INTRODUCTION

From a Catholic perspective the common good is the goal of all politics. This has been expressed in a tradition that stretches from before St. Thomas Aquinas in the thirteenth century to Pope Benedict XVI's encyclical *Caritas in Veritate* in 2009. While the common good is one of those phrases that few would directly challenge, the reality it describes has been under sustained attack for much of the past century. Politicians of one stripe have argued against government's responsibility to serve the common good, while others speak an abstract policy language that obscures our shared moral commitments to one another. In the same period of time, changes in the way we live have made our connections to the common good very difficult to see. Our suburban single-family homes isolate us from the supports and responsibilities of community. The consumer economy that supplies our material needs hides from us our fundamental dependence upon the labor of others.

This essay outlines the various forces that over the past century have eroded our appreciation for the ability of government to serve the common good. It considers the predicaments Catholics face in voting because of this, and it offers resources from the tradition of Catholic moral and political thought for addressing them.

A CATHOLIC VISION OF POLITICS

Many are familiar with Machiavelli's handbook on politics, *The Prince*. Few are aware that St. Thomas Aquinas also penned such a text, a treatise, *On Kingship,* written to the king of Cyprus. In it Aquinas offers a fundamental Catholic insight into politics. Following Aristotle, he defines humans as social and political animals. Unlike other animals, we lack the instincts necessary for our survival. Humans rely instead upon reason. Reason in this account is intrinsically social. Humans cannot flourish alone. We depend upon the broader community both to learn what we need to know to survive and to fulfill the needs that no individual can address by himself or herself. Society requires a government to structure and order these shared undertakings. For Aquinas, unlike much modern political thought, government is not a correction for human fallenness; it is an essential part of human social life. Government is a "general ruling force within the [social] body which watches over the common good of all members."[1]

Aquinas also followed Aristotle in a rather negative assessment of democracy as a form of mob rule. The Catholic Church continued this suspicion of democracy until late in the modern era, but eventually came to embrace democracy and responsible citizenship as an essential part of politics, "founded on human nature and hence belong[ing] to the order designed by God."[2] Benedict XVI reaffirmed the importance of participation in modern forms of political life in his social encyclical *Caritas in Veritate*. Commitment to the common good requires both the responsible use and careful preservation of "that complex of institutions that give structure to the life of society, judicially, civilly, politically and culturally." Benedict deepened Catholic reflection on this topic, describing such action for the common good as not only a requirement of justice, but also as an exercise of Christian charity, and indeed a contribution to and prefiguration of the eschatological city of God. "Every Christian is called to practice this charity, in a manner corresponding to his vocation and according to the degree of influence he wields in the *pólis*. This is the institutional path — we might also call it the political path — of charity, no less excellent and effective than the kind of charity that encounters the neighbor directly, outside the institutional mediation of the *pólis*" (*Caritas in Veritate*, no. 7).

THE DISAPPEARANCE OF THE COMMON GOOD

These are the ideals that Catholicism brings to its engagement with political life. Such ideals are always enacted in particular cultural and historical contexts. Our own context is marked by several dynamisms that make it particularly difficult to embrace and act upon these ideals. Three clusters of problems stand out: the loss of a sense of government as shared service to the common good, our living in a form of life that isolates us from one another, and the turn from policy to values.

Loss of a Positive Imagination of Government as a Service to the Common Good

One of the most profound obstacles to a full engagement of the Catholic vision of public life is the loss of an imagination for the positive work of government. Certainly there can be poor, illegitimate, and even outright evil forms of governance. But government itself is an essential part of human social existence. The decisions of rulers, the laws and policies drafted by legislators and carried out by executives are essential services to the common good. A variety of factors over the past several decades has conspired to erode this positive imagination of government and policy.

The generations that lived through the Depression, World War II, the Cold War, and the civil rights movement experienced, in a variety of ways, the importance of government action and the significance of the details of specific laws and policies. The generation formed in the instability of the Great Depression viscerally understood the chaos that unregulated markets can unleash and for that reason counted on government to protect the common good. They experienced the New Deal and Great Society programs as profound improvements in the social safety net. Social Security provided a guaranteed minimum retirement and life and disability insurance. Medicaid and Medicare ameliorated the lack of health care among the poor and eliminated fears of being unable to afford care in old age. These policies fundamentally changed life for those generations in a manner that their children and grandchildren now take for granted.

Likewise the civil rights movement provided profound experiences of the importance of government. The Supreme Court offered redress for injustices that were ignored and abetted by state and local courts. The federal government enforced these decisions over against the intransigence of local authorities. Finally, the Civil Rights Act of 1964 was a climactic moment in the generations-long struggle to secure equal political and economic rights for African Americans. These laws and policies formed generations in a positive imagination of the role of government in society. They had a clear sense that policies and their details matter.

This positive imagination began to erode in the 1970s. Supreme Court decisions and civil rights legislation could undo legal exclusion but were less able to impact pervasive racism and even ran the risk of hardening racist attitudes as the push for equality moved into bussing and affirmative action programs. Here pursuit of the rights of minorities revealed fractures in the common good that could not be quickly healed. If these government policies illuminated long-standing and deep social fractures of racism, other actions, such as the *Roe v. Wade* decision, created new ones. At the same time, the economic stagnation of the 1970s was proving resistant to the economic policies that had dominated the post-Depression era. These various crises undermined confidence in government policy and fractured the sense that the government served the common good.

POLITICAL PARTIES AND THE LOSS OF THE COMMON GOOD

In the midst of these crises, the political and economic vision of neoliberal economic theorists such as Milton Freidman and Friedrich Hayek was advanced as a solution to the economic malaise of the decade. Embraced by the Republican Party in the United States and the Conservative Party in Great Britain, it provided the economic and policy ideas behind the Reagan and Thatcher "revolutions." Unlike the economist so influential in the response to the Great Depression, John Maynard Keynes, who saw government intervention as essential for stabilizing the market and orienting it to the national common good, these economists presented markets in themselves as the most rational and effective form of collective human activity. From this perspective, the common good is reduced to whatever outcome Adam Smith's "invisible hand" produces from the aggregate of individual economic decisions. Thus, government regulation was seen as a destructive distortion of market decisions. Taxation for government programs was portrayed as a transfer of capital from efficient markets use to less efficient bureaucratic programs. Markets would more efficiently and rapidly address the range of human need if only government would get out of the way. Ronald Reagan gave voice to this belief in his first inaugural address: "In this present crisis, government is not the solution to our problem; government is the problem."

These revolutions were far more than mere electoral victories. They were part of a broader reorientation of commonsense assumptions away from a positive imagination of government as a form of collective agency to promote the common good to a private, individualized focus on economic activity. Thus, even the opposition figures Bill Clinton and Tony Blair shared their assumptions. In his 1996 State of the Union address, Clinton pronounced that "the era of big government is over." It wasn't, of course, no matter which party was in power, but the assumption that the government was an essential servant to the common good had been fundamentally undermined. This ideological shift was the product of a decades-long ideological program promoted by enormously well-financed foundations and think tanks such as the American Enterprise Institute and the Heritage Foundation. These funded and deployed countless pundits, experts, and editorial writers in the press nationally and regionally, who tirelessly highlighted whatever government inefficiencies and errors they could find and preached the virtues of market-based solutions. All the while, social inequality grew profoundly, as tax cuts favored the wealthy and hyperwealthy, and wage earners' income stagnated. The combination of these factors produced our current situation, where it is common sense for many to think of government as the enemy of the common good and for many more who don't accept this view to lack persuasive language to express the classic and Catholic view of the common good.

Ours is an age when even a traditional statement of the Catholic view of the responsibility of government for the common good, such as these words from Benedict XVI's encyclical *Caritas in Veritate*, seems radical:

> Economic activity cannot solve all social problems through the simple application of commercial logic. This needs to be directed towards the pursuit of the common good, for which the political community in particular must also take responsibility. Therefore, it must be borne in mind that grave imbalances are produced when economic action, conceived merely as an engine for wealth creation, is detached from political action, conceived as a means for pursuing justice through redistribution. (no. 36)

While this political program was being carried out on the political right, an equally important tendency of the left was unwittingly eroding the connection between government and the moral imagination in a different way. The massive policy initiatives of New Deal and the Great Society involved countless actuarial and cost-benefit calculations, but they were presented in deeply moral and communal terms. America was a community with the power to govern the economy for its common good. The nation had a responsibility to take care of its poor and powerless. Poverty in old age, in rural areas, and in inner cities was presented as a national scandal and call to action.

The demands of crafting policies to address these problems, however, drew Democratic rhetoric away from moral visions toward wonkish policy talk of cost-benefit analysis, demographics, and regulatory language. The moral commitment to the common good was lost amid the administrative bureaucratic language. Political appeals were too often couched in terms of individual benefits—e.g., Bill Clinton's holding up his health access card to illustrate his plans for health care reform. In Liz Cohen's words, this gave rise to an era of the "Citizen as Consumer."[3] From this perspective, the collective goods that government programs served were viewed in purely individualistic terms. For example, the broad social safety net provided by Social Security (protecting children against the death of a parent, workers against disability, and an entire nation against absolute poverty in retirement) was reduced to an argument about return on investment for the individual retiree. Democrats too often confused the policy details with the political and moral work of tending our shared commitment to the common good. As a result, government was too easily parodied as a detached, amoral bureaucracy. As we shall see below, the political urgency of the moral went elsewhere.

The Common Good and the Way We Live Apart

These contributions to the loss of an imagination for the common good by both political parties took place while two important shifts in society and the economy were undermining it in our everyday lives. The post-war suburban exodus eroded the ties of community and extended family. The rise of the global economy and the devolution of state power over the domestic economy took away an important dimension of political agency to work for the common good.

THE SINGLE-FAMILY HOME

The suburban form of life with the nuclear family in a single-family home is a space in which the common good does not easily appear. It limits the scope of our moral imagination by separating us from others' needs and leaving the nuclear family to face its own needs and crises solely on its own income.

Extended families have long since ceased to be networks of mutual support and responsibility. Rather than depend on family for support in times of illness and financial crises the nuclear family is left to handle such needs through individual financial instruments such as mortgages, life and disability insurance, savings accounts for retirement and education. In crises help comes not from our broader families, community, or government, but from that much more fickle friend in times of need—the credit card.

Just as we cannot rely upon our extended families to step into the breach to pay our mortgage should we lose a job, we likewise have little sense of deep responsibility for those outside our immediate family. This is a cash-flow intensive form of life, and the vast majority of stable families are but a few paychecks from bankruptcy. We are all too busy struggling and seeing to our own separate flourishing to spend much time thinking of others.

With little experience of responsibility or support outside of our nuclear families, the sense of a community-wide common good erodes profoundly. With so many unable to properly save for retirement, not to mention for their children's education, anti-tax rhetoric will always find a ready audience. Thus George W. Bush's simple justification for tax cuts: "It's your money." The Church should answer with John Paul II (*Sollicitudo Rei Socialis*, no. 42) that there is a "social mortgage" on private property. But that teaching falls on deaf ears, as we lack the ability to imagine the collective good within which "we" might act together to spend that money for anything more than the support of our individual families.

As communitarian political thinkers have long argued, we need communities of commitment in which to form our moral imaginations and to learn the habits of concern for others. Community is necessary to forge the character that is able to sacrifice for others' needs. For much of human history, this was learned in the extended family, clan, and village. In the suburban family home we lack these. The needs of others outside of our immediate families are not readily apparent to us. The lives of people next door, behind their automatic garage doors, might as well be miles away. We know our newscasters better and see the grocery store cashier more often. In this space, we are too often on our own—encountering others neither in their support for us nor in our obligation toward them. It is no wonder that tax cuts so easily became the default government policy initiative in the past thirty years.

Something must be said here about the use of the Catholic principle of subsidiarity. This holds that higher levels of authority should not intervene in situations adequately handled by lower ones; and conversely that they should assist when a problem cannot be addressed on a lower level. It is one of the few dimensions of Catholic social teaching enthusiastically promoted by supporters of the small government doctrines of Reagan and Thatcher. While such an application is not unwarranted, it has derived its force from the excesses of the Eastern Bloc communist nations, where totalitarian governments often usurped the rights of families. That system is gone. Our situation is quite different. Here the danger is the opposite: that the family and the private good become completely closed off from broader responsibility to the common good.

CONSUMER CULTURE AND COMMODITY DISTANCING

Our lives may be isolated, but we nonetheless still depend upon one another to survive. Our economy, however, systematically hides these connections from us. Capitalism is far from new. During most of the time of its existence, however, consumers were also producers, and consumption did not take place far from the site of production. With the rise of global capitalism and the decline of direct experience of producing goods, we lose any sense for the connection between production and consumption.

Our economic system does not provide any ready means for us to think about our relationships with others. Other socioeconomic systems provide this information quite directly. Even the exploitative system of the slave plantation made clear the owner's reliance upon the labor of the slaves. A subsistence-oriented family farm, of the sort that a large percentage of people lived on just a few generations ago, provided feedback concerning consumption. The fall harvest had to last until crops became available again in late spring. Thus a desire for bourbon, for example, had clear limits. If you feed too much of your corn to the still, your family would go hungry and you might not have any seed corn. Our economic system provides us no ready feedback. We don't know what too much is. We never really know when we're taking more than our share from the commonwealth or when we are eating our seed corn. This, of course, is one of the reasons we consume so much. But this forms our imagination more broadly. Things seem to come from nowhere, and each act of consumption forms us to imagine the world as a place without consequences or condition. In the political realm, this erodes the kind of balanced thinking that policy requires. Higher Medicare prescription benefits and fighting multiple wars are incompatible with tax cuts. But we choose them all nonetheless. The hard-nosed decisions and debates necessary for serving the common good are neglected, and through our deficits, we eat our grandchildren's seed corn.

Our contemporary form of life isolates us from one another and deprives us of knowledge of the relationships that sustain us. Benedict XVI speaks to the essential need for human relationships. Not only do these constitute the common good, these relationships open us to relationship with God as well. "As a spiritual being, the human creature is defined through interpersonal relations. The more authentically he or she lives these relations, the more his or her own personal identity matures. It is not by isolation that man establishes his worth, but by placing himself in relation with others and with God. Hence these relations take on fundamental importance" (*Caritas in Veritate*, no. 53)

Economic Deregulation, the Decline of Political Power over the Economy, and the Turn to "Values"

There is debate among scholars regarding whether globalization involves a loss of state power over the economy or whether the very creation of a global economy is an action of state power. Both positions, however, accept that national governments exercise less and less control over their domestic economies. The neoliberal economic policies that have been pursued by governments on the right and the left for the past forty years have entailed the systematic abandonment of traditional state means of stewarding national economies. Free trade agreements and the rise of the World Trade Organization have virtually eliminated governments' abilities to preserve employment in specific industries or in the entire manufacturing sector. (Whether such actions are wise, effective, or efficient is not our concern here.) Thus, as blue-collar manufacturing jobs have been decimated in the heartland of the United States over the past forty years, governments had little to offer to staunch the decline. The manufacturing jobs that once provided a secure livelihood for the American working class have been outsourced to cheaper labor markets. Furthermore, the very complexity of global economic policy makes it difficult to render it into compelling politics. As a result, the economy, which is such a crucial element of human flourishing and the common good, is seen to be a force outside of political reach. There is less and less that politicians can propose or that governments can do to impact the economic lives of communities.

These two facets of contemporary life combine to further undermine the policy imagination. We are trained by our daily consumption to not think about the costs and conditions of what we enjoy. Our experience of the productive side of the economy furthers this disconnect. We experience it as a realm beyond political influence.

Catholicism sees politics as an intrinsically moral undertaking, and the common good is at the center of this moral project. With the decline of this fundamental moral anchor, a more narrow understanding of morality and politics has emerged in the last few decades. This moral politics centers on the term "values."

"Values," in this sense, stands for the constellation of moral concerns that most distinguish conservative religious voters from others: abortion, stem-cell research, and same-sex marriage. The term received enormous attention on the basis of an ambiguously worded CNN exit poll after the 2004 presidential election, which asked voters to choose the "most important issue" in their decision. Eighty percent of those who chose "moral values" voted for George Bush. Certainly many who voted for George Bush did so in opposition to John Kerry's support for abortion rights and embryonic stem-cell research. It is equally certain that many religious people who voted for Kerry did so for a different set of moral reasons. They were voting against the Bush administration's decisions to conduct an unjustified war of choice and its reinterpretation of long-standing laws and policies to allow the use of torture—both of which fed into the global scandal of Abu Ghraib. Indeed 73 percent who chose "Iraq" as their most important issue voted for Kerry. The wording of the poll rendered issues as these something different from "moral values," doing violence to the fullness of Christian moral concern. The ambiguity of this poll illustrates the ambiguity of the term, which is used by some in a classic ideological fashion: to claim for a small group a universally valued good—in this case, moral concern.

Whatever its meaning, the turn to values rests upon the deeper political and economic changes we have been discussing: the loss of a sense of government as a servant of the common good and the vast narrowing of the sense of the range of problems that politics can solve. With the government's ability to yoke the market to the common good deeply in question, the very real challenges to the common good of abortion on demand and embryonic stem-cell research loom large, often without any clear counterbalance from the collection of common good policies that defined Democratic politics in the twentieth century.

Furthermore, values issues such as abortion and same-sex marriage provide a clarity that contemporary economic policy with its millions of shades of gray cannot. This clarity is not simply a matter of right and wrong, but of a clearly imaginable political path and policy goal. This is the dimension of our situation that Thomas Frank seems to miss in his much-discussed *What's the Matter with Kansas?*[4] He wonders why those counties that have been hardest hit by decades of Republican economic policies become ever more conservative in their voting. His account of the "Summer of Mercy" action by Operation Rescue emphasizes the "movement culture" experiences of the protest, and the subsequent organization of prolife activists for a grassroots takeover of the Kansas Republican Party. He argues that the material goal of the movement to stop abortion is "almost, by definition, beyond achieving" (p. 96). This overlooks the significance of a fact at the center of his account. Abortion clinics closed during the week of the protests. The participants had a concrete experience of successful political agency: they stopped abortions (or delayed them for a week). Even if a pathway to a complete cessation of abortion in this country is far from clear (overturning *Roe v. Wade* will return the matter to the states and leave the majority of abortions untouched), it is clearly imaginable. A clear goal undergirds the movement, even if the means to achieve it are unclear.

Likewise, whatever the significance of same-sex unions in the larger scheme of things, voters who oppose it had a clear experience of agency as they went to the polls (always timed to coincide with national elections) to support amendments that permanently prevented legal recognition of such relationships in their states. These issues provided a clear experience of political agency. People's votes made a difference. It's been decades since voters were offered a similarly clear and specific opportunity to impact the economy in the ballot box. This is not to say there is no difference between the parties on this front (although there is much less than there should be). My point is that outside of these "values" issues, it's not at all clear what policies people should demand.

This use of values contributes to political polarization. Politics gets reduced to a duel over irreconcilable sets of values. As a result, our ability to imagine common ground withers. It leads to increasingly apocalyptic language by both sides of the culture war. Each portrays any victory of the other side as an absolute moral catastrophe. It brings with it the other dimensions of apocalyptic as well—the impossibility of cooperation or concessions.

There is a deeper problem with this political configuration of values. Although it is oriented toward issues that are ultimately a matter of the public common good (e.g., protection of human life in all of its forms), they represent a reduction of politics to issues that are located very close to areas of life commonly held to be private: matters of sexual and medical ethics. This political turn toward the private has been undertaken by the same Republican Party that has done so much to undermine the essential role of government for the public common good.

RESPONDING TO THESE DYSFUNCTIONS FROM THE CATHOLIC TRADITION

This essay has argued that the current political culture in the United States is marked by a severely impoverished imagination of the common good and that political action within this culture is likely to become dysfunctional. There are elements within the Catholic tradition that are valuable for engaging public life in a way that avoids these extremes. The remainder of this essay will focus on two: catholicity as the fullness of the faith and prudence as a way of relating morality and politics.

Catholicity

Catholicity is one of the classic "marks of the church" handed on in the Nicene-Constantinopolitan Creed professed by Catholics and many other Christians in their liturgies. "Catholicity" has many meanings, but the root from which it is derived means "on the whole." Its earliest theological meaning meant the "fullness of faith." This meaning is the dimension of Catholicity that is most endangered in the current political context. We face two interrelated dangers. First, that partisan divisions will rend the body of the Catholic Church; that the fullness of the faith will be compromised as its members selectively emphasize the dimensions of the faith that best fit with their political inclinations. There is ample evidence that this is happening, that the Catholic Church like various denominations and other religious groups is being torn asunder by our broader cultural divisions. While these are not simply partisan, they are encouraged and exploited by politicians.

The second danger is that, due to the strong and effective polemics of conservative and Republican Catholics in claiming that theirs is the only authentic form of Catholic public engagement, many Catholics will construe their political decisions as a choice between their Catholicism and their deepest moral sensibilities and political judgment. A well-educated, deeply Catholic friend conveyed to me what she saw as a crisis of conscience in the 2004 presidential election. Speaking with a priest she had said, "I know I am a Catholic, and I'm supposed to vote for the pro-life candidate, but I just can't bring myself to vote for George Bush." Her bald statement of the conflict is quite similar to what I sense among many Catholic undergraduates I have taught. They don't find such a simplistic reduction of political responsibility to a single issue compelling, but they take it to be the authentic Catholic one. Thus, when they decide to vote or act otherwise, they understand their own actions to be ignoring or to even to be acting against their Catholicism.

In this case, the priest counseled my friend to follow her conscience. This is an acceptable response. But within this context, it runs the risk of accepting this frame of a choice against Catholic doctrine. In this circumstance, a voter with such a conflict was not torn between orthodox Catholic doctrine and something else. They were facing an election in which both candidates held positions fundamentally at odds with Catholic principles and held other positions that Catholics could legitimately embrace. What my friend needed to hear was that she should make sure her conscience was fully formed by the range of Catholic moral teaching relevant to the vote, and that her decision in conscience (no matter how fraught) would thus be clearly and explicitly motivated by her Catholic faith—not one undertaken aside from or against her faith.

The U.S. Conference of Catholic Bishops have long addressed these two challenges in their quadrennial statements on political responsibility, most recently in *Forming Consciences for Faithful Citizenship* (2007). The bishops have consistently presented a broad range of Catholic moral principles and concerns relevant in voting decisions. They describe seven themes from the Catholic moral tradition that should guide political decisions: the right to life and the dignity of the human person; the call to family, community, and participation; the correlative relationship of rights and responsibilities; the option for the poor and vulnerable; the dignity of work and the rights of workers; solidarity; and care for God's creation. They note that this framework does not easily fit the ideologies of "liberal" or "conservative." This is evident in the elaboration of these themes. To take but the first—the right to life—the bishops apply it to the issues of abortion, euthanasia, embryonic research, torture, unjust war, the death penalty, and starvation (no. 40–no. 56).

They noted that "no party and too few candidates fully share the Church's comprehensive commitment to the life and dignity of every human being from conception to natural death." As a consequence they called for deeper Catholic engagement in the political process, from lobbying and advocacy to working within political parties and running for office, in order to transform both the parties and the public square (no. 16).

John Paul II modeled this complexity of Catholic public engagement in the encyclical *Evangelium Vitae*. Within this document he invokes the now famous distinction between a "culture of death" and a "culture of life." Less well known is that "culture of death" was already in use, and the pope made a classic Roman move in balancing its negative apocalyptic assessment with the more positive vision of a "culture of life." At first glance this is hardly an exit from apocalyptic thinking—a polar contrast between death and life. But the details of the encyclical make clear its Catholic approach to public life. John Paul was concerned to promote the possibility of moral reasoning amid skepticism and a disengaged pluralism that breeds a lazy relativism. In this sense he was very concerned with what are called moral values in the American political scene: "skepticism in relation to the very foundations of knowledge and ethics." His analysis, however, made clear that these were social matters of the common good, not just issues of personal morality. Moral confusion is "made worse by the complexity of a society in which individuals, couples, and families are often left alone with their problems" (no. 11). Responsibility for abortion lies with those who promote its legalization as well as an "attitude of sexual permissiveness, and a lack of esteem for motherhood, and with those who should have ensured—but did not—effective family and social policies in support of families" (no. 59). John Paul articulated a comprehensively Catholic approach to politics. Unfortunately, his message was frequently shoehorned into divisions within American values politics, often by bishops who, in their passionate commitment to values they see as endangered, overlook their responsibility to the Catholic whole.

Morality and Politics, Cooperation and Prudence

Politics is an essentially moral undertaking, but "values" as they are currently construed do not adequately guide us. How can we think about the relationship of politics and morality in a way that attends to the truly social and political responsibility to the common good? The Catholic moral tradition offers a range of resources for addressing the relationship between morality and politics. We will consider two here: the principle of cooperation and the notion of prudence.

COOPERATION

The principle of moral "cooperation" embodies two important Catholic commitments: the significance of evil acts and the imperative to be involved in the world despite its sinfulness. Evil actions are destructive of both victims and perpetrators. For that reason, our relationship to these actions is tremendously important. Cooperation recognizes that the fallen world is a messy place. Our Christian obligation to act within the world will bring us into situations where the pursuit of important goods becomes entangled with evil. Thus, we will often find ourselves implicated in evil actions, even though we do not directly undertake them ourselves. Implication in such actions can be described as "cooperation." But what is the exact nature of such "cooperation"?

The tradition distinguishes between formal and material cooperation. In formal cooperation, although we are not the principal agents of the action, we fully intend the outcome and we act in some manner to assist the outcome. In such a circumstance, we are full moral accomplices to the act.

The real value of the framework is evident in those situations where we don't in any way support the evil action, but find ourselves unwillingly part of a larger structure of evil. This is termed "material cooperation." The cab driver coerced into providing a getaway for armed robbers, the anesthesiologist asked to assist in an immoral surgical procedure, the corpsman ordered to fuel a plane for an immoral bombing mission—these people may not intend the evil act itself, but are caught up in situations in which they are called to assist. The morality of such circumstances depends on how near and essential one's assistance is to the act itself. The nearer our assistance to the act, the more our cooperation is drawn toward consent. The getaway driver for an armed robbery can be an accomplice to murder, despite never having held the gun. More "remote" forms of cooperation are permissible, but in such cases we must have as a "proportionate reason" another good that we are working to achieve in order to justify our cooperation.

Cardinal Ratzinger (now Pope Benedict XVI) invoked this notion in 2004 in the context of debates regarding Catholics' voting for pro-choice candidates. This brought a much-needed traditional perspective to this issue. One can indeed vote for a candidate without embracing or even countenancing every position that he or she espouses. Yet on many issues—abortion, torture, unjustified war—the moral issues at stake are so profound that one must have a compelling proportionate justification for such a vote. The principle of cooperation pulls conscience into the public realm. One should be able to give an account of one's reason—to oneself and to others.

Yet for all the clarity this application of cooperation brings, it remains ill suited to the circumstances of contemporary democratic citizenship in the United States. It envisions a moral space where one is able to abstain from cooperation, where there is a choice between action and inaction. This is not to say that such choices are without cost. They may be severe: loss of livelihood, exile from public life, bodily harm. Indeed, the martyr St. Thomas More suffered all three.

Contemporary voters do not face this sort of choice. Rather they must choose between two political parties, both of which hold positions fundamentally at odds with Catholic moral principles. This is not a momentary crisis, but a constitutive element of the contemporary moral landscape. In such a context, to focus cooperation on one particular issue, no matter how severe, inevitably aids the other party. If cooperation is to be invoked, it must be invoked for all options. And here we face its inadequacy.

Cooperation is oriented toward questions of how one cannot act, more than how one should. As a result, it leads to a focus on saying "no" to various policies and politicians. Recent presidential elections have presented voters with a choice between two options, both of which could easily be ruled out by strict application of the principle of cooperation. Certainly one can imagine elections that should be boycotted. But recent U.S. presidential politics were far from such moral extremes, and they offered serious choices about the future direction of our nation. Is it proper to simply not vote in such a situation?

The inadequacy of the principle was manifest in the recent health care reform debate as well. Some bishops were careful to broaden the range of their moral concerns beyond abortion. But these other issues were still deployed as moral hurdles that had to be cleared in order to support the legislation. So a hypothetical possibility that the legislation could fund abortion, lack of universal coverage, no coverage of immigrants (or even allowing them to purchase their own coverage in the exchanges) were all summoned as reasons to oppose passage of the bill.

The principle of cooperation does not help us weigh the truly political questions raised by the legislation. Efforts to provide universal coverage have failed in the United States for nearly a century. This was the closest our nation had ever come to that ideal, and failure to pass it would have doomed it for a decade, perhaps forever. Furthermore, politics would continue after its passage. How to weigh what the bill accomplished against the fuller ideals we hope to achieve down the road? A broad or narrow list of its defects was not enough to judge what should be done.

The analytic of moral cooperation is a fundamental component of the Catholic moral tradition and will rightly continue to play a part in Catholic moral reasoning concerning public life. But it must be augmented with a fuller, multidimensional political imagination, one that can better attend to the complexity of political decisions.

PRUDENCE

The traditional way of addressing such questions has been in terms of the virtue of prudence. Although in popular usage it is equated with caution and hesitation, its classical meaning preserved in the Catholic moral tradition centers on moral and political action. The *Catechism of the Catholic Church*, following St. Thomas Aquinas, defines the virtue as what disposes "practical reason to discern our true good in every circumstance and to choose the right means of achieving it" (no. 1806). In Catholic moral thought, prudence came primarily to be understood as the virtue operating in moral decision-making that enables us to discern the principles at stake in a situation. That is, given the context (grandmother's house or the aisle of a grocery store), eating a cookie might be an acceptance of hospitality or a theft. Once we perceive the good at stake, prudence then guides our discernment for how to respond morally.

The term was, however, originally political as well. Following Aristotle, St. Thomas Aquinas located prudence within practical situations where principles had to be put into action. In addition to knowledge of moral principles, this requires knowledge of the contingent situation. It is helpful to contrast prudence with art here. Art is the knowledge of how to do a predictable practice well. A woodworker or a chef understands wood or food and draws upon the knowledge of their craft to find artful solutions when problems occur. In human affairs, however, our materials are not so easily known. In politics, we have no certainty how others will respond to our actions, of the motivations of our partners and opponents, how a policy will really play out in society. Thus, we deliberate. We draw upon our past experiences, our own and experts' knowledge of the law and of the legislative process, of the current political and cultural context. We use these to envision the likely outcomes of the options available to us and to choose the one that seems most likely to succeed.

Prudence is a much more adequate guide for engaging in politics than cooperation because it better locates morality in relationship to politics. We must be guided by moral principles, but the political task is the prudential evaluation of how to best enact these principles. Politics as the "art of the possible" does not mean simply accepting the inadequacies of the status quo and getting on with life. At its fullest, politics is the prudential struggle to creatively and doggedly enact moral principles in public life. Rather than take the status quo for granted, prudence surveys it with an eye for the possibilities of transformation that are at hand.

Prudence connects principles with context. Thus in addition to the evaluation of proportionate reasons for voting for a candidate with problematic policies as the principle of cooperation leads us to do, we must also survey the political and cultural terrain. What is the status of the problematic issue? Is it deeply entrenched in legislation and court decisions? If so, what are the most likely options for changing it? How realistic are proposals against it? Is the problematic moral stance well entrenched or new? Are we wrestling against a long-established injustice or facing a new temptation on which people's minds are rapidly changing? How do candidates' views on specific issues comport with their overall approach to government? What at this moment in time seems most in play? What can one best accomplish with a vote in this election?

An example of such a prudential approach to politics can be found in various "abortion reduction" policies that have been proposed in the House and Senate, portions of which were incorporated into the 2010 Patient Protection and Affordable Care Act. In the current, highly polarized, and gridlocked politics of abortion, lawmakers sought to carve out common ground that many pro-life and pro-choice citizens could agree upon. These policies focus on giving support to pregnant women in difficult circumstances. This is a model of a prudential policy because it finds a way to advance concern for life in a deeply polarized context. It required the difficult political work of finding policies that both pro-life and pro-choice politicians could agree upon.

Abortion reduction policies also reinforce the common good by challenging the reduction of abortion to a personal "value." These policies portray women's fraught choices facing an unplanned pregnancy as taking place within the context of broader societal values. Are we a society that leaves women to face such difficult challenges on their own? Or do we stand with them, collectively acting to welcome life in even the most difficult circumstances? The latter is required if we really believe that abortion is a matter of the common good. This is an integral requirement of what John Paul II described as a "culture of life."

CONCLUSION

Catholicism views politics as an essentially moral undertaking in service to the common good. Such service is never easy, but in America at this moment in time it is difficult for specific reasons. We live in a manner that hides our reliance upon and obligations to one another. Decades of Republican rhetoric and policies have undermined our ability to imagine government as a servant of the common good. During the same time, Democratic rhetoric has obscured the moral component of government policies and regulations. Political morality is in danger of being reduced to a few important, but narrow "values" issues. Matters such as abortion and fetal stem-cell research are serious threats to the common good. Yet any attempt to address these issues politically must contend with the fact that many politicians who oppose them are part of a party committed to reducing broader government service to the common good and furthering the legacy of the past forty years in which a shared sense of responsibility for the common good has declined precipitously.

Voting, in our time, is a very difficult choice. While Catholics of all positions in the Church must strive to avoid importing the deep political divisions of American culture into the Church, we should understand that we will likely continue to disagree on our prudential evaluation of political policies, parties, and candidates. Our unity in the political realm will be found in our shared commitment to moral principles. We should not expect to find it in our prudential judgments. We should approach such decisions with humility and openness. Such decisions are products of our best deliberations taking place within the ongoing course of history. While they are matters of conscience, they are not private. We should be willing to share our reasons with one another in order both to be open to mutual correction in our unavoidably fallible judgments of history and politics and to convince others of the best path to common good as we see it. Even our disagreements can school us in the importance of our shared political work of building the common good.

QUESTIONS FOR FURTHER REFLECTION

1. What was St. Thomas Aquinas's notion of government? How has this notion been developed in Pope Benedict XVI's *Caritas in Veritate*? How does the idea of "the common good" fit into the Catholic concept of government/politics?

2. What role should government play in establishing the common good? How has this happened historically in the United States according to the author?

3. How does the author think we have lost the notion of the common good in our politics? What has caused this loss?

4. What, if anything, has replaced the notion of "the common good" as the goal of society? Is government capable of helping society to reach that goal, or is there another engine better able to drive this process, such as economic action or activity? What has Benedict XVI said about the need for the political work of the common good to correct the inequalities caused by the market?

5. The author writes of the way that Americans live apart. What does he mean by that? Do you agree or disagree with that description of modern

American society? What effect does the author think that living apart has had on the notion of the common good?

6. What does the author mean by "consumer culture"? What effect does he think that it has had on the common good? Do you agree or disagree? Why? How has economic deregulation affected the government's ability to work for the common good?

7. What does it mean to be a "values voter"? How does the use of "values" often ignore important moral dimensions of the common good? If you were to think of the reasons why you vote for or against a political candidate, would you consider yourself a values voter? What would those values be that are important to you when you vote? Do you agree with the author that seeking to be a values voter has replaced seeking to achieve the common good in our society?

8. The author writes of the concept of "Catholicity as the fullness of faith." What does he mean by that? How would a comprehensively Catholic approach affect the way that Catholics participate in the political process? What effect would it have on the range of issues that Catholics should focus on when they vote?

9. What does the author mean by the principle of moral cooperation? Are there different types of moral cooperation? What problems does the author see in using this principle in making political choices? What does he mean when he says that cooperation is oriented more toward questions of how one cannot act than toward how one should? Is not acting ever a valid choice for a Catholic in a political question?

10. How is the virtue of prudence understood in Catholic moral thought? Does the virtue of prudence have a political application as well? Why does the author think that prudence is a better decisional tool for Catholics in the political process than an analysis focusing on permissible levels of cooperation? Do you agree or disagree? Why?

NOTES

1. Thomas Aquinas, *On Kingship to the King of Cyprus*. chap. 1, no. 8. *http://dhspriory.org/thomas/DeRegno.htm.*

2. Second Vatican Council, *Gaudium et Spes*, no. 74.

3. Lizabeth Cohen, *A Consumers' Republic: The Politics of Mass Consumption in Postwar America* (New York: Knopf, 2003).

4. Thomas Frank, *What's the Matter with Kansas?* (New York: Henry Holt, Metropolitan Books, 2004).

TWELVE

Can You Sin When You Vote?

Maureen H. O'Connell

DECISIONS BEHIND THE CURTAIN

When I was a child, my parents often brought me and my two siblings with them when they voted. Greeting neighbors while waiting in line, watching the feet below the curtains of the voting machines, and reading the faces as they emerged after pulling the lever instilled in us the significance of this civic ritual. We learned that voting is an expression of personal and civic responsibility, a means of participating in community or taking inventory of personal values and acting with conviction; a private choice, but one that is expressed and witnessed by others in a public space.

Although they let me pull the lever to cast their choices, I never knew exactly for whom my parents had voted. The reckoning that went on behind that curtain was sacrosanct; it was almost as sacred, it seemed to me during my childhood, as whatever happened behind the curtain of the confessional. Now, as an adult fully inducted into the communities of citizens and communicants, and as someone who attempts to integrate my spiritual life or relationship with God into my political life or my relationships with others in my communities, I can easily identify similarities between these two confessional spaces. Here we wrestle with our consciences, we take inventories of our personal values, we desire to participate fully in community, and we emerge with a renewed sense that change is possible.

But the connection between the moral obligations for voting and the sacrament of reconciliation is not as simple and straightforward as the title of this essay suggests. Certainly, we might answer the question "Can I sin when I vote?" affirmatively if we fail to inform our consciences properly, if we vote in a way that violates or contradicts our conscience, or if we vote for someone who actively contradicts the "fundamental and inalienable ethical demands" of the Catholic faith.

Then again, several variables involved in the act of voting suggest that quite the opposite may be the case. The *Catechism of the Catholic Church* indicates that sin is "a failure in genuine love for God and neighbor caused by perverse attachment to certain goods" and "wounds the nature of [persons] and injures human solidarity" (no. 1849). As my childhood experiences attest, voting is an act that nurtures the person and human solidarity by fostering communal life. How can this expression of participation and empowerment—promoted by the institutional Church as essential for upholding human dignity and life in community—be an occasion of sin? Moreover, if we rightfully acknowledge that no political party or candidate fully upholds the laws that the Magisterium claims "do not admit of exception, compromise, or derogation"—including abortion, euthanasia, protection of the embryo and families, the inalienable right to education and religious freedom, an economy "that is at the service of the human person," and "absolute and radical rejection of violence and terrorism" in the name of peace—then sin would seem an unavoidable consequence of voting.[1] If that is the case, then how can we truly sin, or freely choose not to choose the good, if we are presented with nothing but bad options?

This ambiguity, as well as the potentially divisive nature of faith-based discussions of both voting and sin, compels me to rephrase the underlying inquiry at the heart of the essay. That is not to say that our contemporary reality does not call for critical reflection on the condition of human sinfulness. I'm just not certain that the voting booth or the confessional are the appropriate loci for that reflection, since a preoccupation with either misses the depth and breadth of the Christian moral life. So rather than ask if we sin when we vote, I suggest that we consider instead if when we vote we might also uphold the divine law to love God and love neighbor, as well as the moral law to promote the full dignity of persons and the common good. In other words, if we ask ourselves, "Can we love when we vote?" we might discover a positive approach to the essay's original question, an approach that encourages us to consider constructive ways in which we might integrate our spiritual and political lives.

In what follows I will attempt to answer the question about voting and loving in four stages, and indirectly illuminate connections between voting and sinning in the process. I will (1) overview contemporary approaches to the moral life that reorient the moral life, and likewise sin, toward our capacity to love; (2) examine traditional and contemporary ideas about sin in order to identify its potential to empower moral agency rather than suspiciously restrain it, (3) explore the moral concept of conscience as the capability for a particular kind of vision of self and others, and (4) propose ways that we might inform our consciences so that the spaces behind the voting and confessional curtains of our lives remain in creative tension.

MORAL LIFE ON BOTH SIDES
OF THE CONFESSIONAL CURTAIN

In order to discover the potentially rich relationship between faith convictions and political commitments, we might begin by considering the evolving understandings of the moral life in the Catholic tradition.[2] Generally speaking, the last century brought with it at least four significant shifts in Catholic moral theology. They share common characteristics, including a turn away from a defensive suspicion of the social reality toward a positive engagement in socioeconomic life, and away from a legalistic or confessional approach to the moral life toward a model that emphasizes discipleship.

First, on an institutional level, Pope Leo XIII ended the Church's isolating preoccupation with dogma and definitive truth claims in the wake of modernism with the first of the modern social encyclicals, *Rerum Novarum,* in 1891. In this document, the pope couched socioeconomic questions about the plight of the working poor as moral questions with significance for Christian employers and owners of production. Since that first document, popes, synods, and conferences of bishops have attempted to articulate the practical implications of Catholicism for a variety of political questions from religious freedom and reproductive technology to economic development and state-sponsored violence. A more recent installment in this tradition, *Caritas in Veritate*, written by Benedict XVI in 2009, reaffirms the synthesis of social and moral questions in a far more complex economic reality characterized by a financial and environment crisis and the dominance of technology in science and communication—all on a global scale. "Globalization," he notes, for example, "is a multifaceted and complex phenomenon which must be grasped in the diversity and unity of all its different dimensions, including the *theological* dimension."[3] So long as human beings remain at the heart of the social reality, then social questions will remain moral questions.

Second, in the theological academy the "turn to the subject" or the recognition that persons are capable of discerning and responding to the self-disclosure of God in our respective lives served as a catalyst for a similar turn in moral theology toward the moral capabilities and potentialities of persons. Moral theologians shifted the emphasis away from reactive or negative approaches to the moral life characterized by a preoccupation with evil acts to be avoided and privately confessed toward a more proactive and positive approach that reflected active discernment on the part of individuals and communities. "Faith, as it is lived, is not produced by concepts and norms," explains Bernard Häring, SJ, one such moral theologian. "It is far more than subscribing to a code of dogmas. . . . One of the most uncreative approaches in the Church is to stress fidelity to certain negative commandments to such an extent that fidelity to Christ and his great affirmative commandments of justice, love, and mercy is seriously neglected."[4] Moral theology was no longer solely concerned with moral codes, but rather relational faithfulness to Christ.

The *resourcement* theology of Henri de Lubac, SJ, and Hans Urs von Balthasar offered a third shift in moral theology, which resurrected original but largely forgotten resources for contemplating the moral life such as Sacred Scripture and the writings of the early Fathers of the church. These sources of the tradition, narratives of God's ongoing invitation to love—love of self, love of God, and love of neighbor—challenged the reward-and-punishment approach to morality that had prevailed for most of Christian history in no small part as a result of the prevalence of moral manuals in the confessional as early as the thirteenth century. The manuals, and the scholastic analysis of the moral life that they encouraged for centuries to follow, dissected the components of sinful actions often in isolation from the relational context in which they occurred. A return to biblical stories that captured various persons' responses to Christ's invitation to discipleship or the biographical accounts of early Christians such as St. Augustine of Hippo in North Africa or the Cappadocian bishops in the fourth century, for example, suggested that it was insufficient to think about morality merely in terms of rendering a proper confession or properly absolving sins. Far from being a dry and analytical science, morality began to attune itself to what von Balthasar deemed the provocative "theo-drama" of our personal response to God's invitation to love in a world created by a dramatically loving God.[5]

Finally, the *aggiornamento* spirit of the Second Vatican Council, epitomized in *Gaudium et Spes*, the Pastoral Constitution on the Church and the World, articulated a radically humble self-understanding of the institutional Church and an empowering view of the lay faithful. In this and subsequent social encyclicals the Church accepts its social location as one of many members of civil society, rather than as the pinnacle of civil society or the source of state authority as had been previously promulgated. Moreover, laypersons are encouraged to assist the Church in achieving its central mission to make the grief and suffering of the poorest persons on earth the Church's very own grief and suffering. The *Compendium of the Social Doctrine of the Church* notes that "Complying with the different demands of their particular area of work, lay men and women express the truth of their faith, and, at the same time, the truth of the Church's social doctrine, which fully becomes a reality when it is lived concretely in order to resolve social problems" (no. 551). In other words, the laity are no longer interminably lost sheep in need of paternalistic care but rather capable members of the Body of Christ who give witness to the Kingdom of God in their various vocations.

In short, moral life in the last century has evolved away from singular concerns with personal salvation earned in the confessional and toward complementary concerns with justice taken up in this world, away from negative admonitions against evil acts and toward positive responses to God's invitation to a deeply personal relationship, away from actions that we ought to avoid and toward the good we are capable of doing, away from moral restraint to moral engagement, away from a preoccupation with the state of one's soul in the confessional and toward attention to the stirrings of one's heart in our everyday lives. The primacy of love in the moral life is a common denominator in each of these shifts, whether a love for the least or the marginalized in the tradition of social teaching, or God's incarnational love for humanity, which renders the person the focal point of all moral reflection, or the love of and for God reflected in biblical narratives that offer resources for moral reflection. Benedict XVI expresses the ethical implications of Christian love in *Caritas in Veritate* when he describes it as "the extraordinary force which leads people to opt for courageous and generous engagement in the field of justice and peace" or "the force that builds community" by embodying the self-gift of Christ, which is the truth that brings fullness, integrity, and freedom to persons.[6]

I see two implications of this evolution in understanding of moral life for our inquiry as to whether we can love when we vote. First, acknowledging that human dignity stems from being made in the *Imago Dei,* or in the image of an Incarnational and Trinitarian God, reminds us that we are created with certain kinds of agency or capabilities: the capability for meaningful relationships with ourselves, with God, and with others; the capability to know or understand ourselves and our reality through reason, or the cognitive intellect and the intuitive intellect, logic and imagination, minds and bodies; the capability to freely respond to what is going on around us with our individual gifts and vocational skills; the capability to be delighted by and desire goodness, and to care for created things. "God created [humans] rational beings," notes the *Catechism,* "conferring on [them] the dignity of a person who can initiate and control [their] own actions" (no. 1730). This self-awareness encourages us to accept that we are created for a purpose, but not necessarily with a plan. The former encourages moral agency and responsibility, a commitment to honest discernment and attention to the world around us; the latter can foster apathy and blind obedience or an acquiescence of responsibility in the name of resolve. Both have implications for either side of the confessional and voting curtains.

Second, since love is an inherently relational experience and one that ought to be expressed in our vocational lives, then our contributions to the various public spaces in the "ordinary time" between election years are morally significant. This claim rests on the foundational idea that "the human person needs to live in society. Society is not for him an extraneous addition but a requirement of his nature" (*Catechism of the Catholic Church,* no. 1879). As such we have a responsibility to ensure that we live in communion with others and that all persons are able to do the same. The Catholic tradition defines this responsibility in terms of the common good—our responsibility to ensure the minimum conditions for flourishing life in community.

Since this responsibility springs from our social natures—from *our* need for and capacity to love—creating the common good is not solely the responsibility of the state or the government, but rather the responsibility of collectives or associations of persons, or what the tradition calls "civil society," that is, "the sum of relationships and resources, cultural and associative, that are relatively independent from the political sphere and the economic sector (*Compendium* no. 417)." The common good is cultivated not necessarily by political leaders but rather by Catholic youth organizations, interfaith coalitions, the Knights of Columbus, Christian Life Communities, and countless other organizations that encourage a discipleship lived in the context of civil society. Therefore, it makes little sense to dissect the morality of political choices in the privacy of the voting booth if we are not willing to analyze whether these choices reflect an active commitment to those values in the various circles of civil society in which we operate every day.

SIN AND WHY IT'S MORE THAN PERSONAL

There is no way of getting around the fact that sin is a "non-starter" when it comes to religion and politics. Sin is something to avoid at all costs—whether in practice or in polite conversation. For some—such as generations of Catholics who came of age before or in the wake of Vatican II and who are well versed in the Church's doctrine of sin if only because they tend to kneel behind the confessional curtain far more frequently than they step into the voting booth—sin should be avoided because it postpones or precludes eternal reward. Younger generations of Catholics, who are more likely to step behind the polling curtain than into the confessional, avoid sin because it reflects what they identify as a method of manipulation on the part of ecclesial authority or institutional religion, which many of them wish to cast off in order to seek God in more experiential and nonjudgmental venues.[7]

These unreflective assessments indicate that most Catholics could use a refresher when it comes to the concept of sin. Developments in moral theology mentioned above indicate that we should not try to avoid sin in order to sidestep an uncomfortable reckoning of past actions; nor should we ignore it in order to avoid uncomfortable judgment of actions in the here and now. Reflecting critically on sin rather than uncritically rejecting it gives us important insights into what it means to be human, how we ought to live in community, or what it means to flourish. That is to say, examining sin in its personal and social manifestations reveals information we need to integrate our faith convictions and political commitments in a meaningful way.

PERSONAL SIN

Scripture scholar Bruce Vawter notes that the Hebrew word for sin, *hattah*, means "to miss the mark" as when on a journey.[8] Anyone who heads out for an unknown destination armed with a global positioning system has most likely experienced this way of thinking about sin. The moment we inevitably find ourselves disoriented and turned around, a pleasant voice calmly announces, as if to confirm this state of confusion, "Recalculating route." In reality, the point of the GPS announcement is not to add to our confusion but rather to create clarity: we are going to miss our end destination if we continue in the direction we are headed. We need to rethink things.

The writers of the Hebrew Bible understood sin in a similar way. In these stories sin was an action that would have derailed the people of Israel, wandering in the desert for an entire generation, from reaching the promised land. What's more, Yahweh and later Christ reveal that the promised land or the Kingdom of God is not simply a physical place on the map but more precisely a space in which we palpably experience God's immanence.

Classic definitions of sin in the Christian tradition identify any number of reasons as to why we might miss our final destination, that is, union with God. Our actions may violate the right ordering or harmony of the cosmos as God created it: relationships of persons to themselves, persons to God, persons to others, persons to the created world. Moreover, Aquinas notes that sins are acts with a wrong object that encourage excess rather than balance, or that violate the divine law to love God and neighbor. As such, they separate us from communion with God and with others. According to the *Catechism*, "sin is an offense against reason, truth, and right conscience; it is a failure in genuine love for God and neighbor caused by perverse attachment to certain goods. It wounds the nature of [persons] and injures human solidarity (no. 1849)."

Contemporary moral theologians build on this notion of sin as missing the mark in order to present sin in a more constructive way, insisting that it is more than something simply to avoid. Attention to sin illuminates tendencies in human nature that threaten our ability to live fully human lives. Häring understands it as a failure of creativity or a refusal to accept the creative responsibility that comes with being made in the image of a Creator God. *In Human Values and Christian Morality,* Joseph Fuchs, SJ, considers sin in terms of its impact on the disposition of persons and not simply on the moral order, noting that ultimately it is a withdrawal from our liberty to give fully of ourselves to God and others.[9] Pope Benedict XVI presents sin as personal denial of self-gift or gratuitousness, or in terms of a conviction that we are the "sole authors of [ourselves], [our] lives and society" which justifies a selfish "closing in upon [our]selves."[10]

Perhaps most helpful for our discussion about the relationship between sinful acts and our public responsibility to life in community is James Keenan, SJ, who claims that we ought not think about sin simply in terms of acts that we do and their various effects, but rather in terms of the good we fail to do. He suggests this failure often is a result of the fact that we fail from our strengths: "Our sin is usually where you and I are comfortable, where we do not feel the need to bother, . . . where we have found complacency, a complacency not where we rest in being loved but where we rest in our delusional self-understanding of how much better we are than others."[11] This approach has import for politics, where we have to walk a fine line between active engagement in social change and an ideological zeal that compels us to disregard persons with different perspectives or to judge others before judging ourselves.

SOCIAL SIN

In March 2008, Benedict XVI formally introduced the notion of social sin into the Catholic moral lexicon when he promulgated an updated list of the seven "deadly" sins. Several of these new expressions reveal the social dimension of their sixth-century counterparts articulated in the moral manuals previously mentioned. Genetic modification and human experimentation, for instance, reflect a type of vanity with social implications. Polluting the environment offers a contemporary expression of a sloth or extreme laziness when it comes to care of creation. Social and economic policies that induce poverty reflect a kind of financial gluttony. Sin is no longer personal; it's also social.

Peter Henriot, SJ, defines social sin in three ways.[12] First, social sin is our direct and indirect, knowing and unknowing participation in structures that oppress and dehumanize. Paying taxes serves as a classic example. This requirement of life in community sustains public services and goods necessary for individuals to flourish in community such as education, clean water, or Medicaid. But through our taxes we also support two wars, which have claimed literally countless civilian lives, or a criminal justice and corrections system that incarcerates Americans of color at an astounding rate, or an immigration policy that separates children from their undocumented parents in deportation processes. Social sin seems an unavoidable cost of life in community.

Henriot also suggests that social sin involves situations that promote selfishness or egocentrism. These two values and the practices that stem from them seem equally unavoidable in American socioeconomic culture driven by materialism, consumerism, and narcissism cultivated by online social networks and instant communication, or moral therapeutic deism that demotes God to just another member of our entourage or fan club. When understood in these terms, sin has political implications insofar as it prevents us from imagining a more inclusive and far-reaching vision of what the world might be or what it means to flourish, since it traps each of us at the center of our own respective universes.

Finally complicity in others' sufferings or experiences of injustice, whether through voluntary ignorance and apathy, is also an expression of social sin. For example, some suggest that in this age of globalization, we live in a "runaway" world that seems to have a logic, a power, and an end goal that lies beyond human control.[13] To the extent that we resign ourselves to this kind of thinking, we fail to accept our own moral agency, which comes from being made in the image and likeness of God. As co-creators who do indeed possess the intellect, passion, and abilities to imagine alternatives and bring them into being, we sin when we fail to accept our agency and responsibilities as co-creators.

So what does all of this talk of sin mean in terms of answering the original question of the essay, that is, can we love when we vote? I see three possible implications. First, the moral life requires that we acknowledge our sins—both personal and social—and not simply avoid them. If we claim to be created in the image of God, then we must accept that we are also created with the wisdom to recognize that we are not God—we are finite, limited, conditioned by the circumstances of our bodily existence. Moreover, moral maturity expects that we acknowledge sin in a way that moves beyond guilty paralysis toward a spirit of renewal that inspires us to resist these tendencies as individuals and communities. To do so, we need to ponder the power of God's forgiveness and then participate in the radical freedom of that forgiveness through our own acts of forgiveness. This is the sacramental point of the confessional: personal atonement and recommitment to life in community, to life in civil society, to the vision of what could be.

Second, attention to the pervasiveness of sin in ourselves and in our communities brings a much-needed sense of humility or critical realism to Christian engagement in politics. No platform, candidate, or policy will ever overcome the inherent brokenness in the human condition or the pervasiveness of social sin in our social reality. This is not to say that we should not work diligently for the charity and justice that Christ embodied in his ministry. His command to the disciples after the parable of the Good Samaritan to "*go* and *do* likewise" reminds us that Christianity is not a set of beliefs but a tradition of practices through which we come to know God's love on our shared journeys down to Jericho. Attention to sin can remind us to be wary of ideology or strident overconfidence that cannot acknowledge limits in one's position or that sees one's own position as unquestionably superior. We can find evidence of this in the *Compendium*: "When reality is the subject of careful attention and proper interpretation, concrete and effective choices can be made. However, an absolute value must never be attributed to these choices because no problem can be solved once and for all" (no. 567).

Finally, acknowledging the pervasiveness of sin both personal and social underscores the importance of conversion in our personal and public lives. We must constantly assess our values, our desires and passions, and our vocations in light of their impact on others and their connection to structures and systems of oppression. While the Church does not seek to change unjust social structures it does seek to change the human hearts that create and sustain such structures. It does this by encouraging conversion or a return to the original path to God marked by the covenant with the Israelites or the Way of Christ made evident in his ministry. In order to avoid missing the mark we must constantly ask ourselves questions that keep our focus on the future or which help us to recalculate continually the route between who we are and who is it that we hope to become as individuals and as communities. The confessional and voting booth are places where this recalculation occurs.

THE CATHOLIC CONSCIENCE
AND THE LONG VIEW

In his best-seller *God's Politics: Why the Right Gets It Wrong and the Left Doesn't Get It*, evangelical minister and editor Jim Wallis suggests that politics is about having a vision—a sense of who it is we hope to become as communities and as a nation. To that extent, the biblical prophets were politicians, reminding both the kings and people of Israel that "without a vision the people will perish." The prophets understood their mission as one of creating social change by converting people's hearts or reorienting them to their relationship with Yahweh mediated in the covenant outlined in the Ten Commandments.

In the Catholic tradition, conscience plays a similar prophetic role insofar as it helps us to discover and in some cases rediscover that vision of the covenant—renewed by Christ and outlined in the Sermon on the Mount—and to orient ourselves to it. In fact, we might best understand the conscience as the twin capabilities of discerning a vision—of self and others—and of constantly committing ourselves to that vision in a pattern of action that will ultimately bring it to fruition.

The *Catechism* explains that "conscience includes the perception of the principles of morality; their application in the given circumstances by practical discernment of reasons and goods; and finally judgment about concrete acts yet to be performed or already performed" (no. 1780). Moral theologians have done much innovative work to explain these three components.[14] As *synderesis* conscience is foremost our ability through our capacity for reason to know inductively the difference between the good or the right and the bad or the wrong. Second, as a *process* of discernment and deliberation, conscience involves the skills of self-awareness, reflection, meaningful conversation, and humility. This is a place where we come to know and serve God, since "[Our] conscience is [our] most secret core and [our] sanctuary. It is the place, in the words of John Paul II, where 'the relationship between [our] freedom and God's law is most deeply lived out.'"[15]

And finally conscience involves *judgment* or courageously committing oneself to the vision of self and life in community that one has deduced in the previous two steps. Richard Gula suggests that these three components of conscience reveal it as a dynamic capability to respond to the invitation of the covenant rather than as static obedience to commands. Conscience appeals to central values rather than to authority figures. It is oriented toward the future with hope rather than guiltily obsessed with past wrongdoing.[16] Häring adds to this: "A mature Christian conscience will not think of faith as a catalogue of things and formulation. . . . Indeed, an over-emphasis on control of doctrines and a militant theology about doctrines can become obstacles to an integrated faith."[17]

This capability for self-awareness, for discernment, and for committing ourselves to a vision that offers integrity and fulfillment is an expression of human dignity and the source of the obligations we have to ourselves and to others. In fact, one of the most significant changes in Church teaching involves the obligation to protect the freedom of conscience. *Dignitatis Humanae*, or the Declaration on Religious Freedom, promulgated during Vatican II, claims that the Church will always respect an individual's choice of religious expression; states are to do the same. We are obligated to obey our conscience, to commit ourselves to the vision we have of self and life in community; and we are obligated to inform our conscience or to constantly sharpen our vision, since as we travel through life the contours of our horizons will undoubtedly change.

What are implications of this approach to conscience for voting and loving?

First, voting is an expression of conscience since it is an act of freedom, one by which we commit ourselves to our central values through active engagement in community and discernment of sources of authority. Therefore, voting is indeed a moral act—an expression of our vision of ourselves and a commitment that forms our character. Just as conscience is not about blind obedience to moral law or magisterial authority but rather a "religious submission of will and of mind"[18] to these resources for the moral life, so too should the act of voting be an expression of faithful fidelity to an informed set of values. Gula describes this submission as a "serious effort to reach intellectual agreement that what is taught is an expression of truth" and an attempt to "strive for personal appropriation of the teaching so as to live by it out of personal conviction."[19] The *Compendium* notes that the point of conscience is to avoid "slavish acceptance of positions alien to politics or some kind of confessionalism" as well as blind "political allegiance" that is more ideological than critically conscientious (no. 566).

Second, conscience reminds us that the moral view is a long view, one that does not merely consider acts in isolation or in the immediate but rather evaluates patterns of action over time since these patterns structure and orient our moral character. That is not to say that individual actions are not significant; rather, it considers their significance in light of whether or not they keep us moving toward an ultimate end that brings personal integrity, authentic freedom, and communion with others. Voting therefore is not an isolated act but rather one that fits into a larger picture comprised of a variety of actions that keep us striving for that end. In the Catholic tradition, this vision is union with God in this life through respect for persons and the promotion of the common good of all persons.

Third, Gula explains conscience in terms of "me coming to a decision *for myself* but not *by myself.*" In other words, for any choice of conscience to truly reflect or embody me, I need others to assist me in sharpening and constantly refocusing my vision of myself since any number of factors can blur my vision. I can fail to seek what is true and good. I can neglect to consider whether my choice is consistent with my personal character or social and cultural values. I can be distracted with immediate consequences of my choice and not consider its long-term impact on me or others. Communities—neighborhood associations, church social ministry teams, political parties—face similar liabilities when it comes to making sound choices. This leads me to my final point.

VOTING WITH VISION

In 2002 the Congregation for the Doctrine of the Faith, a department of the Magisterium, issued a statement on voting which notes that "Christian faith has never presumed to impose a rigid framework on social and political questions, conscious that the historical dimension requires men and women to live in imperfect situations, which are also susceptible to rapid change."[20] The same document also notes that while a "a well-formed Christian conscience does not permit one to vote for a political program or an individual law which contradicts the fundamental contents of faith and morals,"[21] that same Christian conscience might enable a person to give support to proposals or those who "support proposals aimed at limiting the harm done by such a law and at lessening its negative consequences at the level of general opinion and public morality."[22]

Since our answers to the questions of this essay, as well as the moral aptitude needed to navigate the seemingly contradictory guidance offered in the above doctrinal statement, hinge on an informed conscience, how ought we to go about informing it? Catholic moral theology offers four general sources to which we might turn for assistance in coming to a decision for ourselves but not necessarily by ourselves. Integrating the act of voting into our moral and spiritual lives encourages us to refer frequently to each of these sources, not only during election cycles but also in the "ordinary time" of the political calendar when moral life and political life are far more likely to intersect.

1. *Revelation.* While we would be hard-pressed to find any texts that explicitly address the political issues that define our time, or even the act of voting itself, we would be equally hard-pressed to deny the centrality of the sacredness of life, our mandate to love our neighbors, or the significance of the covenant for personal and communal salvation in biblical texts. Wallis goes so far as to say that if we were to take a pair of scissors to every passage dealing with poverty, the Bible would be left in shreds. Certainly, to inform our consciences we need informed methods of biblical interpretation that move beyond a narrow biblical literalism or historical criticism that leave no room for the moral imagination toward a complex and nuanced engagement with texts. While scholars have developed a variety of hermeneutical approaches for appropriating biblical texts into moral theology, a common denominator among them is the ongoing biblical invitation to see persons and the world as God does, and

then to relate to persons and the world accordingly.[23] After telling the parable of the Good Samaritan, Jesus enjoined his disciples to "Go and do likewise" and not simply to imitate him. Conscience discerns how to be *like* Jesus, an act of humility, rather than how to *be* Jesus, an act of idolatry.

2. *Tradition.* This is an expansive and therefore rich category that includes the content of the Catholic tradition—official doctrine, dogma, encyclicals—as well as the witness of those who have carried that content forward in a variety of forms whether written, spoken, or embodied. For example, in each election cycle for nearly two decades, the U.S. Catholic Bishops have written a pastoral letter, *Forming Consciences for Faithful Citizenship*, whose purpose is not to "tell Catholics for whom or against whom to vote" but rather "to help Catholics form their conscience in accordance with God's truth."[24] Central concepts from those documents—preferential option for the poor, common good, dignity of persons, and perhaps more importantly the lived example of persons who have embodied or incarnated those principles throughout history, saintly or otherwise—offer invaluable resources for informing consciences.

3. *Social sciences.* We cannot identify possible solutions to complex issues such as immigration or health care reform, abortion policy or stem-cell research without knowledge of the causes of injustice at the root of these problems or their connections to other injustices. Nor can we make normative judgments about political platforms or social policies that seek to redress these injustices without practical information from the field or frontlines—statistics, firsthand accounts, analysis, financial estimates, ethnographical studies. While finding this kind of information may be less challenging in our high-speed digital age, finding reputable sources is increasingly difficult. The Catholic lobby and a variety of social service agencies committed to these issues such as the United States Conference of Catholic Bishops, NETWORK, Jesuit Relief Services, Catholic Relief Services, and CARA (Center for Applied Research in the Apostolate) continue to validate particular research in the social sciences—economists, sociologists, psychologists, political scientists—in order to inform their own advocacy work and policy recommendations. They, in turn, can be a helpful resource to laypersons.

4. *Experiential wisdom.* The growing agency of laypersons in the Catholic moral tradition discussed in the first section of this essay stems from an increasing confidence in the virtue of prudence to mine human experiences for the wisdom needed to make good decisions. With increasing frequency, the moral questions we consider behind the curtain of the voting booth or the confessional are not abstract concepts with little connection to our personal lives but situations we ourselves have experienced in one capacity or another: friends or loved ones without health insurance, hospitals in our neighborhood

that perform abortions. We need to reflect on these experiences so as to identify the wisdom in them that might shape our visions of ourselves and our connections to others, and that might be shared more widely. The *Compendium* recognizes this wisdom as the contribution of individuals in terms of "forming individual consciences and a country's culture" (no. 550). Likewise, the *Catechism* notes that we strive "to interpret data of *experience* and the signs of the times assisted by the virtue of *prudence*, by the advice of competent people, and by the help of the Holy Spirit and her gifts" (no. 1778).

CONCLUSION: A TALE OF TWO CURTAINS

"It helps, now and then, to step back and take the long view," wrote Bishop Ken Untener of Saginaw in 1979 in a poem titled "Prophets of a Future Not Our Own," often attributed to Archbishop Oscar Romero. "The Kingdom is not only beyond our efforts, it is beyond our vision." While this might seem to contradict the moral optimism I have attempted to convey throughout this essay in terms of the tension that ought to exist between the spaces of the confessional and the voting booth, in fact this quote underscores the freedom that comes with acts of conscience such as voting. No platform will be complete, no candidate ideal, no policy the definitive answer to injustice, no single vote a condemnation or absolution for human brokenness. And yet, freed from the expectations of religious ideology or political idealism that suggest the contrary, we might approach our civic responsibility to vote as just one of many ways of actively saying "Yes!" in our spiritual and political lives: "Yes!" to a deeply personal and socially invigorating relationship with God and others; "Yes!" to our central values, "Yes!" to our vision of what life in community could be, "Yes!" to our own potentials to effect change on the other side of the curtain. After all, "We are workers, not master builders; ministers, not messiahs," Bishop Untener reminds us. "We are prophets of a future not our own."

QUESTIONS FOR FURTHER REFLECTION

1. Why does the author think that the question, "Can You Sin When You Vote?" states the issue too narrowly? Have you ever thought, in the voting booth, that you might be committing a sin when you pull the lever? How would you state your moral obligations in the voting booth?

2. The author writes about four significant shifts in Catholic moral theology. The first is Pope Leo XIII's ending the Church's preoccupation with dogma and definitive truth claims. How do you understand this shift? What may have caused it?

3. The second shift that the author describes is the "turn to the subject" in moral theology. What do you understand by this? What was behind this shift? What effect has it had? The third shift is *resourcement* theology. What do you think this means? Where did it come from? What has been its effect?

4. The fourth shift was the *aggiornamento* of the Second Vatican Council. What do you understand by this? What effect has it had on the Church's moral teachings? What has been the cumulative effect of all four of these shifts? What are the implications of these changes or adaptations in our understanding of the moral life?

5. The author writes that "it makes little sense to dissect the morality of political choices in the privacy of the voting booth if we are not willing to analyze whether these choices reflect an active commitment to those values in the various circles of civil society in which we operate today." What do you think the author means by this? Would you agree or disagree? Do you think of how you vote in the context of everything else that you do in your life? Why or why not?

6. Why does the author think that the term "sin" is a non-starter when it comes to religion and politics? How does the author say we should think about sin today? What does she mean by personal sin? What are some examples that you can think of?

7. What does the author mean by social sin? Where does this concept of social sin come from? What are some examples of social sin? How does an individual become morally responsible for social sin?

8. What kind of conversion do personal and social sin call for? How would you do this? What roles does conscience play in this process? What does it mean for conscience to take the long view? Is this an abdication of conscience?

9. What does the author say are the implications of this approach to conscience in voting? Do you agree? Is this a very clear standard for you? Why or why not?

10. How should we go about forming our consciences before we vote? What sources should we use to do this? Are all of these sources equally important?

NOTES

1. Congregation for the Doctrine of the Faith, *Doctrinal Note on Some Questions regarding the Participation of Catholics in Political Life* (2002), no. 4.

2. For a full historical overview, see John Mahoney, SJ, *The Making of Moral Theology: A Study of the Roman Catholic Tradition* (New York: Oxford University Press, 1988), as well as James F. Keenan, *History of Catholic Moral Theology in the Twentieth Century* (New York: Continuum, 2010).

3. *Caritas in Veritate*, no. 42, emphasis mine.

4. Bernard Häring, *Free and Faithful in Christ: Moral Theology for Clergy and Laity*, General Moral Theology 1 (New York: Seabury Press, 1978), 63 and 75.

5. Hans Urs von Balthasar, *The Glory of the Lord*, vol. 1, *Theo-Drama*, trans. Graham Harrison (San Francisco: Ignatius Press, 1988).

6. *Caritas in Veritate*, no. 1 and no. 34.

7. For an examination of the beliefs and practices of four generations of American Catholics, see *American Catholics Today: New Realities of Their Faith and Their Church*, ed. William V. D'Antonio et al. (Lanham, MD: Rowman & Littlefield, 2007).

8. Bruce Vawter, "Missing the Mark," in *Introduction to Christian Ethics: A Reader*, ed. Ronald P. Hamel and Kenneth R. Himes (New York: Paulist Press, 1989), 199–205.

9. Joseph Fuchs, SJ, *Human Values and Christian Morality* (Dublin: Gill and Macmillan, 1977).

10. *Caritas in Veritate*, no. 34.

11. James F. Keenan, *Moral Wisdom: Lessons and Texts from the Catholic Tradition* (Lanham, MD: Rowman & Littlefield, 2004), 57.

12. Peter Henriot, SJ, "Social Sin and Conversion: A Theology of the Church's Social Involvement," in *Introduction to Christian Ethics: A Reader*, ed. Ronald P. Hamel and Kenneth R. Himes (New York: Paulist Press, 1989), 217–26.

13. Anthony Giddens, *Runaway World: How Globalization Is Reshaping Our Lives* (New York: Routledge, 2003).

14. Most notable is Richard Gula's treatment of the subject in *Reason Informed by Faith: Foundations of Catholic Morality* (New York: Paulist Press, 1989), 123–35.

15. *Veritatis Splendor*, no. 54.

16. Gula, *Reason Informed by Faith*, 127.

17. Häring, *Free and Faithful in Christ*, 223–84.

18. *Lumen Gentium*, no. 25.

19. Gula, *Reason Informed by Faith*, 156.

20. Congregation for the Doctrine of the Faith, *Doctrinal Note on Some Questions regarding the Participation of Catholics in Political Life* (2002), no. 7.

21. Ibid., no. 4.

22. Ibid.

23. Richard B. Hayes offers paradigms of biblical hermeneutics, as well as theologians who have employed these approaches in their respective attempts to articulate the contemporary significance of biblical teaching, in *The Moral Vision of the New Testament: Community, Cross and New Creation, A Contemporary Introduction to New Testament Ethics* (New York: HarperOne, 1996).

24. United States Conference of Catholic Bishops, *Forming Consciences for Faithful Citizenship* (2008), no. 7.

ADDITIONAL BIBLIOGRAPHY

Himes, Kenneth, et al., eds. *Modern Catholic Social Teaching: Commentaries and Interpretations*. Washington, DC: Georgetown University Press, 2005.

Heyer, Kristin. *Prophetic and Public: The Social Witness of U.S. Catholicism*. Washington, DC: Georgetown University Press, 2007.

——, Mark J. Rozell, and Michael A. Genovese, eds. *Catholics and Politics: The Dynamic* ervaas Wijsen, Frans Jozef, Peter Henriot, and Rodrigo Meja. *The Pastoral Circle Revisited: A Critical Quest for Truth and Transformation.* Maryknoll, NY: Orbis Books, 2005.

Spohn, William. *What Are They Saying about Scripture and Ethics?* New York: Paulist Press, 1995.

Wallis, Jim. *God's Politics: Why the Right Doesn't Get It and the Left Gets It Wrong.* New York: HarperSanFrancisco, 2006.

Wijsen, Frans, Peter Henriot, and Rodrigo Mejía, eds., *The Pastoral Circle Revisited: A Critical Quest for Truth and Transformation.* Maryknoll, NY: Orbis Books, 2005.

THIRTEEN

Lessons from the U.S. Bishops' Economic Pastoral Letter: Modeling the Way of Holiness

Anthony J. Pogorelc

INTRODUCTION

The Second Vatican Council called all Catholics to "full, active, conscious participation in the liturgy." Holiness was not to be achieved through passivity but through engagement. The same council placed social action at the core of the Church's ministry and described the Church as the People of God with a mission to serve the world.

November 2011 marks the twenty-fifth anniversary of the U.S. bishops' pastoral letter on Catholic social teaching and the U.S. economy: *Economic Justice for All*. This pastoral letter, often called the Economic Pastoral, applied the teachings of Vatican II to economic life and modeled the spirit of Vatican II in the dialogical process used in its composition. For those who place a priority on dialogue, it represents a zenith in the manner in which teaching authority was exercised by the U.S. bishops. It has implications for both inter- and intra-Catholic relationships today.

Many changes have occurred in U.S. and world Catholicism since the pastoral was written. The inclusion of a process of wide consultation in the manner of exercising teaching authority did not persist. The widespread desire for dialogue was criticized when it appeared in efforts such as the Common Ground Initiative. The desire for clear identity has led some groups to define themselves in opposition to others. *America* (March 8, 2010: 4) reports the introduction of "tea-party" tactics by a small, vocal group of conservatives. They have particularly aimed to discredit leaders on the USCCB staff such as John Carr and the Catholic Campaign for Human Development. Ironically they have attacked some of the individuals who have been most effective in advancing the church's pro-life ethic in the public square.

In the face of such challenges, the Economic Pastoral presents us with a vision of what is possible and calls to resist temptations to join in the shouting. It is a vision of hope for those Catholics who as individuals and groups want to engage in respectful dialogue.

In this essay I will highlight some key themes of the pastoral that call Catholics to lives of holiness through the promotion of social justice. Second I will show how they are modeled in the letter's process of composition and serve as a model for the civil engagement of Catholics in the world today.

THE MESSAGE OF THE PASTORAL

The Economic Pastoral called Catholics to link the practice of faith and daily life, proclaiming boldly that moral values have a role in shaping the way people use and share their economic resources. Ethics is not a private matter but a public matter that must be applied in every dimension of personal and social life. Drawing on the theology of covenant from Scripture, it reminds us that our relationship with God impacts our relationship with every other human being, especially those who are least in this world. Justice is measured by how we treat the poor and vulnerable, and there is a floor beneath which social and economic rights must not descend. The Church carries out its mission by promoting family life and social stability by advocating just wages, the alleviation of poverty and hunger, and a global order that furthers human dignity. Everyone, especially the poor, must have a role in shaping their destinies. Every voice must be heard.

In the pastoral, the bishops advocate a "new American experiment." This means a broader sharing of economic power and accountability to the common good. The challenge of the pastoral is not only to think differently but to act differently. Catholics must become informed and active citizens. Study of the text of the pastoral should be followed by prayer and culminate in service.

In the final chapter, "A Commitment to the Future," the bishops discuss conversion as a process that transforms the heart and is fulfilled in action. "Full, conscious and active participation" in the liturgy enables the laity to live out their holiness in the world. The bishops write (*Economic Justice for All*, no. 332):

> Holiness is not limited to the sanctuary or to moments of private prayer; it is a call to direct our whole heart and life toward God and according to God's plan for this world. For the laity holiness is achieved in the midst of the world, in family, in community, in friendships, in work, in leisure,

in citizenship. Through their competency and by their activity lay men and women have the vocation to bring the light of the Gospel to economic affairs, "so that the world may be filled with the Spirit of Christ and may more effectively attain its destiny in justice, in love and in peace" (Dogmatic Constitution on the Church, no. 36).

Scripture must influence not only personal life but the social policies established by communities. Catholics are likewise called to be prophetic and to engage in social critique. They must critique consumerism and the waste of resources so embodied in the "throwaway society." This foreshadows the message of Pope Benedict XVI to be conscientious stewards of the environment. Parents must transmit this message in their words and through the lifestyles they establish in their families. Individuals must transcend self-interest, and institutions must serve the common good. The church itself must embody justice in its institutional practices. Dialogue with the world must be ongoing.

In the composition and promulgation of *Economic Justice for All* the bishops demonstrated that the content of what is said and the manner in which that content is communicated are both of great importance. The bishops reflected the spirit of *Ad Gentes*, the Second Vatican Council's document on missionary activity, which endorsed an incarnational model for the Church's activity. This means that the Church needs to integrate the mores of a people into its manner of interacting in a particular culture.

American Catholics, formed in a democratic ethos, want to participate in deliberations about the life of the Church. Studies of American Catholics by William D'Antonio and others bear this out. Even conservative voices called for consultation and collaboration by the hierarchy and laity within appropriate bounds. The process used to compose the 1986 Economic Pastoral presented a model of a successful process of consultation, collaboration, and participation. The late Monsignor George Higgins called this process of composition the most extensive and open-ended ever used in the Church and predicted that the process used to compose this pastoral letter might even overshadow the content itself.

ROOTS OF THE PROCESS

The process used in the Economic Pastoral followed earlier attempts to employ consultation in the exercise of pastoral teaching. In preparation for the national conference to mark the 1976 U.S. Bicentennial, known to many as the Call to Action Conference, the bishops incorporated an extensive and open process of consultation, but it did not continue beyond the conference. The 1983 Peace Pastoral employed a consultative process only after the initial work had begun. With the Economic Pastoral a consultative process was intended right from the start. Even those Americans who disputed the contents were pleased with the process and its use of consultation in the exercise of teaching authority. Of recent efforts by the bishops to employ a consultative process, the Economic Pastoral provides an example of effective collaboration from inception to completion.

The bishops used this process because they wanted to effectively engage Catholics and all people of good will; they also learned from their previous efforts. In November 1980 they completed a pastoral letter on Marxist communism, a theoretical document that avoided the discussion of the political and military activities of then-communist regimes. Some bishops believed capitalism and its effects deserved attention as well, but to be effective a more engaging presentation would be required. Bishops' pastorals tended to by written by staffers in the national offices, perfunctorily discussed by the bishops, voted on, and promulgated. With the Economic Pastoral, the concern for effective communication became a prime consideration; the bishops realized the intimate connection between medium and message. Their concern to compose a pastoral letter that would speak to a general audience shaped how they went about composing the letter. By proceeding in this way the bishops were breaking new ground and responding to the challenges posed by modern communication technology.

In November 1980 the bishops voted to establish the U.S. Bishops' Committee on Catholic Social Teaching and the U.S. Economy, which began meeting in July 1981. Milwaukee Archbishop Rembert G. Weakland, OSB, headed the committee. Attempts to produce this document compelled the bishops into a learning mode. They soon realized they needed greater technical expertise to address the issues, so they studied economics and consulted with experts. As they did in preparation for the Bicentennial Conference, they called for a series of hearings to help them grasp economic issues, their complexity and effects. They sought testimony from a wide spectrum of sources that included theologians, economists, sociologists, congressional staffers with specializations in economics, representatives of social justice organizations from the United States and third-world countries, business leaders, representatives of organized labor, and persons representing rural and farming interests. In addition, the hearings were supplemented by correspondence with a similar variety of persons.

As a result of the hearings and discussions among the bishops and their staff, a preliminary text was drafted and made public on November 11, 1984.

The first draft became the focus of a wide variety of programs and discussions within the Catholic community; this was unprecedented. In response to the variety of interested parties, the bishops altered their time line and extended the time for public discussion. Archbishop Weakland said he noticed over this time that the quality of the dialogue improved. At first the replies seemed more like commentaries on what was being said about the document. As time went on, it became evident that respondents were interested in the text itself, commenting on it directly.

The bishops' committee received more than ten thousand pages of comments on the first draft, carefully read them, and produced a synopsis to circulate among the body of bishops. The draft was also made public in the National Catholic News Service weekly, *Origins*. Bishops discussed the draft at their summer 1985 meeting and had the opportunity to offer written commentaries as well. The committee processed this material and integrated it into the second draft, released in October 1985. The process of dialogue continued until the spring of 1986 when the committee formulated the third draft, which was submitted for the final vote in November 1986.

According to Archbishop Weakland, the process changed the project. The original idea of writing a more theoretical document on Christianity and capitalism gave way to the desire to produce a more concrete document on the U.S. economy and Catholic social teaching. This was an unprecedented move by the bishops to open themselves to the Catholic laity and others. It spurred both enormous enthusiasm for the bishops and the project as well as immense criticism. This criticism came especially from those who held more libertarian views of the economy, and from those, primarily outside of American culture, who did not see this process as appropriate to the way the bishops ought to exercise their teaching authority.

RESPONSES ORGANIZED BY CATHOLICS

The American Catholic laity responded enthusiastically to the bishops' invitation to participate in the process of composition of the Economic Pastoral. Catholic universities throughout the country in collaboration with their local communities took the initiative to organize conferences on it. Conferences held at universities such as Georgetown, Marquette, Notre Dame, and Santa Clara brought together professionals of varying disciplines and perspectives to discuss the drafts.

These conferences occurred at different stages of the process of composition. The Notre Dame meeting preceded the first draft and was organized to help the bishops think about how Catholic social teaching could be applied to four areas: employment, poverty and welfare, trade and third-world countries, and principles for cooperation.

The conference sponsored by the University of Santa Clara's Institute on Poverty and Conscience occurred in January 1985, following the release of the first draft. A range of Catholics and those with other religious and humanist stances gathered to discuss the substance of the pastoral. Academicians and specialists in business and economics, both liberal and conservative, debated the issues; critics and supporters of the document had their say. Dr. Michael Harrington of the Institute for Democratic Socialism saw the pastoral letter as an important document because it insisted on measuring economic progress in moral and social terms, not just statistical norms. Both he and Dr. Gregory Baum of the University of Toronto focused on the devastating effects of the structures of economic marginalization for society and how it leads "people to define themselves with growing elements of blindness and ideology."

Michael Novak of the American Enterprise Institute praised the bishops for their courage in using such an inclusive process: "There has not been any branch of the Church in history whose bishops would willingly put before the rest of the country the first draft of a term paper and ask everybody to mark it up, and then in all humility, go back and reconsider and do it again." He then proceeded with his critique of the contents saying that the first draft placed too negative a cast on the U.S. economy.[1]

It was the bishops' response to these critiques that demonstrated their commitment to the dialogical process. The laity saw the effects of its input. For example, the second and third drafts noted successes in the American economy, while they also challenged structural factors that enabled poverty to persist.

Taking advantage of the climate of dialogue created by the bishops, a group of influential Catholic political and business leaders, who held that government intervention in economic life should be kept to a minimum, organized their own committee. They declared that they were meeting the obligation assigned to the laity by the Second Vatican Council to reflect on their own experience in the light of the Gospels. As the bishops were releasing their first draft, the committee issued a document: *Toward the Future*. Like *Economic Justice for All*, it began with a reflection on Scripture and Catholic social teaching, but its interpretation of these texts and of their experience led to conclusions contrary to those of the bishops. Interestingly, the chief theological spokesperson for the lay committee, Michael Novak, was also the single most frequent participant in the bishops' hearings.

The bishops were listening to all voices. The conferences offered the bishops insights from specialists to help them in their revisions. The process gave all Catholics, especially the laity, an unprecedented role in the process of composing and refining a pastoral letter. One participant in the Notre Dame conference said, "The future dynamism of the church depends on the possibility of the whole Body of Christ being heard."[2] The conference demonstrated the interest of the Catholic academic and business communities in Catholic social teaching as well as their commitment to participate in the life of the church.

THE PASTORAL AND THE MEDIA

It was not only the lay Catholic community that initiated responses to the invitation for dialogue. This open process stirred the curiosity of the American public; it was covered by almost every newspaper and major television network. The pastoral was controversial, and the media loves controversy.

The conservative journal *National Review* published seven articles on the pastoral between December 1984 and April 1985. Editor William F. Buckley addressed it in his columns; in one series he discussed the interest of non-Catholics in the pastoral. Buckley's own views were similar to those expressed in *Toward the Future. Business Week* and the *Wall Street Journal* also covered the developing pastoral.

As early as the initial planning stage the business press showed interest in the project. In December 1983, Daniel Seligman, a senior editor at *Fortune,* wrote that he expected the bishops' document to be "a paean to planning." Acknowledging that the bishops consulted from a broad range of perspectives, Seligman concluded that the bishops' bias favored national planning, and their conclusion would reflect this bias no matter what data the consultations netted because a planned economy could offer them a role while the impersonal market forces ruling capitalism could not. Almost a year later, Seligman wrote that the first draft lived up to his expectations and held forth on his own amoral approach to economic issues. He concluded that those, like the bishops, who connect ethics and economics could only do so because they really don't know economics.[3]

Letters from *Fortune* readers challenged Seligman's approach to economics. One asserted the existence of a moral dimension to the economy. Another criticized Seligman for conveying an attitude of pontifical infallibility and preventing issues of justice from reaching the public eye. A third reflected a post–Vatican II understanding of the church and affirmed the bishops' role of challenging the status quo and the laity's of influencing the economy by critical examination and ethical action.

As it continues to do today, *Sojourners* magazine insisted that economic documents are moral documents and praised the pastoral as good news for the poor. It also exposed the resignation of two labor leaders from the committee that produced *Toward the Future* because they said its ideological agenda was preset.[4] An article in *The Humanist: A Magazine of Critical Inquiry and Social Concern* encouraged the bishops' efforts to promote social justice.[5]

By and large in the United States criticism was aimed at the content of the document, while the process was considered one of the finest examples of inculturation into the democratic culture.

Yet from other quarters of the Church critical voices were raised. Some, especially in Europe, saw the extensive consultative process as weakening the authority of bishops because they had publicly entered into a learning mode. This was perceived as a confusing role reversal because in such a model of ecclesiology the bishops are considered the teachers—*ecclesia docens*—while the laity are considered the learners—*ecclesia discens*. To these critics Archbishop Weakland replied,

> The model adopted by the U.S. conference believes that the Holy Spirit resides in all members of the church and that the hierarchy must listen to what the Spirit is saying to the whole church. This does not deny the teaching role of the hierarchy, but ultimately strengthens it. Discernment, not just innovation or self-reliance, becomes a part of the teaching process. (*Origins* 13:46, p. 759)

LESSONS OF THE PASTORAL

The Economic Pastoral contained a message and modeled a process that challenges Catholics today. The bishops sought to promote ethical action in the public sphere and to exercise effective, Gospel-centered leadership. They were attentive to the process and allowed it to transform the project. They opened themselves to critique from a variety of quarters, seriously responding, but also remaining steadfast in their prophetic stance. They were attentive to the theological import of the process as an expression of the inculturation called for by Vatican II.

The Economic Pastoral made a claim on all Catholics, inviting them to study, pray, and act. The process of dialogue and collaboration employed in the composition of the Economic Pastoral is a model for how Catholics together can exercise their mission to serve the world. The content of this pastoral letter was embodied in its process, which reflected respect for human dignity, a concern to listen to a range of voices, and the encouragement of participation and good communication.

In the last decade massive conflicts have been created by terrorism, an ongoing state of war in Iraq and Afghanistan, battles over immigration, health care reform, abortion and same-sex marriage, bank and industry bailouts, and the loss of jobs. Powerful media outlets have framed these conflicts as irresolvable while at the same time profiting from them. In some cases, the creative leadership and unity exercised by the Catholic episcopate has given way to condemnation, punishment, and silence. Segments within the Church are acting without coordination.

Cardinal Newman wrote in *On Consulting the Faithful* that at critical moments in the life of the Church the laity saved the Church from becoming a people adrift. Without a vision the people perish. The Economic Pastoral connects us to the vision of Vatican II, which gives us a positive direction as we navigate in troubled waters. It reminds us of what is possible. When he called for a Second Vatican Council in 1962, Blessed Pope John XXIII said: today the Church "prefers to make use of the medicine of mercy rather than that of severity." This vision calls us to resist the temptation to condemn; it calls us to listen to every voice, especially those that represent differing perspectives. It calls us to present ourselves as dialogue partners. The content and process of the pastoral are an encouragement for Catholic individuals and groups who want to follow this way to holiness. In a manner that was concrete and evident the Economic Pastoral manifested the Body of Christ functioning as a living organism in the service of the Gospel in the modern world. This is what it means to respond to the call to holiness.

QUESTIONS FOR FURTHER REFLECTION

1. What lesson does the author say that we should draw from the Second Vatican Council's call for full participation in the liturgy by the laity? How does this lesson apply to holiness? How does it apply to voting?

2. Describe the consultative process that the U.S. bishops used in drafting their 1986 pastoral letter on the U.S. economy, *Economic Justice for All.* Who did the bishops consult in the process of drafting this pastoral letter? Is it a good idea that the bishops actually changed their draft of this pastoral letter based on critiques they received of the draft documents?

3. Does such widespread consultation by the bishops weaken or strengthen their teaching authority? What, if anything, does this widespread consultation teach us about the process by which the bishops should teach?

4. Do you think that the topic on which they are teaching makes a difference as to whether the bishops should use such a consultative process?

5. Do we, as Catholics, have a right to be consulted by our bishops when they attempt to apply Gospel values to a situation as complex as the American economy? Do we, as Catholics, have a right to be consulted by our bishops when they attempt to apply Gospel values to a situation as complex as American politics and elections?

6. What did the U.S. bishops' pastoral letter on the American economy have to say about holiness? How would this definition of holiness apply to Catholics' participation in the political process today?

7. The Economic Pastoral called Catholics to link faith and daily life, stating that moral values have a role in shaping the way people use economic resources. What lesson does this have for Catholic participation in the political process? Should Catholic moral values have an effect on the way we vote? How so?

8. One criticism of the process that the bishops used to draft their pastoral letter was that those who, like the bishops, connect ethics and economics, could do so only because they really don't know economics. Is this a fair criticism? What if the same criticism were applied to the bishops' pastoral letter on Catholics and politics, *Forming Consciences for Faithful Citizenship*? Is it fair to say that the bishops can only connect ethics and politics because they don't know politics?

9. Cardinal Newman said that at critical moments in the life of the Church the laity saved the Church from becoming a people adrift. How would you apply that insight to the role of the bishops and the role of the faithful in contemporary American political life?

NOTES

1. Carl Zablotney, SJ, "Key Speakers Debate Pastoral Letter," *National Jesuit News* 14, no. 5 (February 1985).

2. Interview with Professor Thomas Bausch, dean of the Business School at Marquette University and participant in the Notre Dame Conference, June 1987.

3. Daniel Seligman, *Fortune*. First article: December 12, 1983; second article: December 10, 1984.

4. Danny Collum, "The Bishop's Moral Capital," *Sojourners,* January 6, 1985.

5. *The Humanist,* January 7, 1985.

FOURTEEN

President Kennedy and Archbishop Chaput: Religion and Faith in American Political Life

Stephen F. Schneck

The Church is a depository of a teaching, of a religious message that it received from Jesus Christ. It can be summarized with the following words from Sacred Scripture: "God is love" (1 John 4:16) and throws its light upon the meaning of the personal, familial and social life of man. The Church, having the common good as its objective, asks nothing other than the freedom to be able to propose this message, without imposing it on anyone, in respect for freedom of conscience.[1]

—Benedict XVI

His Holiness's understanding of the role for the Catholic faith in the political and public world, as expressed in the comment above and as elaborated more completely in his 2009 encyclical, *Caritas in Veritate*, does much to illuminate the way forward from recent criticism of John F. Kennedy's well-known 1960 Houston address on the role his Catholicism would have in his future presidency.[2]

The criticism, largely confined to Catholic circles on the politically conservative side of the politics spectrum, was ignited originally by the archbishop of Denver, Charles J. Chaput, OFM Cap., who in 2010 declared Kennedy to be "sincere, compelling, articulate—and wrong." The archbishop's remarks were (not coincidentally) also offered in Houston, anticipating the fiftieth anniversary of Kennedy's speech. The remarks were intended to be provocative. Indeed, he insisted that the future president's campaign speech was more than erroneous; it was civilizationally catastrophic. In the archbishop's assessment,

John F. Kennedy "wasn't merely 'wrong,'" his "Houston remarks profoundly undermined the place not just of Catholics, but of all religious believers, in America's public life and political conversation. Half a century later," he warned, "we're still paying for the damage." Tough words . . .

Archbishop Chaput maintained that Kennedy in Houston promoted a virus of secularism and Continental-inspired *laïcité*, a virus that in succeeding decades contaminated and colonized the American public square, destroying thereby the finely balanced architecture for faith and public life crafted by America's Framers. That's a damning indictment, if true. But, not to put too fine a point on it, I find the archbishop's thesis to be "sincere, compelling, articulate—and wrong." While the archbishop was correct in identifying aspects of Kennedy's Houston address to be at odds with traditional Roman Catholic teaching about the role of faith in public life, he erred in his history of religion and the American Framers, in his analysis of the contemporary status of faith in American public life, and his anti-Kennedy remarks reflected an impoverished understanding of what role faith properly should play in the public square, colored worrisomely by a pessimistic appreciation of politics and governance.

In what follows, I pursue a number of quick investigations: noting where Kennedy was wrong (as well as where he was right) in his Houston address; noting where the archbishop went off-track in his assessment of the American Framers' intentions for religion in public life; noting and appreciating the positive role that religion has played and increasingly plays in American public life (not being anything like Europe in this regard); and concluding with a theoretical reflection about the proper role of faith for political and public engagement. In regard to this last point, as indicated, I find the insights of *Caritas in Veritate* to be wonderfully instructive.

KENNEDY'S ERRORS

In September 1960, then Democratic presidential candidate, Senator John F. Kennedy, addressed a gathering of the Greater Houston Ministerial Association. At issue was the role his Catholicism would play should he become elected president. Throughout the spring and summer of that campaign year, nasty anti-Catholic leafleting had dogged his appearances in the South and Midwest. He'd prostrate America before the Vatican Anti-Christ, the pamphlets warned—punctuated with slurs about "Papists" too crude to believe given our greater appreciation of religion in general and of the Roman Catholic faith in particular in today's America.

Such anti-Catholic bigotry has a long history in the United States and has taken a particularly virulent form in response to Catholic involvement in politics and public life. Indeed, the only Catholic previously to have run on a major party ticket for the presidency, Al Smith, saw his campaign wither and collapse amid similar anti-Catholic attacks a few decades before Kennedy's bid. The candidate knew, accordingly, what was at stake when he mounted the Houston stage in 1960. The then supposedly "solid Democratic South" (and in 1960 it was), which was so much part of the New Deal coalition beneath Franklin Roosevelt's and Harry Truman's electoral success, was crumbling over the issue of Kennedy's Catholicism. The Houston address was a hurried attempt on the part of his campaign to stem a growing flood of "anti-Papist" defections from supporting the Democratic ticket.[3]

That political context needs to be weighed carefully, lest the words of what was in large part a campaign sortie be freighted with more theoretical heft than appropriate. Charged by Kennedy's famous charisma, more than a few lines of that speech still speak across the decades to our own generation's questions about denominational religion and public life.

The speech began with a pointed complaint by the future president that the issue of his confessional denomination should pale before the truly critical issues of the day: communism and "the hungry children I saw in West Virginia, the old people who cannot pay their doctor bills, the families forced to give up their farms—an America with too many slums, with too few schools. . . ." Issues such as these, Kennedy thought, transcend divisions between Catholic and Protestant denominations, "for war and hunger and ignorance and despair know no religious barriers." A candidate's religious denomination should never be a point of contention in an American election. As Kennedy put it, "What kind of church I believe in should matter only to me." The right question to ask, he insisted, is "what kind of America I believe in." Arguably, a faith-formed conscience should indeed illuminate assessment of the moral imperatives for governance and politics, as signaled in this speech by the candidate's concern for hungry children, elderly without health care, slums, and communism. But the specific interest of one religious denomination are not what any president should seek to advance.

Understood in this way, Kennedy's oft-quoted remarks from the speech—those that seem most to have incensed Archbishop Chaput—are colored quite differently from depictions rendered by contemporary critics:

I believe in an America where the separation of church and state is absolute, where no Catholic prelate would tell the president (should he be Catholic) how to act, and no Protestant minister would tell his parishioners for whom to vote; where no church or church school is granted any public funds or political preference; and where no man is denied public office merely because his religion differs from the president who might appoint him or the people who might elect him.

The "church" that Kennedy would separate from the state here is that of immanent denomination, not of transcendent faith. The state should not be used as an instrument to advance the interests of one or another denomination.

The archbishop looked at these matters quite differently. In his 2010 criticism of Kennedy, he struggled to grasp the future president's acute concern about denomination. That struggle to understand Kennedy is hinted at from the archbishop's opening comments, wherein he noted that while he's "a Catholic bishop, speaking at a Baptist university in America's Protestant heartland," he nevertheless felt "welcomed with more warmth and friendship than I might find at a number of Catholic venues" which is as he admits "a fact worth discussing." Such shared warmth and friendship between the archbishop and his Baptist hosts stands in marked contrast to the denominational tensions swirling around Kennedy's speech. From the recorded footage of the 1960 audience, tensions and even antipathy (in my opinion) seem evident on the faces of the assembled ministers. Accordingly, where Kennedy's 1960 reflections about religion in America focused on the acute problem of *denominational* division between Catholics and Bible-Belt Protestants, the archbishop's 2010 reflections focused on a very *different* division that he perceived at the heart of the contemporary question of religion for public life. As will be argued subsequently, I'm convinced that the archbishop's worries about an emerging American *laïcité* are unfounded and that his efforts to trace such a notion to Kennedy's Houston address are entirely groundless.

This does not mean, however, that I have no issues with the presentation that Kennedy made in Houston long ago. I do. For while I understand the future president's insistence that politics and governance be conducted within the authenticity of moral conscience and not used to advance the interests of a given religious denomination, I think Kennedy (at least here) did not fully appreciate the proper and evident role of religion in the formation of that same conscience. Included in his address, for example, is the following:

Whatever issue may come before me as president—on birth control, divorce, censorship, gambling or any other subject—I will make my decision in accordance with these views, in accordance with what my conscience tells me to be the national interest, and without regard to outside religious pressures or dictates.

Kennedy, of course, is not alone in making such pronouncements. In 2007 at Villanova University's law school, the Catholic Supreme Court Justice Antonin Scalia echoed Kennedy and insisted that "there's no such thing as a

'Catholic judge,'" that "the Catholic faith seems to me to have little effect on my work," and that "just as there's no 'Catholic' way to cook a hamburger," so . . .

> I am hard-pressed to tell you of a single opinion of mine that would have come out differently if I were not a Catholic.[4]

But these arguments of Scalia and Kennedy about the workings of their consciences in their public service are ridiculously flawed. Epistemologically, conscience is not and could never be a blank slate or John Locke's *tabula rasa*. Our moral sensibilities require formation, and our prudence requires mature reflection developed through education and experience. Kennedy's own conscience surely was formed in part by his family background, by his famous wartime trials in the South Pacific, by his formal education, by his years of public service, and no doubt much more. It was also formed by the teachings and practices of his Catholic faith. Scalia's has no doubt been similarly formed. To speak of conscience divorced from such formation is futile at best and dangerous at worst. Authorities as diverse as Alexis de Tocqueville and Max Weber identify religion as among the most influential of factors in the shaping of moral understanding and reasoning. What Kennedy's conscience might counsel regarding the national interest and what Scalia's does jurisprudentially would always reflect (in part) the role of their respective Catholic upbringings, the Church's formal teachings as presented in various venues, their encounters with Scripture and liturgy, and the integration of all such religious elements in their Catholic practices.

Similar but definitely larger difficulties are evident in the Kennedy address's oft-remarked aspiration for an America "where there is no Catholic vote." To be sure, he went on immediately to qualify this understanding by adding that he also looked forward to an America where there would be

> . . . no anti-Catholic vote, no bloc voting of any kind—and where Catholics, Protestants and Jews, at both the lay and pastoral level will refrain from those attitudes of disdain and division which have so often marred their works in the past, and promote instead the American ideal of brotherhood.

Once again, Kennedy's sensitivity to denominational tensions presents itself. Moreover, his objection to the idea of denominational bloc voting—as for example, denominational political parties—is one well-informed by historical lessons. Such blocs inevitably exacerbate denominational differences, splintering the polity into fractious sectarianism, as evident for example in the denominational consociationalism of today's Lebanon. But Kennedy's language still goes too far, implying perhaps that a conscience formed in the Catholic religion would or should be invisible or indistinguishable among voters generally. Or, worse, perhaps the suggestion here is that Catholics should strive in political life to block or suspend their faith's imprint on conscience, as if it were desirable to vote areligiously. If so, that's wrongheaded, because inescapably faith informs a believer's conscience and conscience informs all efforts to do right in political life.

In current politics, Catholics are Republicans and Democrats, Tea Partiers and Greens. Political scientists strain to identify measurable distinctions between Catholic voters and American voters generally, noting that gender, income, education, race, and geography all appear to trump religion in analysis of Catholic voting patterns. For many analysts this means what is imagined that Kennedy wanted—i.e., no Catholic vote. Some explain this as demonstrating the success of Catholic assimilation in American culture and others explain it as the failure of the Church in conscience formation. In fact the phenomenon is much more complex than such analyses appreciate. What would be completely wrong, however, would be to interpret political science's difficulty in measuring the Catholic vote as due to the raging effects of secularism. So those opposed to an active role for religion in American public life would be wrong to imagine that due to secularism's appeal Catholics do not vote as Catholics. Likewise, those frustrated with American Catholics for not deploying their politics to advance one or another set of presumed Church interests would also be wrong to imagine that religion is no longer politically meaningful to Catholic voters.

Roman Catholics are profoundly influenced by their faith when they engage in political life. This is certainly evident in the activism of Catholic elites. Witness the political involvement of the bishops, the plethora of Catholic public interest and even Catholic partisan organizations involved in policy and political activities. Notice the vibrant political discussions on the pages and websites of Catholic publications like *America, First Things, Commonweal, Our Sunday Visitor, National Catholic Reporter, Catholic Standard, National Catholic Register;* in news services like CNA and CNS; in the monthly periodicals of Catholic service organizations; and in dozens of diocesan newspapers around the country. More ink and electrons are spilled in the so-called Catholic press on political topics than on any other societal concern. Such elite activism is revealing of the way in which Catholics approach American politics more broadly. Perhaps even more telling is the close attention American political parties and mainstream media pay to the shifts and currents of Catholic voting patterns.

Why, then, doesn't the connection between faith and public life for Catholics seem to show up in the polls? It's because there is not a singular and monolithic Catholic vote, but rather there are multiple and often countervailing Catholic votes. Studies show that, in comparison with the electorate generally, Catholics are more motivated by moral and value factors and correspondingly less by self-interest or pragmatism in voting (which is a big hint for anyone courting the Catholic vote). For some those values play out as deference to ethnic traditions, which inevitably have a significant religious component. For others such values reflect careful consideration of specific Church teachings—as evident in the militancy by which some Catholics embrace the pro-life cause, or social justice, or environmentalism. For most, though, their Catholicism plays an important but much more mixed influence in their political participation as family and ethnic traditions, Church teachings, positive and negative religious experiences, personal faith, and many more factors push and pull conscience. Still, as much as Justice Scalia or some interpretations of Kennedy's Houston speech might argue otherwise, religion remains a large influence on Catholics in the public square.

For believing Catholics that is as it should be. Some Protestant theologies maintain that faith is a matter of private grace between an individual and God and that the public realm is itself intrinsically devoid of divine meaning, thereby leaving Christians a dichotomous choice: either prophetic political engagement to compel divine purpose upon the public realm or else withdraw from politics in order to safeguard salvational grace from the world's corruption. Traditional Catholic theologies, very differently, see the political realm as originally a natural creation of divine purpose, informed by natural law, and a venue wherein participation can lend itself to enriched understanding of divine purpose. Ours is a theology that demands a dialogue of religion and politics, not as a one-way street that perceives religion's role only as speaking truth to power, but rather as a two-way street on which political life is also recognized for the possibility of deepening faith and better understanding of divine purpose. It would be as wrong to say then that there is not or should not be a Catholic vote (if this indeed is what President Kennedy meant) or Catholic jurisprudence (if this is indeed what Justice Scalia meant).

RELIGION AND THE AMERICAN FRAMING

In his own Houston address, Archbishop Chaput sharpened his indictment of Kennedy's (and by implication, Scalia's) promise that Catholicism would not bias his public service by claiming that such a promise was un-American on historical grounds. Where Kennedy argued for separation of church and state, the archbishop asserted bluntly: "The Founders and Framers did not believe that" and the "history of the United States contradicts that." As the archbishop put it:

> Unlike revolutionary leaders in Europe, the American Founders looked quite favorably on religion. Many were believers themselves. In fact, one of the main reasons for writing the First Amendment's Establishment Clause—the clause that bars any federally endorsed Church—was that several of the Constitution's Framers wanted to protect the publicly funded Protestant churches they already had in their states.

Historians blanche at such grand "message of history" assertions. In fact, the period of the 1787 Constitution through the first decades of the republic (a period the archbishop calls "the Framing") was a time in which questions regarding the proper role for religion in American political life were even more hotly debated than now. Moreover, resolution of that strident theoretical and practical debate did not abate (if indeed it ever has) until the remaining few establishment states began ending official state religions in the 1820s. Let me be pointed about this in order to be clear: *Far from anything like a consensus agreement among the Framers about the proper role for religion in public life, they were in fact bitterly divided on the issue.*

Overlooking the many heated differences among the Framers about religion's role, Archbishop Chaput instead described the eighteenth-century attitude to such questions as one of singular and settled consensus. He claimed, for example, that

> America's Founders encouraged mutual support between religion and government. Their reasons were practical. In their view a republic like the United States needs a virtuous people to survive. Religious faith, rightly lived, forms virtuous people.

What the archbishop cherrypicks from history in this statement is indeed one among many of the Framing era's contending arguments about religion. But such cherrypicking entirely misses the important historical debate. Let me identify four contesting arguments about religion in public life from the Framing period to illustrate: American millennialism, civil religionism (the archbishop's pick), religious separationism, and secular deism. [Sorry about all the "–isms" but it's easier reading this way.]

American millennialism took bearings from a belief that with the American Revolution a new and penultimate age in history had begun. The Revolution, when read through a peculiar lens in Scripture, revealed America to be the vanguard for the end of history, understood as the completion of the Christian history that had begun with Adam's sin, was redeemed with Christ's sacrifice, and would be resolved with the Second Coming. Unlike other countries, America was divinely appointed (i.e., "exceptional") for a salvational purpose—that being *to lay the foundation for the Second Coming.* Geographically in the late eighteenth century this account of the connection of religion and public life had its greatest following in New England, with notable political figures like Nathaniel Niles and Fisher Ames among its prominent advocates.

For American millennialists—who evidence a Puritan legacy—government, politics, and public life generally were to be directed and controlled by religion for religious purposes. The state should be an instrument of religious power, serving religious ends. Subsumed under religion, the state's primary task would be to enforce religious beliefs on citizens, instilling righteousness, and thereby hastening preparations for America as ground for the New Jerusalem. In its most dramatic form, such thinking is theocratic. Anyone familiar with American history will recognize that various versions of this eighteenth-century millennialism continued to have effect in American political life, even down to the present day. Arguably, millennialism has proven to be very attractive in times of national crisis. But, in the Framing period, hard on the historical heels of the "miracle" of the Revolution, these arguments had enormous appeal.

Civil religionism, which I believe is the archbishop's preferred interpretation, reverses the millennialists' understanding of the proper relationship between religion and public life. Where millennialists advocated using the state as a tool for advancing religion, civil religionists advocated using religion as a tool for the state's purposes. Promoted by Founders and Framers as diverse as Benjamin Franklin and George Washington, what's critical here is the recognition that religion is wonderfully useful for promoting common values in citizens.

This has two important possible effects. First, religion could be ideal for inculcating civic virtue in citizens, the same civic virtue that republics (especially more democratic kinds) need. Democracies empower citizens with extraordinary but dangerous freedom. Without civic virtue, such empowered citizens could enact all sorts of mischief. The hope was that religion might be used by the state to train citizens to be civically virtuous, thus limiting political libertinism. Second, noting the factionalism and centrifugal effects of self-interest that inevitably accompany more democratic kinds of republics—centrifugal effects that could easily overwhelm the national interest, as no. 10 of the *Federalist Papers* points out—some Framers perceived that a thin, formal, and nondenominational national Protestantism could work to overcome divisions and direct citizen political involvement toward national purposes, thereby building a useful sense of national identity and unity in the citizens. If the state might invest national institutions with religious trappings, this would lend them a sense of gravitas and sacred dignity, elevating the public square above local divisions.

Religious separationism is the theoretical argument of those Framers who applauded Thomas Jefferson's famous Danbury Baptists letter. In the politics and religious history of the times, separationism was advanced by the Jeffersonian Republicans, which was the political party supported by eighteenth- and early-nineteenth-century Baptists, Methodists, and other minority and so-called "new" denominations (as opposed to older and more established denominations like the Congregationalists, Episcopalians, and Presbyterians, who leaned toward the Federalist Party). Besides Jefferson himself, Framers like James Madison and George Mason notably subscribed to this argument. Jeffersonian Republicans gradually grew in size and influence in the early years of the nineteenth century, which is evidence that separationism had a very widespread appeal.

As the name suggests, those associated with separationism wanted Jefferson's wall between church and state. Reading their writings, three rationales seem to be central. First, as wonderfully expressed in the Virginia Statute for Religious Freedom (1777, 1779) these Framers believed that republican government depended on citizens possessing minds free from compulsions or massaging by government. If the state interfered with citizens' conscience (even via state-sponsored religion) they believed it undercut its legitimate basis in free popular sovereignty. Second, these Framers worried that mixing intense religious differences with republican politics was particularly dangerous for fomenting factions that could shatter the polity or even lead to civil war—an argument, for example, that James Madison makes in the *Federalist Papers*. Given the fragile nationalism of the early republic, the thought was that America was vulnerable in this regard. Already religious persecutions of minority denominations (like the Baptists) had led to unrest. Third, among these Framers were those who argued that the blurring of government and religion compromised the authenticity of religion itself. Such reasoning is evident in George Mason's Virginia Declaration of Rights (1776) and in the changes insisted upon in the 1787 Constitution by the Anti-Federalists that ultimately led to the First Amendment—which speaks not only against the establishment of state-sponsored religion (as Archbishop Chaput noted) *but also blocks the state from interfering with the "free" exercise of religion.* Like civil religionists, religious separationists also believed in the necessity of civic virtue among the citizenry for good government and, likewise, believed that religion was an important source for that civic virtue. However, separationists reasoned that this could work only if religion was truly autonomous from the state; otherwise, civic virtue would not grow from the citizens' hearts but be instead a state imposition upon their will at odds with authentic faith.

Secular deism refers to the arguments of those Founders who advocated excluding religion from politics and governance. Among the better-known names associated with this argument are the Revolutionary hero of New England Ethan Allen and the Revolution's chief propagandist, Thomas Paine. Allen in 1784 penned a book, *Reason the Only Oracle of Man*. The title explains it all. With the Revolution, Allen believed that history had entered into a new stage of enlightenment—a *novus ordo seclorum* ("a new order of the ages") as it says on the dollar bill. No longer, he thought, would superstition and dogmatic belief repress the human soul. With the emergence of American independence, pure reason would become the basis for morality, society, and government. It should be the only recourse for legitimacy in the conduct of public life. Religion should be utterly excluded, as should custom, tradition, passions, and so forth. Thomas Paine's *Age of Reason*, published in revolutionary France in 1794, makes similar, albeit slightly less anti-religious arguments. Here in eighteenth-century America are early roots for the *laïcité* that Archbishop Chaput warned us against in his Houston speech. Moreover, just as the aforementioned American millennialists had seen the Revolution as ushering in an end to history, so too these secular deists imagined the Revolution as unleashing an emerging perfect order—in this case one culminating in a final historical stage of reason and freedom.

The Framers were divided about the question of religion and government. Of the four categories I've identified, the two outliers are millennialism and secular deism. While both had some appeal in the young country, both were very much minority arguments in the Framing era. The real debate of that period was between the civil religionists and the religious separationists, which played out in the competing political visions of the Federalists (and later the Whigs) and the Jeffersonian Republicans (later called Democrats). It raged through the Framing Period, through the early years of the republic, and through the Second Great Awakening. I would contend that that debate has never been resolved and remains a structural element of American politics down to the present. What has changed, however, is the rising importance of the two marginal arguments from the Framing era—millennialism and secularism. In fact, among political conservatives, I see an increasing understanding of the debate about the role of religion in American public life as one very much colored by contrasting these two extreme positions—both of which were marginal in the eighteenth century.

In light of the foregoing, it should be apparent that John F. Kennedy's 1960 remark about the separation of church and state is plainly *not* outside the mainstreams of political thought from the American Framing and Founding. As indicated previously, Kennedy's proposal could never be fairly construed as an appeal for *laïcité,* or secular deism. Mapped against the four categories of the Framers' thinking outlined above, Kennedy obviously conforms with what was here called religious separationism—the thinking of Jefferson, Madison, and Mason and the thinking of the Jeffersonian Republicans, who later came to call themselves Democrats. The archbishop's understanding of what the Framers thought about religion oversimplifies things, seeing all the Framers as civil religionists, resulting in an inability to appreciate the historically American provenance of Kennedy's thought.

RELIGION IN AMERICAN PUBLIC LIFE: VIBRANT AND HEALTHY

In his Houston address, Kennedy disclosed the seriousness of his own Catholic faith, professing to the assembled Baptist preachers that he would never "disavow" his church "in order to win this election." In a memorable passage he put this poignantly.

> But if the time should ever come—and I do not concede any conflict to be even remotely possible—when my office would require me to either violate my conscience or violate the national interest, then I would resign the office; and I hope any conscientious public servant would do the same.

Faith, the future president tells us, is more important than politics, more important than government, and more important than the presidency. Archbishop Chaput, though, was not persuaded. Kennedy may have mouthed the words that he would not abandon his faith for mere politics, but as the archbishop saw it,

> . . . in its effect, the Houston speech did exactly that. It began the project of walling religion away from the process of governance in a new and aggressive way. It also divided a person's private beliefs from his or her public duties.

I do not pretend to know what the archbishop's political leanings might be. His analysis of Kennedy's long-ago speech, however, seems in many ways similar to an analysis of our country that is quite common in American conservative political circles. It's an analysis that is premised by a combination of notions: the "decline of the West" and "barbarians at the gate." The analysis has been employed in consideration of many aspects of contemporary American life: mores, art, entertainment, literature, social relations, and public and private institutions of every kind, including religion. It's in application to religion that it seems to inform the archbishop. In a nutshell the claim is that religion in America is in decline, not due to internal institutional failures so much as due to external factors. Secularism is the prime culprit. In the quotation from the archbishop above it is secularism that is aggressively "walling religion away from the process of governance." The claim is made so often it has become accepted as self-evident in many quarters. But is it really true? Speaking of the "decline of the West," is religion really in a tailspin in America? Speaking of "barbarians at the gate," is secularism squeezing religion from the public square? No, no, and no.

Looked at from a historical perspective and assessed by current measures, religion is alive and well in America. And far from being squeezed out of American political life and the exercise of governance, religion plays a prominent and more active role in politics, governance, and public life—and looks to continue to expand in its influence. Let's look first at the claim of religious decline and then come back to the claim that religion is being gradually excluded from politics.

The archbishop's 2010 Houston answer to the question of religious decline follows from his criticism of Kennedy. We're told that Kennedy's speech "clearly fed" "trends in American life" such that "the life of our country is no more 'Catholic' or 'Christian' than it was 100 years ago. In fact," he warned, "it's arguably less so." But comparing American religiosity today with the religiosity during the American Framing—an era that the archbishop valorized vis-à-vis Kennedy—finds a very different picture than that which might be expected given the thesis of decline. Americans today are far more likely to be active church members than they were in the Framing generation.

In their important historical study, *The Churching of America 1776–1990*, Roger Finke and Rodney Stark explore the ups and downs of religion in America over its first two centuries.[5] Revealed are the fluctuations of religiosity and the life cycle of denominations. Catholicism swells with European immigration from the mid-nineteenth century through the fin-de-siècle then rises again with the new immigration from Latin America, Asia, and Africa of our own day. Both periods of Catholic expansion coincide with sharp declines among Mainline Protestant denominations. Similarly, Baptists and Methodists explode in numbers in the early part of the nineteenth century while correspondingly Congregationalists dwindle precipitously at the same time. On historical examination religiosity turns out to be neither constant nor constantly falling—but is instead an up-and-down reality over the course of American history: rising during the First Great Awakening in the first half of the eighteenth century, falling during the Founding and Framing periods, rising again in the Second Great Awakening of the 1820s and 1830s, and so forth. Some important larger patterns, though, do stand out.

Most important for present concerns is the book's analysis of rates of religious attendance. The "decline of the West" understanding of religion so commonplace among political conservatives imagines that religion has been in decline as it is increasingly precluded from a place in American public life. But that decline thesis turns out to be wrong. As analyzed by Finke and Stark, the bigger pattern of religious adherence in American history is quite different. They estimate that in 1776 less than one-fifth of Americans belonged to or regularly participated in organized religion. By the 1860s that fraction rose to more than one-third of Americans. By 1900 religious adherence had risen to one-half of Americans. By 1980 two-thirds of Americans belonged to organized religions. Recent data such as have been released by the Pew Forum on Religion and others suggest that American religious adherence remains close to the high level it had in 1980. What does this mean? It means that things are reversed from the "decline" depiction. Church adherence not only has not declined since the Framing period, the actual pattern is one of continuing growth not only over the last hundred years, but over the whole range of American history. From the perspective that the big picture of American history provides, religious adherence is *not* in decline; it's growing.

A similar but slightly different pattern is evident in polling data asking Americans about their belief in God. With some ups and downs, belief in God rises throughout the twentieth century, peaking in the upper 90 percentile ranks in the 1950s and remaining at 92 percent in the most recent polling. Data from the 1990s indicates, moreover, that the intensity of belief among believers is rising even now. A 1987 Gallup poll found that 60 percent of interviewees "completely agreed" with the statement, "I never doubt the existence of God." But in 1999 Princeton Survey Research found that the proportion expressing a similarly strong belief in God had grown to 69 percent. Compared with shockingly lower numbers that result from European polls on these and similar questions, it's clear that religion is vibrant and healthy in the United States, whatever some may wish to claim to the contrary.

Other patterns in religiosity are also important to mention, drawing from the Finke and Stark analysis as well as other recent analyses of religion in the United States. One pattern is that as denominations become more assimilated into American culture and society, they decline in numbers of adherents and vitality. Religious denominations thrive and grow in problematic relationship with the American public square and correspondingly decline when the relationship becomes complacent or unproblematic. Finke and Stark describe this process in their account of the decline of "5" Protestantism in comparison to upstart sects:

> These historical trends are not oddities of the American religious economy or of recent history—they are not new things under the sun. Rather they reflect basic social forces that first cause successful religious firms to compromise their "errand in the wilderness" and then lose their organizational vigor, eventually to be replaced by less worldly groups, whereupon the process is repeated.[6]

What might be perceived as religious decline in some historical periods, accordingly, might be more properly understood as "denominational" decline as new forms of religiosity and new denominational sects rise to replace denominations that have assimilated.

Let me also note what is seldom appreciated in popular accounts. The time period overlapping the American Framing and Founding was not a period of especially intense religiosity. Already it has been noted that less than one-fifth of Americans were active church adherents during this era. It was not until the Second Great Awakening early in the nineteenth century—driven largely by the enthusiasm of the growing and relatively new Baptist and Methodist movements—that a significant uptick in religious fervor is notable in American history, evidenced in part by the surge in church adherents noted previously. Measuring the importance of religion in the American public square would likely find the contemporary period to be more "religious" than the period of the American Founding. Perhaps evidencing a "decline of the West" worldview, Archbishop Chaput maintained in his 2010 speech that "we live in a country that was once—despite its sins and flaws—deeply shaped by Christian faith." He argued, moreover, that "it can be so again." From the larger historical perspective, though, while religiosity has periods of waxing and waning, the historical pattern is one not of religious decline; it can more accurately be described as one of continued growth.

What of the "barbarians at the gates" argument? Isn't aggressive secularism closing politics and government to religious expression? Aren't we believers losing battles to secularists and atheists who would push us from the public square, denying us voice and participation? No. Believers are winning the battle for such voice and participation. American political life (and even governance) reflects greater religiously branded participation and outreach than at any time in the last half-dozen decades.

Much of the newfound religious political participation should be credited to the extraordinary involvement of the so-called Christian Right in American public life since the rise of the Moral Majority in the 1980s. This involvement has changed the face of American politics and government dramatically. Both political parties in the United States now feature sophisticated religious outreach to all major denominations. State governments and the national government have formal offices for faith-based engagement on issues of public policy, as well as de facto liaisons with religious denominations. Ranging the ideological spectrum are public interest religious organizations advocating religious interests in American political life. These are matched by religiously oriented political action and activist groups working for candidates and public policies that support various denominations' interests.

National candidates are now regularly expected to divulge the specifics of their denominational beliefs and to relate such beliefs to their political and policy agendas. They are scrutinized regarding the congruency of their denomination's religious doctrines vis-à-vis candidates' actual faith practices and policy positions.

Religious media channels, newspapers and magazines, e-zines, blogs, and news services have ready access to the conversation of American public life to express their social, civilizational, policy, and political concerns relevant to denominational positions on such matters. Unlike the situation in many parts of the world, in the United States no denominations are denied voice or possibilities of political participation. America's long-established civil religiosity remains prominent. Officeholders take their oaths with hands atop religious Scripture. Governments are awash with chaplains. More so than ever before, Jewish boys wear yarmulkes to public school, Muslim women wear hijabs to work, and Catholic seminarians wear Roman collars on the subway. Public buildings are regularly adorned with lines from Scripture, sculptures depicting religious lawgivers, and similar religious symbolism. Crosses, crèches, menorahs, and calls to prayer are not denied public exposition. In our lifetime, the place of religion in American public life, governance, and politics has grown. Believers are not being squeezed from the public square.

THE VOCATION OF POLITICAL LIFE:
THE ARCHBISHOP AND THE PRESIDENT

Previously in this essay, I noted a difference between some Protestant theologies and the Church's teachings about political participation. For many Protestants, faith is primarily a private grace between an individual and God. The world and society, in such thinking, are understood not as sources for coming to understand divine meaning but rather are seen as challenges or tests for that relationship with God. The affairs of this world are fallen and compromised by sin, not helpful in understanding our end in salvation. Politics and governance, from this perspective, are held out as particularly pernicious venues for testing the grace of one's relationship with the divine. To engage in the corruption of political life is to risk much. Historically these kinds of theologies have handled the challenge of politics in a couple of ways. Earlier I described this as a dichotomous choice: introspective withdrawal or prophetic engagement. Pietistic Christians, with the Amish being an example, choose to withdraw from active engagement in politics in order to safeguard the purity of individuals' grace. And while few Protestants take this as far as the Amish, other denominations historically—including many evangelicals prior to the rise of the Moral Majority in the 1980s—similarly disdained political involvement for the threat it poses to faith. At the other extreme are those who (like the Puritans of America's earliest days) seek to resolve the danger of corruption from public life by prophetically compelling divine purpose upon the political order. Elements of these different Protestant theological approaches to politics were certainly evident in our discussion of the Framing period.

Via interpretations by Martin Luther, John Calvin, and others, the thinking behind these theologies is one that has its theoretical roots in St. Augustine. It's fascinating that Archbishop Chaput concluded his reflections on what he perceived as the catastrophic legacy of Kennedy's Houston address by turning to Augustine's political thought. At the center of Augustine's thinking, as the archbishop noted, is an understanding of the depravity of the fallen world. Even reason—which for the ancient philosophers was a privileged faculty for moral conscience—was thought by Augustine to be untrustworthy owing to it being compromised by sin. Only faith could be counted on if we were to know anything in conscience—as Augustine put it, *credo ut intelligam* ("I believe so that I may understand"). Archbishop Chaput explained Augustine's perspective this way:

> He doesn't believe human beings can know or create perfect justice in the world. Our judgment is always flawed by our sinfulness.

Moreover, for Augustine, as we move beyond and away from the grace of our own faith and into political life we find ourselves in situations where the wages of sin are multiplied. Again quoting from the archbishop, "errors in moral judgment can't be avoided," and in public life "these errors also grow exponentially in their complexity as they move from lower to higher levels of society and governance."

Given this picture, it's no wonder that one response for believers would be to withdraw from the political realm and its dangers. Many early Christians, indeed, thought that believers should invest little concern in the realm of Caesar and look away from earthly affairs toward the realm of God, whose coming kingdom is not of this world. Augustine though (who really was writing while the barbarians were at the gate) saw that for Christians much that was potentially useful for salvation would be lost should the political order fail. Christians were obliged, he concluded, to bring the gift of their grace to political engagement in order to secure the political order for the benefits it might lend in pursuit of salvation. Speaking God's truth to power enacts some measure of that truth in the political order, however limitedly and however temporally. This is the obligation he imposed on believers in political life. As the archbishop said, "political engagement is a worthy Christian task, and public office is an honorable Christian vocation." "Christian leaders," he proposed, "*can* accomplish real good, and they *can* make a difference. . . . It will never be ideal. But with the help of God they can improve the moral quality of society, which makes the effort invaluable."

However, despite his mention of "humility" and "modesty" in such speaking truth to power, the archbishop's approach—following Augustine—would seem to suggest that proper religious engagement in political life is essentially prophetic, a prophetic exercise of the truth of faith upon what is presumed to be a sinful political order.

If this is indeed the archbishop's position as developed in his Houston address, then I am disappointed. It would be an impoverished understanding of Christians in political life that sells the possibilities of politics short. Differently, following St. Thomas Aquinas, I'm convinced that citizens' reasoning is not so compromised by sin that progress toward the common good in political life is precluded. I'm convinced that the political order is not at heart a construct of sinful power, but a natural order created by God in which human life has an ordained earthly home. Most importantly I'm convinced that like all divinely created things the political order is luminous with divine purpose, a purpose that even through reason alone citizens can partially realize. Such purpose is intrinsic in political life itself and, while it harmoniously complements the divine purpose invested in the Church, it does not depend on Church or revelation for its legitimacy. Unlike Augustine, who saw only fallenness and barbarians in political life—thereby begging for Christians with grace to bring order—following Thomas I see the possibility of public life as not something to be subdued by prophetic militancy but as a realm capable of realizing its own natural order and laws by citizens' rational perception of the common good, all of which dovetails in support of our final end in salvation.

A different relationship between church and state results. Because the state has its own access (however limited) to order and natural law laid down by the

Creator, it is not necessary for the Church to direct believers in the task of governing. A limited, but still good political order is possible by rational recognition of the natural law apart from revelation. Nevertheless, when the Church succeeds in its own task of habituating believers in moral conscience and in magisterially informing believers of revealed truth, harmonies are engendered in political life that raise up the polity's own natural pursuit of the common good. As noted in the introduction to this essay, Pope Benedict XVI's *Caritas in Veritate* speaks to this directly. His Holiness speaks of this as "cooperation between faith and reason" (no. 56), one which should be a "fruitful dialogue" (no. 57) for both church and state. He continues:

> For believers, the world derives neither from blind chance nor from strict necessity, but from God's plan. This is what gives rise to the duty of believers to unite their efforts with those of all men and women of good will, with the followers of other religions and with nonbelievers, so that this world of ours may effectively correspond to the divine plan: living as a family under the Creator's watchful eye.[7]

From this perspective, the relationship between faith and public life and between church and state is not a one-way street. Faith is not the sole source of authority vis-à-vis the common good. The task of Church is not to compel an order of grace upon presumed sinful politics. It is, rather, a two-way street, a cooperative and fruitful dialogue wherein faith can convey something to public life, but where also public life valuably contributes to faith.

> Reason always stands in need of being purified by faith: this holds true for political reason, which must not consider itself omnipotent. For its part, religion always needs to be purified by reason in order to show its authentically human face. Any breach in this dialogue comes only at an enormous price to human development. (no. 56)

A dialogue is not an imposition of one side upon the other. It inevitably must respect the distinct and important separation of both parties. *Caritas in Veritate* (in no. 9) cites from Pope Paul VI's *Populorum Progressio*, "The Church does not have technical solutions to offer and does not claim to interfere in any way in the politics of States.'" So church and state must be separate and distinct. It is that separation which enables each the freedom to progress toward their respective ends, while at the same time such progress dialogically generates mutually advantageous harmonies for both in light of humankind's highest end.

Did Kennedy have such harmonies in mind in his 1960 Houston address when he spoke of the separation of church and state? It would be presumptuous to assume so (although I'd contend that's more likely than contentions he wanted *laïcité*). I do hear echoes of Thomism in many of that president's other speeches. Here is a passage from his famous 1961 inaugural, hinting at the idea of such harmony between church and state.

> With a good conscience our only sure reward, with history the final judge of our deeds, let us go forth to lead the land we love, asking His blessing and His help, but knowing that here on earth God's work must truly be our own.[8]

Many have noted, likewise, that the best-known line from that speech invokes the Thomistic idea of the common good.

> And so, my fellow Americans: ask not what your country can do for you—ask what you can do for your country.

It would be foolish, however, to expect from Catholic politicians a nuanced and theologically informed understanding of the role that faith should play in public life. It seems unfair for Archbishop Chaput to have complained in his Houston criticism of Kennedy that so few politicians can "explain how their faith informs their work" today, as if workaday politicians before Kennedy or at any time should be expected to offer a tidy theological accounting. If the political sphere of human life is aglow with the imprint of the Creator who designed us to be political creatures, and if politics genuinely has access to the order of the natural law, and if politicians engage in an effort to realize the common good, then evidence of the fit between faith and public life should be evident in their vocation. To my mind, despite his humanly failings, Kennedy's presidency does much to demonstrate the kind of dialogical interplay between that president's Catholic faith and the political exigencies of policies in pursuit of the common good that all must hope for. Far from "walling his religion away," as the archbishop describes things, I see Kennedy very much involving his Catholic-formed conscience in the vision he brought to his presidency John F. Kennedy concluded his long ago Houston address with the following statement.

> But if . . . I should win the election, then I shall devote every effort of mind and spirit to fulfilling the oath of the Presidency—practically identical, I might add, to the oath I have taken for fourteen years in Congress. For without reservation, I can "solemnly swear that I will faithfully execute the office of President of the United States, and will to the best of my ability preserve, protect, and defend the Constitution . . . so help me God."

"So help me God. . . ." Yes, exactly.

QUESTIONS FOR FURTHER REFLECTION

1. Does Kennedy's assertion that it should not matter to voters what kind of church he believes in, but rather what kind of America he believes in, mean that voters should not consider how a candidate's faith has formed his conscience? Is it fair to look at what a candidate's church teaches in order to evaluate the candidate? What if the candidate professes no faith? What if the candidate's faith is one that the voter considers to be bogus?

2. In Kennedy's speech to the Houston Ministers Conference was he saying that denomination was unimportant in making political decisions or that faith was unimportant in making political decisions? Is there a difference between denomination and faith? If so, what is it? As a Christian, do you look more favorably on candidates of other Christian denominations who share your Christian faith than you do on non-Christian candidates? If so, why? Are there some fringe Christian denominations whose teachings you find more troubling than those of non-Christian faiths? What if a candidate for political office was from one of these "fringe" Christian denominations? Do you feel comfortable talking about a candidate's denomination or faith or lack thereof in deciding to vote for him or her? How about talking about whether a candidate is a more or less loyal adherent to his or her faith?

3. Do you think that when Kennedy says that as president he would make decisions in accordance with what his conscience tells him is in the national interest or that when Scalia says that his Catholic faith has little effect on his judicial decisions, they are saying the same thing? Do you agree with the author that they seem to be implausibly denying the role of religion in the formation of conscience? Do you think that it is possible to abstract from conscience when making political/judicial decisions?

4. Do you find that you hold Catholic political candidates to a different test of faith than you do non-Catholic political candidates? Are you more likely to vote for someone you consider to be an unfaithful Catholic than for someone you consider to be an unfaithful Protestant? Does the faith of a political candidate affect how you vote at all? To what extent? Is it only one factor among many, not a factor at all, or a predominant factor? How do you judge any candidate's faithfulness to his or her professed faith?

5. Do you accept the proposition that Catholics have become so assimilated in American culture that there is no reliable, predictable Catholic vote? Is Catholic bloc voting a good idea? If so, who would direct that vote? Is there a role for the hierarchy here?

6. Do you agree that Catholic theology, by its nature, requires that faith and politics mix? If so, what would that mix be? How would it work out in its practical details?

7. The author identifies four different approaches to the interrelation of religion and politics at the time our nation was formed which he calls "isms." How do you understand each of these "isms"? Do you see any of these "isms" having a current effect on American political life? How? Which of these "isms" most influenced Kennedy in his Houston speech? Which "ism" most influences Chaput's criticism of Kennedy's speech? Which "ism" best reflects your own views?

8. Do you believe that religion in America is declining? Do you believe that it is under attack from secularism? Or do you believe that religion plays an important role in American public life? Cite examples to back up your position. Is it proper for religious people engaging in politics to endeavor to impose the truths of their faith on the political realm? What should be the role of religion in the public life of a multicultural, pluralistic democracy?

9. What has been the effect of the so-called "religious right" in American public life? Has this effect been good, bad, or neutral in your estimation?

10. Do you agree with the author that the political order is not at heart a construct of sinful power but a natural order created by God in which human life has an ordained earthly home? How is this position of the author reflected in the relationship of church and state?

NOTES

1. Address of His Holiness Benedict XVI to H.E. Mr. Charles Ghislain, Ambassador of Belgium to the Holy See (Vatican City, April 24, 2010).

2. President John F. Kennedy's address to the Houston Ministers Conference (Houston, Texas, September 12, 1960) can be found in both video and transcript form at the Kennedy Library website: *http://www.jfklibrary.org/Asset-Viewer/Archives/IFP-140.aspx*. Archbishop Charles J. Chaput's address, "The Vocation of Christians in American Public Life" (Houston, Texas, March 1, 2010), can be found in both video and transcript form at the Archdiocese of Denver website: *http://www.archden.org/index.cfm/ID/3489*.

3. Much of the Houston address was composed on-board the campaign plane *Caroline* while en route to Houston, purportedly a rough flight through the famous East Texas thunderstorms.

4. Antonin Scalia, keynote address: Scarpa Conference on Law, Politics, and Culture, Villanova University (October 16, 2007) as reported in the *Philadelphia Inquirer*, October 17, 2007.

5. Roger Finke and Rodney Stark, *The Churching of America 1776–1990* (New Brunswick, NJ: Rutgers University Press, 1992).

6. Ibid., 237.

7. His Holiness Pope Benedict XVI, *Charity in Truth* (*Caritas in Veritate*) (Vatican City: Libreria Editrice Vaticana, 2009), as released by the United States Conference of Catholic Bishops (Washington, DC, 2009).

8. President Kennedy's inaugural address (Washington, DC, January 20, 1961) can be found in both video and transcript form at the Kennedy Library website: *www.jfklibrary.org/Asset-Viewer/BqXIEM9F4024ntFl7SVAjA.aspx*.

FIFTEEN

How Would Jesus Vote? or The Politics of God's Reign

Terrence W. Tilley

Over the last two decades, some Christians have sought guidance for their lives by asking, "What would Jesus do?" This motto, first propagated over a century ago, has been mocked for its triviality. It easily mutates into questions like the title for this essay. Those who use the motto are also challenged in various ways. "How can you ask that? You're no Jesus." The only response can be, "Indeed I'm not," Another challenge is "How would Jesus vote? How silly! Jesus never voted."

The problem is that there seems no way to discern the difference between good and bad answers to WWJD and similar questions. Sometimes WWJD seems nothing other than a rather bogus way of legitimating one's own opinion. After all, since Jesus never voted there is no real control from Scripture or Tradition on how to answer the question correctly.

Yet somehow WWJD and its clone, HWJV ("How would Jesus vote?"), seem to capture something important. Christians have an obligation to consider political issues in light of their faith. Religious leaders frequently instruct their congregations about the moral and practical implications of political issues. The United States Conference of Catholic Bishops offers a guide to voting in each election cycle. A Christian voter may cast the same ballot as a Jewish voter or a humanist voter or any other voter. What difference does being a Christian make? HWJV?

All too often we hear that Christians cannot in conscience vote for certain politicians because of their positions on difficult political issues like school vouchers, abortion rights, marriage among gay or lesbian people, or the use of military force. We hear that Christians are to be "countercultural" and oppose the disgusting, even demonic, tendencies in our culture. We are to resist the tide of culture. We are to provide an alternate stream, a politics of God's reign, rather than the partisan politics prevailing in our country.

However, there is a fundamental problem with this approach. The first part of this essay shows what the problem with "counter-cultural Catholicism" is, at least for the United States. The second part of this essay then provides an alternative view, one that values engagement and communication over seeking confrontation and proclaiming non-negotiable positions.

THE DEPTHS OF DIVERSITY

The United States is now and has been *intrinsically* religiously diverse. But this diversity is not merely external. It is also internal to particular religious communities and persons. While commentators frequently recognize the *external* fact—that there are hundreds of religious denominations and faiths in this country, they frequently are blind to the *internal* fact—that people who live in the United States have internalized that diversity. Culturally and religiously, we are hybrids.[1]

Americans have often been proud of the fact that we have managed to learn how to cope with religious diversity in our history. Sociologist Robert Wuthnow found that this "history has affected our laws, encouraging us to avoid governmental intrusion in religious affairs that might lead to an establishment of one tradition in favor of others. And it has taught us a kind of civic decorum that discourages blatant expressions of racist, ethnocentric and nativist ideas."[2] Yet this decorum may mask a grudging tolerance, a merely pragmatic coexistence that recognizes that members of all religious traditions have civil rights, including the right to worship. Such decorum is a refusal of engagement with religious others.

Crucial to authentic engagement is conversation across and between religious traditions. Conversation is not debate. Rather, as Jonathan Sacks put it, it is a

> disciplined act of communicating (making my views intelligible to someone who does not share them) and of listening (entering into the inner world of someone whose views are opposed to my own). Each is a genuine form of respect, of paying attention to the other, of conferring value on his or her opinions even if they are not mine.[3]

Conversation is how we learn to live together peaceably in a pluralistic society. Only then can we engage in the needed "sustained act of understanding andf seeking to be understood across the boundaries of difference."[4] To engage in such conversations, we must recognize not only that we may have some things to teach, but some things to learn. We may even have to learn to change.

Our diversity does not call for us to water down our views or prohibit us from seeking to change others' views. Wuthnow, Sacks, and Hill Fletcher,[5] in various ways, provide patterns for communication in the context of religious diversity. Communication may include efforts at persuasion directed to overcome disagreements. But to persuade those of a different faith tradition—a political necessity in a pluralistic society—one must communicate effectively with them in ways that they can accept.

ENGAGEMENT WITH DIVERSE TRADITIONS

We cannot refuse engagement with other traditions. We cannot isolate ourselves. We cannot simply be countercultural because the culture is ineradicably within us. Refusing to speak with or ignoring others is not a live option for Christians. A religiously isolated community simply cannot fit in the United States. There is no place isolated enough on which to build such a community. This is not to deny that monasteries or religiously homogenous communities can be built in dense forests or on high mountains or in barren deserts or even behind high walls in the heart of teeming cities. Trappists, Zen Buddhists, Carmelites, some Mormons, and others build such communities. Nor is it to deny that a relatively homogenous neighborhood can be built in the midst of a bustling metropolis. Orthodox Jews in Brooklyn and Muslims in Detroit have developed neighborhoods with distinctive cultures fitting their religious communities in the midst of busy diversity. Yet no such localized community is impermeable to the forces, for good or ill, characteristic of the broader American culture. And one of those forces is the reality of genuine religious diversity, an implicit challenge to the finality and sufficiency of one's own religious way of life. A living faith tradition can survive only on this site if it has a way of coping with the fact that it is one of many traditions on the site, all of which have some good reason for being here. Communication and engagement are essential.

Religious diversity is not merely external to a particular tradition. It can be "internal" in at least two ways, geographic and ethnic. The Roman Catholic tradition, presumably the most extensive and seemingly rather "monolithic," provides a good example of both.

The Catholic Church comes in various "flavors" in the United States. The ways of "being church" vary by location. In the cities of the eastern United States, such as Boston, Philadelphia, and New York, the Roman Catholic Church has been a political and cultural powerhouse; in the South and the rural sections of the plains and mountain states, it has been politically and culturally marginal. In the middle of the twentieth century, newspapers in Chicago and

Milwaukee, for example, grouped their real estate advertisements in the classified sections of newspapers geographically by Catholic parish, not by town or other neighborhood designator. This indicates a powerful cultural position for the Roman Catholic Church, one that it did not have in North Carolina, for example, where Catholics have historically been less than 1 percent of the population or in Utah where the dominant Mormon tradition demands Catholics must make sustained efforts to maintain and nourish distinctive Catholic communities.

The ways "the same faith" is lived out in these and other varied contexts are quite different. To treat the matter somewhat simplistically, we can say that, in the areas with dense Catholic population and a culturally visible institutional structure, the Church as "institution" shapes the way people live in and live out the tradition; in those with a thin population where other churches, e.g., Southern Baptist or Methodist, are the culturally dominant religious institutions, "the Church as remnant community" characterizes the practical ecclesiology of the other faith communities. In the former, the Catholic Church can be powerful enough to function politically as if it were established (save for the lack of tax support). In the latter, the Catholic Church can be practically persecuted (save for the tax exemptions given to all "charitable institutions"). A map showing the proportion of students in Catholic school systems and the distribution of Catholic colleges and universities would give a rough depiction of the distribution of such different population densities and different ways of being church. The denser the distribution of such institutions, the more likely a church is experienced as institution. There are numerous other factors involved, of course, and there are no "pure types" of either situation. The point is simply that geographical location makes a real difference in social location of faith communities and in the way their members live in and live out their faith tradition.

Ethnically, the Catholic Church is becoming increasingly "Hispanic." It has become a commonplace (whether entirely accurate is yet to be seen) that sometime in the next decade or so a majority of members of the Roman Catholic Church in the United States will be Hispanics, but Hispanic conversion to Evangelical, Holiness, and Pentecostal Protestant traditions is also significant. Moreover, there is cultural diversity within "Hispanic" Catholicism. In the Southwest United States, Mexican American culture is strong, while in the Southeast, Cuban American patterns are distinctive, and in the Northeast, Puerto Rican and Dominican Catholics tend to be more visible. Yet all these populations have the census designation "Hispanic," although their religious practices and devotions vary widely.

Groups of migrants may carry their own particular devotions with them. For example, Mexican and Mexican American migrants to the rural South kept their devotion to Our Lady of Guadalupe. Santería is a live option for some Cuban and Cuban American Catholics, but less so for Mexican American Catholics. Devotional and institutional patterns in Roman Catholicism continually evolve. There is no one homogenous, nationwide ethnic pattern even among Hispanics, at least not yet. The penetration of pan-Hispanic media like Univision and Telemundo may change this.

Varying geographical density is not limited to the various Hispanic communities. Filipino and Vietnamese Catholics are strongly represented in San Francisco and in other major metropolitan areas. Historically, Irish Catholics have held sway in Boston, Irish and Italians in New York and San Francisco, middle Europeans in the Midwest (Polish Chicago in the heart of the German triangle from St. Louis to Cincinnati to Minneapolis), Bohemians and Czechs in parts of Texas, and French-derived Catholics in the southern tidewater regions and northern New England. The French and Irish traditions are shaped in part by Jansenist tendencies brought from Europe; Hispanic Catholicism is relatively untouched by such a heritage.

While each of the diverse geographical sites retains some local characteristics and while ethnic groups maintain their traditions insofar as they can, these patterns are relativized by the overwhelming processes of ecclesial centralization under Roman jurisdiction and internal migration in the United States. Cuban American theologians write critically and constructively about Mexican American devotion to Our Lady of Guadalupe, which is not part of their traditional Cuban heritage. Various Roman offices work to make the practice of the faith, especially the liturgical practice, consistent from place to place. The Roman Curia advises the pope to move bishops from Rome to St. Louis to Philadelphia, from New Jersey to Florida and back, from Philadelphia to Hawaii to Virginia (in three recent cases). Vowed religious, other than those committed to "stability of place," can be and are moved from coast to coast and border to border and beyond. Additionally, Catholics, like all Americans, migrate internally to pursue educational opportunities, to take better jobs, to accept military assignments, to live in more suitable climates, and for a host of other reasons. Some traditional or ethnic local devotions fade and are replaced in significance. Robert Orsi shows this in his examination of the growth of the cult of the patron of "hopeless causes," St. Jude, which emerged as a national devotion in the middle third of the twentieth century among the children and grandchildren of immigrants.[6] Problems like the "sexual battery and episcopal complicity" scandal are national problems. People moving from one place to another may be delighted or disillusioned by the way a church operates in a new town or city; they may then engage in parish shopping until a relatively satisfying way of being church is found. Anyone who has been active in the church and migrated internally—the common wisdom is that 20 percent of U.S. residents change residence in any year—can recognize the significant differences in ways of being church in these various locations, and yet also recognize that it is the "same church."

INTERNAL DIVERSITY AS HYBRIDITY

Internal diversity is a key factor in the religious culture of the United States. Hill Fletcher notes that this diversity means that each person is a "hybrid." Since we are "shaped by a multiplicity of stories, the conditions for conversation across difference are in place. Because our frameworks are created intertextually from out of many stories, while two people might not share the story of their religious community, they may have in common some additional stories . . . of culture or ethnicity, of profession or generational outlook."[7] These other stories or traditions in which we live are part of who we are and may be the places that we can meet those who are "other" than us religiously. The key point for present purposes is that we are "composite." We are not shaped merely by our religious tradition, but by a whole host of communities to which we belong. Diversity is internal to our communities and to each of us.

Such communication is possible *because* we are hybrids. We are identified not only by a singular feature like our religion; we also have other aspects to our identity. We have ethnic, economic, political, and other constituents in our identities. We are Irish (or Italian or African American or Mexican or Puerto Rican or English or Chinese). Most of us are hybrids ethnically. We may be part of labor (or management or ownership or unemployed or underemployed). Many of us have been in many—or even all—of these categories. At times in our lives we may not have known where our next meal was coming from, while at other times we are imagining a secure retirement. We may be parents, cousins, Republicans, Democrats, single, divorced, straight, gay, etc. Though we differ in politics and religion and ethnicity and prosperity, we may share enthusiasm for model railroading or knitting. Our identities are composite. As Hill Fletcher put it:

> Overlapping concerns can spread wider the net of solidarity. Yet, while working alongside persons of other faiths, the distinctiveness of their religious perspective is not erased, and communication does not take place on some newly found sameness within the two religions. Rather, as members of multiple communities simultaneously, each possesses a multilingualism through which a shared language can be found.[8]

Even as we recognize our religious differences, we live together in local communities. We can and do come to learn and appreciate, even while we may disagree with, each other's perspective, on everything from zoning regulations to hiring police, from what actions our civic government should take about homelessness or about raising property taxes. In our local civic lives, we know that if we communicate well with others, we might even convert them to our views.

Religious diversity is also "internal" in a very challenging way, but one that is really a component of hybridity. Diversity is found within every religious structure built on this site. Interethnic, interfaith, and interracial marriages are becoming more common. Education at public schools and universities means children of parents from one faith tradition rub elbows and may even live with other good people who do not share their parents' traditions. Work environments are prohibited by law from religious discrimination, unless belonging to a specific religion is a bona fide occupational requirement. Hence, one normally encounters people of other faith traditions in the workplace. The same neighborhood may have a Catholic church, a Jewish synagogue, a Mormon temple, an Islamic cultural center, and a variety of Protestant houses of worship. Buddhist meditation centers and Hindu temples are increasing in number as well. Any of these institutions may anchor or co-anchor a neighborhood. Any may be a civically important place where neighborhood concerns are addressed and action plans formulated.

This internalization of external diversity is also seen in some exemplary individuals. Some Jesuits practice yoga or Zen meditation. Pope John Paul II prayed at Assisi in 1986 with other religious leaders. Women called to ordained service migrate from the Roman Catholic to Episcopal or Lutheran Churches. Married Anglican males who were ordained as priests in the Anglican Communion have been accepted into the Roman Catholic Church and (re)ordained as Roman priests despite the hierarchy's supposedly unwavering commitment to a celibate, all-male clergy. What seem to many to have been hard and fast walls between traditions are being broached in a wide variety of ways. Specific identity markers are slipping in significance, new ones are emerging, and the harsh light of internal diversity banishes illusions of isolated purity. One cannot live in and live out a faith tradition in isolation from the diversity of multiple faith traditions. And that diversity is not only at the institutional level but the individual level as well.

DIVERSITY AND SECULARITY

This pattern of internal and external religious diversity may not be unique, but it is distinctive of the United States. The significance of this pattern is that practicing *one of many* living faith traditions other than the one into which one is born and bred is a cultural "live option" in the United States. The "live option" in most countries is to participate either in the faith tradition endemic to the region or to become secular. That is, the *only* live option for those who cannot or will not practice their inherited faith tradition in most places is secularism (or perhaps being a persecuted minority). Secularization is not the only option to living in a specific faith tradition in the United States, but merely one of many possibilities for those immigrants who need to figure out how to live in and live out a religious tradition in this country, as well as those of their descendants who are afflicted with spiritual wanderlust.

Religious leaders in Canterbury, Rome, Lynchburg, Jerusalem, Teheran, and a host of other locales seem to engage in unending rhetorical warfare against secularization and modern secular humanism. These leaders seem to fear that anti-religious "secularism" will seduce adherents of the various faith communities away from their religious homes. The attacks on secularism in the United States, where a quarter of the population or more participates regularly in worship, seem to have a different object and audience from those in France, where perhaps a twentieth of the population engages regularly in worship.

The religious rhetoric protesting against secularism is often vehement. Vehement rhetoric reflects the perceived power of secularism as the enemy. As terrorism is seen as a threat to the stability and power of the United States, secularism is seen as a threat to the politically or culturally established faith tradition. At times, as in renascent Islamic movements, secularism seems to be the "defining other" that sharpens the cultural identity of the battling faith tradition. However, "the secular" is no one thing that can be attacked straight on any more than terrorism is. Each type of enemy, whether called terrorist or secularist, is particular to the place that cultures it. And, yes, we do think there are some similarities between rhetorical opposition to terrorism and to secularism—the rhetors and the target differ, but the rhetorical attacks are similarly structured.

In the United States, however, no single opponent undermines the allegiance of the faithful. Multiple faith traditions and a variety of secular philosophies vie with each other on the pluralistic playing field. Various forms of secular humanism, egoism, or religious indifferentism are only some of the many live options available, not the only alternative to one's natal tradition. However pernicious the various religious traditions and their theological elite find secularism and secularity, in the United States it occupies a cultural place very different from that in the rest of world. Like the various living faith traditions, the patterns of secularity are many ways among many ways on the cultural landscape. Secularity is not a single *other* to be opposed. It is too diverse to be the opponent that defines who we are, despite the fact that some religious integralists and fundamentalists attempt to paint the secular as demonic, as unified, and as monolithic as patriots painted the so-called "worldwide Communist conspiracy" that was the defining opponent politically and militarily for the United States half a century ago.

The notion that there can any longer be "one way," one political position, that we can proclaim as loudly as possible against all who disagree is, at best, difficult to maintain. Within the church there is diversity. We cannot but have heard other voices. We have internalized diversity in a host of ways. We cannot ignore the other. We can only engage the other.

The implications of this for our political views are huge. Not only can we no longer pretend to be countercultural; we can no longer refuse to engage the political and religious other because the network of internalized connections means that the "other" is "us." In this sort of situation, we cannot ask the question, "How would Jesus vote?" but we can ask, "What would bring us closer to the reign of God that Jesus proclaimed and embodied?"

THE POLITICS OF THE REIGN OF GOD

Our responses to internal diversity are to participate in the practices that help to make a community of diverse people. These are the practices of reconciliation. Reconciling practices are the hallmark of the Jesus movement, past and present.[9] The very sharing of devotion, prayer, and table fellowship in the context of diversity is a reconciling practice.

The devotion to St. Jude characterized by Orsi and noted above was a reconciling practice. Prayer to Jude enables women (and men) to negotiate the seemingly impossible demands placed on them. Orsi notes repeatedly that Catholics from the Great Depression forward were caught between profound role conflicts: to be a good wife and yet a breadwinner, for example. The old roles for women in immigrant communities—roles that women had internalized as good—were in conflict with the new roles women had to play. Prayer to St. Jude and sharing the results of those prayers with others created a realm in which it became possible to reconcile the old and the new.

Demanding conformity in a space of diversity can be a divisive practice. The classic way to promote unity has been to demand theological conformity. Those who cannot say the Nicene Creed or who reject on principle the authority of the pope or the bishops are not engaging in diversity of belief. Rather, they are writing themselves out of the Catholic Church.

Those who do not have a profound devotion to Mary or who cannot accept contemporary magisterial teaching regarding contraception remain Catholics, but diverge in various ways from the contemporary norms, either informal or formal. To demand conformity on all these matters is to make demands that would divide the church, not reconcile God's people.

Our response to external diversity must be dialogue. With regard to religious diversity, the practices recommended by the Pontifical Council for Inter-Religious Dialogue in 1991 remain a useful guideline. Dialogue among faith traditions and proclamation of our tradition "are both oriented towards the communication of salvific truth" (*Dialogue and Proclamation* no. 3).[10] Dialogue takes four forms. The *dialogue of life* is the very practice of living together and supporting each other in a local context of religious diversity. The *dialogue of action* is the practice of collaboration across faith traditions to work for justice and development for all people. The *dialogue of theological exchange* is the practice of scholars seeking to understand more clearly their own heritage and to appreciate others' heritages as well—and, clearly, we can learn much about our own tradition by listening to and appreciating the testimony and criticism of others. The *dialogue of religious experience* emerges in the practice of sharing spiritual values and practices across traditions, as when Tibetan Buddhist and Western monastics share their traditions and practices (cf. *Dialogue and Proclamation,* no. 42). We may not be able to explain the mystery of God's universal salvific will regarding all the faith traditions. But we can hope in God's care for all and enact it in our own small way by continuing the dialogue.

The most effective form of dialogue and proclamation is witness. Our practices, including the practice of believing, are our primary form of witness. The saying attributed to St. Francis of Assisi, "Preach the Gospel always; if necessary, use words," is relevant here. Yet even if there may be times that explicit proselytizing is counterproductive or productive of impasse, as with proselytizing Jews, witness is always relevant and proper. The practice of dialogue is the kind of witness that is "staying at the table" in cooperation with those who differ despite our disagreements with them.

DISCIPLES AND POLITICS

We start as disciples. We live in a tradition that enabled us to encounter Jesus the Christ. We must begin telling stories, sharing our faith. We are called to engage in the practices that constitute living in and living out the reign of God that Jesus instantiated and preached, the *basileia tou theou*. We share the practices of healing each others' wounds and the wounds of the world, of teaching as Jesus taught, of forgiving those who have sinned against us, of praying together, of sharing table fellowship, especially the table fellowship of the Eucharist.

But the key practice is communication. If we are to represent our faith adequately, we must first communicate it adequately. If we cannot communicate the faith adequately to others, how can we represent, even to ourselves, what that faith is?[11] And if we do not communicate our faith to others who do not share our faith, even our children, they cannot understand and accept or reject our faith. We must say and show what we believe. Representing what discipleship means begins and ends in communication.

So how do these reflections help understand how we are to participate in the political process? The answer in principle is simple: we are to do what disciples do, that is, we are to engage in the diverse reconciling practices that are characteristic of the reign of God. Do we engage in practices that empower us to be the eternal God's temporal agents in scattering the proud, putting down the mighty from their thrones, exalting the lowly, filling the hungry, and sending the rich away (cf. Luke 1:51–53)? Do they enable us to love our enemies, do good to those who hate us, bless those who curse us, pray for those who abuse us, and do to others as we would wish they would do to us (cf. Luke 6:27–31)? What do they enable us to do for others, especially the poor, and enable others, especially the poor, to do for themselves (cf. *Economic Justice for All*, no. 24)? The test of good theology is how well it communicates performatively to empower communities of disciples to live in and live out God's reign here and now. We may each have different ways of engaging in these practices, but this diversity is healthy—and so St. Paul's First Epistle to the Corinthians, chapter 12, makes clear: we have diverse gifts, but form one body.

How do we put these kinds of *religious* practices into *political* practice? Thomas Patrick Melady, former U.S. ambassador to the Vatican, contrasted two styles of putting Catholic principles into political practice, engagement and confrontation. He wrote, "Engagement emphasizes the use of strategy to convince the other side about the validity of a position and being civil about it. Confrontation, on the other hand, represents firm opposition to any civil discussion of the issue on the basis that the issue is nonnegotiable."[12] Engagement is certainly preferable to confrontation. Engagement involves an attempt to get others to understand one's own position and to accept it as their own. Engagement is communication. Even if engagement does not convince another, engaging with others may get them to move off their positions and to consider alternatives. Confrontation involves stating one's position and demanding that others come over to one's own side.

Engagement is a communicative practice that seeks both dialogue and proclamation. Three of the practices for interreligious dialogue provide a model for political dialogue. A *dialogue of life* recognizes diversity on political strategies and calls for support of those whose strategies we can support even if we disagree in principle. For example, some of those who refuse to criminalize all abortions and fail to see that abortion is an intrinsic evil might yet promote programs that would likely result in a reduction in the number of abortions. A practice of engagement would find cooperation on this very limited ground a chance for dialogue. A practice of confrontation would refuse to cooperate on principle. The former is an opening to further dialogue; the latter closes off dialogue. A *dialogue of action* is the practice of collaboration to work for justice and development for all people. Even if one disagrees with a politician about a particular issue, e.g., the morality of war, one might support that politician because overall she or he has a commitment to justice and development. Engagement on important issues where there is agreement in principle and strategy can be a platform for authentic dialogue on issues where there is diversity. The *dialogue of principled exchange* is the practice of scholars seeking to understand more clearly their own heritage and to appreciate others' heritages as well. The dialogue of just exchange is engagement. A respectful debate between those who find nuclear deterrence or contraception morally tolerable and those who find deterrence or contraception morally intolerable exemplifies such exchange. Such engagement recognizes that others have reasons for their views even if we do not share the views or find the reasons compelling. But we can learn about our own tradition and possibly how better to communicate it by listening to and appreciating the testimony and criticism of others. In the situation of diversity, dialogue is the beginning.

CONCLUSION

In a situation of internal and external religious and political diversity, the key thing is to recognize which practices reconcile us with others and ourselves and which practices separate us from others and our true selves. I have argued here that the diversity of the United States is unique and deep. While agreeing on the tenets of the faith, Catholics disagree with each other on particular issues, especially issues of political judgment. Even bishops are not united on every issue. Hence, we cannot merely withdraw into our own protective shells. We are too diverse and too deeply involved on every level with others to maintain a pure countercultural community. We are shaped by diversity in our own tradition and others' traditions, even secularity, in a host of ways. Neither can our institutions nor our very selves avoid diversity and hybridity entirely.

In this situation of diversity, no vote is pure because no politician is pure. To think that there is one right way to engage in politics or one right way to vote is folly. Why?

First, the Christian tradition puts it simply: we are all sinners. This does not mean that we can be indifferent to sin. Far from it. But to paraphrase an old motto, "hate the sin, love the sinner," so "hate the position, love the politician" is a possibility. But if we want to encourage a politician who is "good" on a number of issues, but "bad" on some others, the principle is engagement, not confrontation. Why? Because even if we cannot say how Jesus would vote in practice, we can recognize that the politics of the reign of God is a politics of reconciliation. Reconciliation cannot occur by confrontation alone, but only by engagement with others that may include confrontation as part of our engagement and only at the level of principled exchange. But engagement is always first as we need to discover how to live in and live out the reign of God when we are not only diverse, but diverse sinners.

Moreover, only on the basis of established communication can constructive criticism be heard as constructive rather than oppositional. To attend to an accusation of sin, we have first to recognize that we are sinners—but sinners who are redeemed and recovering. Only then can we hear criticism constructively. Only then can criticism have a chance of leading to real change.

Second, Jesus would have voted for a sinner. He would and did "vote for" sinners like Peter, who denied him; the Zebedees, who fought over political prestige; and Mary and Martha, who doubted he could raise their brother from the dead. Jesus made sinners into disciples not because they were perfect, but because they were willing to live as *disciples* who engaged in the reconciling practices that constitute the reign of God. The reign of God will not be fully realized before the eschaton; all we can do here and now is to work however minimally to advance it where we can.

But we can say who Jesus would vote for in principle. In principle, Jesus voted for sinners; in practice, so must we. That someone is a sinner is not reason not to vote. If that were a criterion, no one could receive a vote. The question is *which* sinners can we vote for. The answer is that those sinners who work for reconciliation deserve our vote, because working for reconciliation and peace—even in flawed ways—is working for God's reign, even if the sinners for whom we vote do not always agree with the sinners who vote for them.

QUESTIONS FOR FURTHER REFLECTION

1. Does the question, "How would Jesus vote?" capture something important for you, or does it trivialize the issue? How does the author understand this question? Do you agree?

2. The author says that the United States is religiously diverse in both an internal and external sense. What does he mean by that? Do you think that Catholicism in the United States is internally diverse? Should it be?

3. Conversation, the author says, is not a debate. How does the author define "conversation"? What does he see as its value in dealing with the religious diversity of America? When was the last time you had a conversation with a person of a different faith tradition about the way your faiths affected a particular issue? Describe that conversation if you can. Can Catholics admit there are values to be learned from other faith traditions?

4. The author writes that there are different ways that the Catholic faith is lived out in different parts of the United States. Do you agree? Have you ever participated in parish life in a different part of the country than where you live now? Was it a different faith experience? How was it different? How was it the same? Did the context of your faith in any way affect how you practiced your faith?

5. What effect will increased Hispanic immigration have on the Church in the United States? What cultural diversity exists within "Hispanic" Catholicism? What other immigrant groups are having an effect on U.S. Catholicism? Are these seen by the hierarchy as centrifugal forces? What does the author mean, do you think, when he says that these different immigrant and local patterns are "relativized by the overwhelming processes of ecclesial centralization under Roman jurisdiction"? Is that relativization and centralization a good thing?

6. What does it mean to say that every person is a hybrid? Do you agree with that? How is this characterization reflective of diversity? How does being a hybrid affect how we communicate with others?

7. What does it mean to internalize diversity? What examples does the author give of this internalized diversity? What effect will such internalized diversity have on different faith traditions?

8. What does the author mean by secularism? How do you understand that term? Is secularism the enemy of faith? How does the author say that secularism in the United States is different than secularism as it exists in other parts of the world? How does the author's description of American secularism and how faith relates to it support the notion of America as a "space of diversity"?

9. What does the author mean when he says that there can no longer be "one way," one political position, that we can proclaim as loudly as possible

against all who disagree? Do you agree with this conclusion? What evidence has the author given to substantiate that conclusion?

10. What makes the Jesus movement a reconciling movement? How can demanding uniformity in a space of diversity be divisive, i.e., non-reconciling? What should our response to diversity be? How do the concepts of dialogue and witness fit into this response?

11. How should a disciple of the Lord engage in contemporary American politics? How do your own actions stack up against this standard?

NOTES

1. This section distills insights from Terrence W. Tilley et al., *Religious Diversity and the American Experience: A Theological Approach* (New York: Continuum, 2007).

2. Robert Wuthnow, *America and the Challenges of Religious Diversity* (Princeton: Princeton University Press, 2005), 4.

3. Jonathan Sacks, *The Dignity of Difference: How to Avoid the Clash of Civilizations*, rev. ed. (New York: Crossroad, 1993), 83.

4. Ibid.

5. Jeannine Hill Fletcher, *Monopoly on Salvation? A Feminist Approach to Religious Pluralism* (New York: Continuum, 2005).

6. Robert Orsi, *Thank You, St. Jude: Women's Devotion to the Patron Saint of Hopeless Causes* (New Haven: Yale University Press, 1996).

7. Hill Fletcher, *Monopoly on Salvation?* 110.

8. Ibid., 93.

9. This is the core of the argument in my book *The Disciples' Jesus: Christology as Reconciling Practice* (Maryknoll, NY: Orbis Books, 2008).

10. As at *http://www.vatican.va/roman_curia/pontifical_councils/interelg/documents/rc_pc_interelg_doc_19051991_dialogue-and-proclamatio_en.html*.

11. This insight from the philosophy of language regarding the priority of communicative practice over representation—from Wittgenstein and Austin in the Anglophonic world, adapted by Habermas in the German-speaking world, debated among the post-structuralists so influential today—is crucial. That is, if we try to communicate our faith in Jesus Christ as "truly human, truly divine," using terms like "nature" when "nature" in the present does not mean what *physis* did in the past, we cannot effectively communicate what *physis* did in the past and so necessarily fail to represent the mystery of Christ accurately and adequately. The Council of Chalcedon tried to solve the problem of affirming the mystery of Christ by attributing properties to two different natures in his one person. In our culture, however, we attribute properties to persons, not to "natures." We don't have the robust concept of human nature and the incommensurable concept of divine nature as the ancient Christians did. Hence, if the Chalcedonian doctrine fails to communicate the mystery for contemporary people (and, I think for many, it does fail), then we cannot communicate in a way our interlocutors—both Christians and others—can understand sufficiently well to represent the mystery of Jesus the Christ, the truly divine and truly human one.

12. Thomas P. Melady, "Signal from Rome: Engagement and Confrontation" (October 6, 2009), at *http://ncronline.org/news/politics/signals-rome-engagement-and-confrontation#*.

Contributors

Nicholas P. Cafardi is Dean Emeritus and Professor of Law at Duquesne University School of Law. He is also a canon lawyer. Cafardi was the founding chair of the Pennsylvania Supreme Court's Commission on Racial and Gender Bias in the Justice System, and he was an original member of the United States Catholic Bishops' National Review Board for the Protection of Children and Youth, serving as its chair in 2004–5. His book *Before Dallas* (2008) is a history and analysis of the child abuse crisis in the Catholic Church.

Lisa Sowle Cahill is the J. Donald Monan, SJ, Professor of Theology at Boston College. Her areas of teaching and research include Christian ethics, Catholic moral theology, Catholic social teaching, bioethics, and ethics of sex and gender. She is a past president of the Catholic Theological Society of America and of the Society of Christian Ethics. Recent works are *Theological Bioethics: Participation, Justice, and Change* and *Bioethics and the Common Good*.

Cardinal Georges Cottier, OP, is the theologian emeritus of the Pontifical Household. A native of Switzerland and a priest of the Dominican Order, he has taught at the University of Fribourg and the University of Geneva. He was appointed Secretary of the International Theological Commission in 1989 and was nominated Pro-Theologian of the Pontifical Household in 1990. He was made a cardinal by Pope John Paul II in 2003.

William V. D'Antonio has taught at Michigan State, the University of Notre Dame, and the University of Connecticut. He left the University of Connecticut to become the Chief Executive Officer of the American Sociological Association, where he served until his retirement in 1991. He is currently a Fellow at the Life Cycle Institute at Catholic University. His most recent books are *American Catholics Today: New Realities of Their Faith and Their Church*, and *Voices of the Faithful*, a co-authored study of a Catholic lay social movement.

Richard R. Gaillardetz is the Joseph Professor of Catholic Systematic Theology at Boston College. He is the author of *Ecclesiology for a Global Church* (Orbis) and the co-author, with Catherine Clifford, of *Keys to the Council*, to be published by Liturgical Press in 2012.

John Gehring is a Senior Writer and Catholic Outreach Coordinator at Faith in Public Life. He previously served as the Director of Communications at Catholics in Alliance for the Common Good and as the Assistant Director for Media Relations at the United States Conference of Catholic Bishops.

Gregory Kalscheur, SJ, is an associate professor at Boston College Law School. Prior to entering the Society of Jesus, he clerked for the Hon. Kenneth F. Ripple of the United States Court of Appeals for the Seventh Circuit and practiced law in Washington, DC. His primary teaching and research interests include law and religion, constitutional law, civil procedure, Catholic social thought and the law, and the contributions of Ignatian spirituality to the character of legal education at a Jesuit law school.

M. Cathleen Kaveny is the John P. Murphy Foundation Professor of Law and Professor of Theology at the University of Notre Dame. She is currently completing two books, one on prophetic discourse in the public square, and the other on the pedagogical function of law in a pluralistic society.

Gerard Magill holds the Vernon F. Gallagher Chair for the Integration of Science, Theology, Philosophy, and Law at Duquesne University in Pittsburgh. He is a tenured professor in the Center for Healthcare Ethics. His expertise and publications are in Catholic moral theology and Catholic bioethics. His forthcoming book is on imagination and ethics, focusing on the writings of Blessed Cardinal John Henry Newman.

Bryan N. Massingale is a priest of the Archdiocese of Milwaukee and Associate Professor of Theological Ethics at Marquette University. He is past president of the Catholic Theological Society of America and Convener of the Black Catholic Theological Symposium. He is the author of numerous books and essays on the Church's engagement with social and racial justice.

Vincent J. Miller is the Gudorf Chair in Catholic Theology and Culture at the University of Dayton. His book *Consuming Religion: Christian Faith and Practice in a Consumer Culture* considers how religious communities are being transformed from within by consumer attitudes and practices and how they can work to counter this. His current research explores the impact of globalization and the "culture of choice" upon the fragmentation of religious communities and the polarization of religious and political discourse.

Maureen H. O'Connell is assistant professor of theology at Fordham University. She authored *Compassion: Loving Our Neighbor in an Age of Globalization*, which argues for a revival of the virtue of compassion in light of hurricane Katrina and global poverty. Currently she is exploring the arts as a source of ethical wisdom and catalyst for moral action in *If These Walls Could Talk: Community Muralism and the Beauty of Justice* (Liturgical Press, forthcoming 2011). She is a board member of the Society for the Arts in Religious and Theological Studies.

Anthony J. Pogorelc is a Sulpician priest at the Catholic University of America, serving on the faculty of Theological College and as a Fellow of the Institute for Policy Research and Catholic Studies, where he directs the Changing Spirituality of Emerging Adults project. His specialization is the sociology of religion. He is coauthor of *Voices of the Faithful*.

Stephen F. Schneck heads the Institute for Policy Research & Catholic Studies, a public policy think tank at the Catholic University of America in Washington, DC. A political philosopher by training, Schneck is widely published on topics intersecting politics, philosophy, and the social teachings of the Catholic Church. He is currently writing a book on the imperatives for Catholic faith in American political life.

Terrence W. Tilley holds the Avery Cardinal Dulles, SJ, Chair in Catholic Theology and chairs the Department of Theology at Fordham University. He is the author of ten books, most recently *Faith: What It Is and What It Isn't* (Orbis Books, 2010) and *The Disciples' Jesus: Christology as Reconciling Practice* (Orbis Books, 2008). He previously taught at the University of Dayton, Florida State University, St. Michael's College (Vermont), and Georgetown University. He is past president of the College Theology Society and the Catholic Theological Society of America.